THE ART OF
THE PUBLIC GROVEL

THE ART OF THE PUBLIC GROVEL

SEXUAL SIN AND PUBLIC CONFESSION IN AMERICA

SUSAN WISE BAUER

PRINCETON UNIVERSITY PRESS • PRINCETON AND OXFORD

Published by Princeton University Press, 41 William Street, Princeton,
New Jersey 08540

In the United Kingdom: Princeton University Press, 6 Oxford Street,
Woodstock, Oxfordshire OX20 1TW

Library of Congress Cataloging-in-Publication Data

Bauer, S. Wise.
  The art of the public grovel : sexual sin and public confession in America /
Susan Wise Bauer.
      p. cm.
  Includes bibliographical references and index.
  ISBN 978-0-691-13810-7 (hardcover : alk. paper)   1. Sex scandals—
United States—History.   2. Politicians—Sexual behavior—United
States—History.   3. Presidents—Sexual behavior—United States—
History.   4. Confession—Social aspects—United States—History.
5. Evangelicalism—United States.   6. United States—Moral conditions.
I. Title.
  HQ18.U5B34 2008
  17—dc22   2008020570

British Library Cataloging-in-Publishing Data is available

This book has been composed in ITC New Baskerville with
Trajan display

Printed on acid-free paper. ∞

press.princeton.edu

Printed in the Unites States of America

10   9   8   7   6   5   4   3   2   1

CONTENTS

LIST OF ILLUSTRATIONS

ACKNOWLEDGMENTS

THIS STUDY owes a great debt to Maureen Fitzgerald of the College of William & Mary, who consistently encouraged me to look at Protestant and Catholic practices of confession in relationship to each other and not (as was my tendency) in isolation. At William & Mary, Chandos Brown and Susan Donaldson also provided immensely helpful feedback and criticism. Mark Noll did a careful and much-appreciated reading of an earlier draft of the manuscript. Jonathan Gunderlach cleared the permissions and located illustrations with efficiency and expertise. Final thanks go to Fred Appel at Princeton University Press for his willingness to read multiple drafts and his expert editorial advice. Since I didn't take all of the good advice offered me by these excellent scholars, the final form of the book is my responsibility alone.

THE ART OF
THE PUBLIC GROVEL

INTRODUCTION

FROM PRIVATE TO PUBLIC CONFESSION

ON THE EVENING of August 17, 1998, Bill Clinton faced the American public with an embarrassing admission. Despite earlier denials, he had indeed been carrying on with a White House intern twenty years his junior. "I did have a relationship with Miss Lewinsky that was not appropriate," he said. "In fact, it was wrong. . . . I know that my public comments and my silence about this matter gave a false impression. I misled people, including even my wife. I deeply regret that."

He regretted it even more when the House of Representatives impeached him for perjury. But two months later, the Senate voted to acquit him. His approaches to evangelical leaders before and leading up to a White House prayer breakfast succeeded in garnering him public expressions of support from superstar ministers Gordon MacDonald and Tony Campolo, among others. He left office with a 65 percent approval rating, higher than any other departing president in history; five years later, another poll found that he was not only more popular than the incumbent president, but was also considered more honest.[1] His autobiography, released in 2004, sold more than 400,000 copies in hardback; he won a Grammy for the audiobook version, which he read himself. In 2006, he received several honorary doctorates, as well as the Fulbright Prize for International Understanding. In that same year, Hillary Clinton's staff told the *Atlantic Monthly* that the ex-President was encouraged to stay away from his wife's fundraising events, since it was impossible to keep media attention away from him and on the Senator.

Four years after Clinton's admission, an entirely different sort of confession unfolded in front of a much less receptive crowd of listeners. On November 3, 2002, Bernard Cardinal Law faced his congregation at the Cathedral of the Holy Cross in Boston and told them, "I did assign priests who had committed sexual abuse. . . . I acknowledge my own responsibility for decisions which led to intense suffering. . . . I ask forgiveness in my name and in the name of those who served before me."

But this confession did not redeem Cardinal Law in the eyes of either his flock or his colleagues. A public call by other priests for Law's resignation forced him to step down just four weeks after his Holy Cross confession. He also resigned his position as chairman of the board of The Catholic University of America, then left the United States and moved to Rome.

Clinton's success and Law's failure signal the final stages of a massive shift. At the end of the twentieth century, Americans increasingly expected their erring leaders to publicly admit their sin and ask for forgiveness. Even as evangelicals complained about their diminishing influence in America,[2] the evangelical ritual of public confession assumed center stage in secular American culture.

• • •

Apology and confession are not the same. An apology is an expression of regret: *I am sorry.* A confession is an admission of fault: *I am sorry because I did wrong. I sinned.*

In the last few years, public figures have apologized with increasing frequency. But these apologies often serve as red herrings, drawing the eye and ear away from the missing confession. "I got heckled and took it badly and went into a rage," comedian Michael Richards said in 2006, after hurling profanities at black patrons in a comedy club. "I'm deeply, deeply sorry." There was no admission of wrongdoing here, merely a description of the evening's happenings, along with an apology. "My intent . . . was to tell what happened on the mountain as accurately and as honestly as possible," journalist Jon Krakauer wrote, at the end of his best-selling Mount Everest memoir, *Into Thin Air,* "and I apologize to those who feel wounded by my words." This is not confession, but rather apology as self-defense. An apology, as psychiatrist Aaron Lazare has pointed out, can be made when there is no real sin involved ("I am sorry that I tore the sweater you lent me" acknowledges nothing more than misfortune); an apology may even be made by someone who has not erred, on behalf of those who *have* (as when an American president apologizes for slavery, or a German chancellor for the Holocaust).[3]

Confession is harder. Confession requires that the accused give up innocence and self-defense, taking moral responsibility for an evil act. Apologies can be made with ease, but confessions are painful.

The high-profile sinners driven to public confession in contemporary America—Jimmy Swaggart, Bill Clinton, Bernard Cardinal Law—had already been judged guilty by the public, well before their confessions. No one doubted that Bill Clinton's cigars had been where they ought not, or that Cardinal Law had shuffled priests from parish to parish to avoid embarrassment, and worse.

But their followers, already convinced as to guilt, *needed to hear them say, "I have sinned."*

As it evolved in the twentieth century, the public confession came to serve a very particular purpose. It became a ceremonial laying down of power, made so that followers could pick that power up and hand it back. American democratic expectations have woven themselves into the practice of public confession, transforming it from a vertical act between God and a sinner into a primarily horizontal act, one intended to rebalance the relationship between leaders and their followers. We both idolize and hate our leaders; we need and resent them; we want to submit, but only once we are reassured that the person to whom we submit is no better than we are. Beyond the demand that leaders publicly confess their sins is our fear that we will be overwhelmed by their power.

So it is no coincidence that every one of the high-profile confessions occupying front pages in the 1970s and beyond has involved men accused of predatory behavior: Edward Kennedy, Jim Bakker (not Tammy Faye), Jimmy Swaggart, Bill

Clinton (not Monica Lewinsky), Cardinal Law. The search for similar demands made on women to confess reveals that, barring a few admissions of employing illegal immigrants, women have not felt the same pressure to come forward publicly and admit wrongdoing.

Furthermore, these men, all of whom held positions of legal or moral power, were each accused not only of predatory behavior but of predatory *sexual* behavior. Financial misdealings, when folded into the mix, merely intensified suspicion that these leaders were victimizing their supporters. But the *sexual* sins of these men were the offenses that caused followers to fear that they would be deceived and exploited by those to whom they had willingly granted power.

Before the twentieth century, it had been possible for leaders accused of sexual sins to reassure their supporters without resorting to public confession. But by the century's end, confession was a ritual that permeated American public life. Even Catholic priests and secular politicians found themselves pressured into public confession by followers who were neither evangelical nor Protestant. Public confession had become the most powerful means by which leaders acknowledged the power of their followers.

The path from confession as a private act to confession as a public ritual stretches from the Fourth Lateran Council of 1215 all the way to Oprah Winfrey. Confession of sin, an act originally intended to repair the relationship between God and sinner, was at first practiced in privacy; only a priest, bound to secrecy by the seal of the confessional, served as witness. Post-Reformation, confession of sin took up a supporting role in the conversion narratives of English Puritans, where it helped to reassure the Puritan believer of the reality of his faith. As part of a conversion story, confession of sin was done publicly; the whole purpose of the conversion narrative was to testify, before the gathered saints, to the reality of the conversion.

In colonial American Puritanism, and later in the hands of American revivalists, the confession of sin went through additional transformations. It was detached from the conversion narrative to stand alone. It still took place within sacred spaces, but it became increasingly visible: it moved to the front of the church, and was performed not only in front of other saints, but in front of a watching world. The number of confessions made at any given revival became a measure by which revivalists could gauge their success—and proof to unbelievers that the kingdom of God was advancing, pushing back the kingdom of darkness. Public confessions showed that the holy war against the forces of evil was prospering; revivalists were the recruiters of God's army.

In the last half of the nineteenth century and the first half of the twentieth, leaders accused of sinful behavior could reassure their supporters without resorting to public confession. Presidential candidate Grover Cleveland, accused in the 1880s of taking advantage of a single woman and abandoning the child of the affair, and evangelist Aimee Semple McPherson, suspected of having a fling with her married sound engineer, both managed to recover from their scandals without ever confessing to wrongdoing.

Yet the responses of both showed how the expectation of public confession was already on the rise. Cleveland, while avoiding truly *public* admission of wrong, let it be known that he had in fact confessed to a minister, who in turn spoke on his behalf to the public; McPherson used the language of holy war that accompanied revivalist confession to position herself properly within the cosmic battle between good and evil.

After 1925, revivalist preaching on radio and later on television made the sound and sight of public confession increasingly familiar. This sort of programming, originally shut out from national networks, took an enormous leap forward in 1960 when the FCC changed its restrictions on religious programming; over the following ten years, confession-oriented programming became the most visible, the most aggressive, the most familiar of all religious broadcasts. Simultaneously, a secular (but Protestant-sponsored) form of confession had developed greater and greater influence: group psychotherapy, rooted in the Emmanuel Movement, encouraged the practice of confession in a gathering of equals. Therapy took to the airwaves, with radio psychologists offering live counseling to patients who confessed their difficulties and inadequacies to a listening audience of hundreds of thousands.

By 1969, when Edward Kennedy came before the bar of public opinion to defend his actions at Chappaquiddick, public confession had grown thoroughly familiar to the American public. Yet Kennedy, faithful to his Catholic upbringing (and oblivious to the necessity of reassuring his public that he was *not* a political aristocrat who would abuse his power), refused to confess.

Kennedy' partial failure—he lost the presidential nomination (permanently, as it turned out) but remained in public life—stands at a transitional point. Confessional programming was moving beyond the radio to the television screen, as dozens of confessional talk shows followed the debut of Phil Donahue's ground-breaking television talk show in 1967. Even more significant was the fusion of the language of holy war with political agendas in the 1970s and 1980s. This rhetoric, merging spiritual and political dangers into one enemy, turned political leaders into figures of theological importance and ministers into politicians. Evangelicals pleaded for national repentance, echoing the calls of the nineteenth-century revivalists. Confession was not merely a way to rebalance the power between leader and follower; it was a tool that placed the confessing sinner on the right side of the holy war.

In this highly polarized climate, politicians (particularly those who, like Jimmy Carter, identified themselves as Christians) were also forced to locate themselves on the battlefield. Carter, asked for the same sort of reassurance that Kennedy's supporters had craved, used confession in an effort to demonstrate that he would not take advantage of presidential power, but his misunderstanding of the symbols and rhetoric of holy war turned his confession into a catastrophe. The erring televangelists of the 1980s were also pushed into public confession; like Carter, confession offered them an opportunity to reassure their devotees that they were still fighting on the side of divine good. Bakker entirely failed to appreciate this, instead turning on his allies and destroying any chance of forgiveness; Jimmy Swaggart confessed successfully, preserving his ministry until a later refusal to confess reversed his triumph.

Clinton, raised in blue-collar evangelicalism, was able to speak the language of holy war. His admission of sin, which made careful use of evangelical Protestant vocabulary while avoiding any actual admission of legal guilt (or financial misdoing), was intensely reassuring. It showed that, as a leader, he had no intrinsic, inborn superiority, but was simply a sinner among sinners, a man struggling (and sometimes failing) to fight against wrongdoing. It placed him on the right side of a holy war against evil. It granted power to the listeners, by acknowledging their right to judge their leader and allowing them the chance to take part in the cleansing ritual of forgiveness.

In contrast, Bernard Law's Catholic tradition saw private confession as the norm. But when Law refused to admit fault publicly, many American Catholics saw his reticence as both a minimization of the presence of sin—a refusal to recognize the existence of the battlefield between good and evil—and as an intolerable assertion of authority. Furthermore, Law's actions were widely seen as subverting the American legal system in order to victimize the helpless. And Law's resistance to making a public confession, while entirely in line with Catholic practice, denied an increasingly vocal and active Catholic population any role in the administration of their own parishes. Saturated in a culture that saw evangelical-style public confession as normative and the authority between church leaders and their followers as essentially democratic in structure, American Catholics found Law's reluctant apologies troubling, infuriating, and, in the end, entirely inadequate.

Law's failure and Clinton's success show the extent to which evangelicalism had provided a national language for erring leaders. The warnings of the televangelists were wrong; American politics were *not* more secular than ever. By the beginning of the twenty-first century, erring leaders faced a demand that the voters of 1884 never made: the demand to publicly acknowlege sin and receive God's forgiveness.

The rise of public confession was not due to the power of evangelicalism but to the essential likeness between American democracy and American evangelicalism. They share the resemblance not merely of first cousins, but of full siblings, unable, even when hostile, to separate from each other.

PART I

THE SHIFT TOWARD
PUBLIC CONFESSION

1

GROVER THE GOOD, BELSHAZZAR BLAINE, AND THE RAPACIOUS WOMAN

*The policy of not cringing was not only necessary
but the only possible way.*
—GROVER CLEVELAND, 1884

AT THE AGE OF FORTY-SEVEN, Grover Cleveland was just below the top rung of the political ladder. In fourteen years he had ascended from the post of Erie Country sheriff to the mayor's office in Buffalo, and then to the governor's mansion of New York. In early July of 1884, the Democratic National Convention nominated him for the presidency of the United States.[1]

Almost immediately, he faced a career-ending scandal.

On July 21, just days after the convention, the *Buffalo Evening Telegraph* broke shocking news under the headline "A Terrible Tale: A Dark Chapter in a Public Man's History." Cleveland had seduced a helpless woman, made her pregnant, and then forced her to put the baby into an orphanage. Interviewed by the *Telegraph's* reporter, local minister (and Republican activist) George H. Ball warned the public that Cleveland was a predator, stalking the streets of Buffalo on a hunt for victims.

The *Telegraph* was a tabloid, and the tale wasn't given wider play until a *Boston Journal* reporter followed up on the scandal and published his own account. This version of the story also insisted that Cleveland was a relentless womanizer: "Women now married and anxious to cover the sins of their youth have been his victims . . . and well-authenticated facts convict him."[2] From the *Journal,* the story spread across the country.

This sort of scandal was particularly embarrassing for Cleveland, whose political reputation was built on uprightness. In his years as a public servant, the American political scene had suffered through revelation after revelation of financial corruption. In 1873, Democratic senator William Tweed had been convicted of stealing millions of dollars from New York City coffers, and scores of other politicians, from both parties, had been implicated. The Republican administration of Ulysses S. Grant had been tarred by three separate major financial scandals and several smaller ones.[3]

This had given Cleveland, a relative newcomer to the political scene, the opportunity to position himself as a plain dealer and a man of transparent honesty. His term as New York governor was marked by the passage of anti-corruption measures, and his presidential campaign—headlined with the slogan "Public Office is a Public Trust"—promised voters that he would bring accountability back to the national government. Corruption, according to Cleveland's supporters, was "stalk[ing] forth with impunity," and getting honest politicans into office overruled every other political consideration: "Is it of any avail to discuss the interior arrangements of a house . . . while the house itself is on fire?" demanded one supporter, at an 1884 rally supporting Cleveland's candidacy. Cleveland, the speaker concluded, was "unpretending and straightforward; a man who hesitates not a moment to show the door to the friends of corruption . . . [and] has repelled the corrupt elements of his party."[4] Cleveland's stance of righteousness had earned him the nickname "Grover the Good," not only for his financial probity but also for his personal morality; an April 18, 1884, cartoon in *Puck,* titled "Cleveland the Celibate," showed him laboring away over New York state business, shunning the temptations of three beautiful women.

Now his greatest strength had suddenly crumbled. Consulted by panicked Democratic friends, Cleveland told them that the Democratic party should speak for him and "tell the truth." He himself refused to speak of the matter at all. Even

Figure 1.1. "Cleveland the Celibate"

when crowds of Republican voters greeted him by chanting, "Ma, Ma, where's my Pa?", Cleveland held his tongue.

It was a risky decision. But in November, Grover Cleveland—still declining to acknowledge his illegitimate child—was elected to the presidency. His Democratic supporters taunted his detractors with an additional line to the chant: "Gone to the White House. Ha, ha, ha!"

• • •

Cleveland's victory presents us with a double riddle.

A century later, in an America with a much greater tolerance for sexual escapades, Gary Hart was forced to give up his bid for the Democratic presidential nomination when he was photographed with model Donna Rice sitting on his lap. Fifteen years later, the Republican Speaker of the House Robert Livingston resigned his position due to *rumors* that he had committed adultery. How did Cleveland, living in an era when public standards of morality were much stricter, triumph?

From the vantage point of the early twenty-first century, what seems even odder is that Cleveland won without ever admitting to his fault. At the end of 2006, an Associated Press reporter mused on CNN, "Why have public apologies become such a mainstay of our culture?" He was looking back on a year filled with confessions of wrongdoing: comedian Michael Richards's admission that he had gone on a racist rant in a nightclub; actor Mel Gibson's confession that he had spewed anti-Semitic rage; Congressman Mark Foley's apology for sending sexually explicit emails to underage boys; Pastor Ted Haggard's revelation that he had both taken drugs and hired a prostitute. "It seems that the minute a transgression occurs, be it small or large, we wait for penitence," the reporter concluded. "It's the other shoe that needs to drop before we can move on."[5] Yet the voters who put Cleveland in office—voters who expected their public officials to be good Christians, regular church-goers, and moral men—did not insist that Cleveland humble himself and repent.

There is a double answer to the double riddle. Cleveland had committed a moral sin, but he did so in an era when confession was still practiced within sacred spaces. And as he dealt with the repercussions of his sin, he managed to reassure the voters that he was not a man who would take advantage of weakness.

Cleveland's entrance into politics came at a time when the financial misdealings of elected officials (particularly in New York) had come close to shattering the Lockean contract between American voters and their leaders. Elected politicians were using their power—granted to them only by the consent of the governed—to raid public coffers, acting (in Locke's words) as princes who had "distinct and separate interest from the good of the community."[6] Reaction to financial scandals highlighted the helplessness voters felt as they watched their leaders wheel and deal without their consent. "[I]n a democracy," the *New York Times* editorialized in late 1884, "the fragment of political power falling to each man's share is so extremely small that it would hardly be possible . . . to rouse the interests of thousands or millions of men if party were coupled with another political force. This, to speak plainly, is corruption."[7] Corruption—the use of public funds for private gain—lifted one man above his peers; it amplified the "fragment of political power" belonging to a single personality beyond what it should be. It created a sort of aristocracy, a ruling class willing to treat the masses of American voters as "a herd of inferior creatures under the dominion of a master, who keeps them and works them for his own pleasure or profit."[8]

Cleveland, on the other hand, had a history of identifying himself *with* the American people, *against* the rich who hoped to exploit them. "We are the trustees and agents of our fellow citizens," he had told his fellow civil servants after his election as governor in 1882, "holding their funds in sacred trust, to be expended for their benefit . . . [W]e should at all times be prepared to render an honest account to them touching on the manner of its expenditure."[9] This was language he had already used in accepting the nomination: "Public officers are the servants and agents of the people," he had told the nominating committee.[10] Cleveland was no political aristocrat. He was a "fellow citizen," a servant of the people.

At the same time the Halpin scandal broke, Cleveland's Republican opponent, the Maine senator James G. Blaine, was struggling unsuccessfully against accusations that he had used official powers to grant railroad rights that would profit him personally. Even juicy tales about Cleveland's sexual past did not eclipse Blaine's misdeeds. In a *Harper's Weekly* cartoon from August 9, Blaine appears as a knight in tarnished armor, charging full tilt at a bag labelled "Public Money"; the caption reads "The 'Great American' Game of Public Office for Private Gain." In a *Puck* cartoon from August 13, Cleveland stands at the center of a courtroom, striking a heroic pose in front of a jury of voters, while behind him a headline reads "Tell the truth." At the side of the courtroom, Blaine creeps away with his pockets stuffed with stocks and bonds. The caption reads "[Blaine] Instituted the Ordeal—Can He Stand It Himself?"

THE "GREAT AMERICAN" GAME OF PUBLIC OFFICE FOR PRIVATE GAIN.
This is not "*Protection*"; this is very "*Free Trade*" with the people's money.

Figure 1.2. "The 'Great American' Game of Public Office for Private Gain"

Blaine also had to deal with a more subtle accusation: that he was the friend of the rich, a "political aristocrat," enemy of the common man. A huge percentage of Blaine's support evaporated when, on October 29, Blaine allowed a supporter to call the Democrats the party of "Rum, Romanism, and Rebellion." This was widely seen as a slur against Irish Catholics, the poor working men who had once supported Blaine. In a spectacularly stupid act of misjudgment, that very same night Blaine attended a "prosperity dinner" in his honor, with two hundred of the richest men in America. This placed him firmly in the company of the resented aristocrats of capitalism.

The *New York World* responded with a cartoon that placed Blaine in clear opposition to the public good. Blaine and a dozen

Figure 1.3. "He Instituted the Ordeal. Can He
Stand It Himself?"

or so wealthy men sit at a huge and lavishly set table, beneath a
banner that reads, "The Royal Feast of Belshazzar Blaine and the
Money Kings." In front of the table, a ragged working-class family stands, pleading for food, but no one notices their presence.
They represent the poor of the entire country, while Blaine is associated with the biblical Belshazzar, who used his royal status to
throw a feast and get drunk while his city and its people were invaded and conquered by foreign enemies. The juxtaposition
must have brought John Locke's words into many minds:

> If a man in the state of Nature be so free . . . why will he
> part with his freedom, this empire, and subject himself to

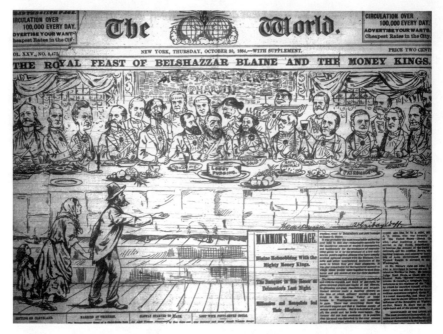

Figure 1.4. "Belshazzer Blaine and the Money Kings"

> the dominion and control of any other power? To which
> it is obvious to answer, that though in the state of Nature
> he hath such a right, yet the enjoyment of it is very uncer-
> tain and constantly exposed to the invasion of others.[11]

American voters yield power to their leaders in order to protect
their own wellbeing and prosperity. A leader who interpreted
election as the acknowledgment of some inborn right to enrich
himself had violated the terms by which he came to power.

By contrast, Cleveland's handling of his scandal kept the
focus firmly on his willingness to accept financial responsibility
for his alleged child. He didn't admit paternity, but he allowed
his friends to broadcast the fact that he was, in fact, paying generous support to the baby's mother, a widow named Maria Halpin. Cleveland also ordered his campaign workers to entirely
ignore the fact that Blaine too had sexual indiscretions that
might have been paraded before the election (in figure 1.3,

Figure 1.5. Grover the Good ("Another Voice for Cleveland")

the closed book labelled "Blaine's Private Life" represents this decision). This kept any head-to-head comparison of the sexual lives of the two men out of the headlines, and the focus straight on their financial reputations: an arena in which Cleveland could clearly triumph.

Set against Blaine's identification with the rich and famous, Cleveland's sexual misdeeds played more as a joke than as a disqualification for public office. On September 27, the New York paper *The Judge* showed "Grover the Good" jumping up and down with frustration, while a baby in the arms of a well-dressed woman yells, "I want my Pa!" The cartoon repeats the assertion that Cleveland was the father of Halpin's child, but there are no true victims in the picture; tears notwithstanding, both the baby and the woman are well-fed and well-dressed.

The prosperous appearance of the figure of Maria Halpin in the cartoon reveals that, throughout the scandal, Cleveland managed to cast himself not as victimizer, but as something closer to a victim. The first stories about Halpin had portrayed him as a wolfish womanizer who had satisfied his own desires at the cost of a helpless widow's health and reputation. In order to keep the Halpin scandal from destroying his carefully constructed financial persona as friend of the common man, the helpless and disenfranchised, Cleveland had to avoid appearing as a predator.

He did this by refusing to address the issue himself, while allowing his friends to construct a different version of events on his behalf. His direction that the Democratic party should "tell the truth" gave party supporters the freedom to investigate Halpin's story. There was no question that Cleveland had been carrying on a sexual relationship with Maria Halpin. But the story of their relationship, as told by the Democrats, removed Cleveland from the role of sexual predator and recast the story as yet another example of his righteousness. According to this version of events, Halpin was a drunkard, possibly the seducer rather than the seduced, and Cleveland had rescued the baby from neglect by paying for it to be raised in a reputable orphanage. The Reverend Kinsley Twining, a well-known Protestant minister, came out in public support of Cleveland: there had been "no seduction," he insisted, "no adultery, no breach of promise, no obligation of marriage," and since the baby's birth Cleveland's behavior had been "singularly honorable, showing no attempt to evade responsibility, and doing all he could to meet the duties involved, of which marriage was certainly not one."[12]

It is difficult to see why marriage to Halpin was so entirely off the table, but for the Reverend Twining to say this, rather than Cleveland himself, implied that there were perfectly good reasons. Cleveland knew that he must not be seen as an exploiter. And so, while refusing to explore Blaine's private life, he *did* allow Halpin's personal life to be made public, to the extent that this assisted him. Halpin was an alcoholic, which made Cleveland's decision to take the child away from her an act of rescue. Even Cleveland's refusal to admit the child's paternity worked in his favor, leaving open the possibility that the child wasn't his—which made his sexual relationship with Halpin appear, paradoxically, less damaging. It turned Halpin into a loose woman, possibly a seducer, not marriage material and certainly neither innocent nor vulnerable.

This was a task made simple by Halpin's absence from the scene. Cleveland's supporters, while investigating her story, never spoke to her; no one could find her.

2

IN THE PRESENCE OF THE ELECT
(WITH THE WORLD LOOKING ON)

Look back into your lives, call to mind thy sins, as many as possible.
—GEORGE WHITEFIELD

THE REVEREND KINSLEY TWINING, having assured the public that Grover Cleveland was "certainly not" obliged to marry Maria Halpin, did not let the matter rest. Cleveland, he explained, was an honorable man, but he was no stranger to wild oats. He had been guilty of an "illicit connection" or two when he was "younger than he is now" (a conveniently vague phrase); in fact, he had fallen into a "culpable irregularity of life, living as he was, a bachelor."[1]

Cleveland supporters cringed at this frankness, but the Reverend Twining's words did Cleveland much more good than harm. Twining did not appear on Cleveland's behalf as a character witness; his role was that of absolving cleric. His presence signals the answer to the double riddle's second half: Cleveland was able to avoid public confession, at least in part, because his public believed that he had already confessed in private.

Public confession of sin was not an unknown phenomenon to Grover Cleveland. As the son of a Presbyterian minister, he had grown up in a church tradition that encouraged the confession of sin in the presence of others.

But the "others" in question were not the larger public; they were fellow believers, members of the Protestant congregation who acted as witnesses. By 1884, the Protestant practice of confession had moved into ever-widening sacred spaces. It had not yet broken through into the profane world of politics—but it *was* on a trajectory that ultimately would bring it into full public view.

• • •

Centuries before, the ritual of confession had taken shape as an intensely private act. The Catholic practice of regular private confession to a priest, with the entire act protected by the "seal of confession" which prohibited the priest from speaking about any of the matters confided to him by a penitent, had been confirmed by the Fourth Lateran Council of 1215.[2]

But Grover Cleveland did not belong to this particular tradition of private confession; nor did the majority of his supporters, who were not Roman Catholic but Protestant. With the Reformation, Protestants had developed a ritual in which confession of sin played an essential (and much more public) role. This was the "conversion narrative," a testimony to the circumstances of a sinner's conversion that *included* a confession of sin, but did not have confession of sin as its primary goal. Rather, the conversion narrative produced a ritual space within which a Protestant sinner might confess in the presence of a crowd.

This was the first point in the trajectory toward public confession. Conversion narratives could not take place in private. The presence of other believers was absolutely necessary if the narratives were to fulfill their goal—to reassure the Protestant believer that his conversion had been real.

The conversion narrative itself grew out of one of the great ironies of the Reformation. Martin Luther's theological rebellion was rooted in his deep sense of inadequacy; no matter how hard he labored at religious duties, he was haunted by the dreadful conviction that he had not yet performed well enough to be justified—to be declared righteous in the sight of God. In 1519, meditating on the Epistle to the Romans, Luther came to a sudden realization of the solution:

[A]s it is written: "The just person lives by faith." . . . I began to understand that this verse means that the justice of God is . . . a passive justice, i.e., that by which the merciful God justifies us by faith. . . . All at once I felt that I had been born again and entered into paradise itself through open gates.[3]

The sinner, declared righteous by divine fiat, should be set free from the fear that he has not done enough to earn God's favor. God's favor comes to those who do not deserve it; righteousness is not a prerequisite, but a result. "The Christian who lives in confidence . . . does all gladly and freely," Luther wrote in his tract *Sermon on Good Works*, "not with a view to accumulating merit and good works, but because it is his great joy to please God and to serve Him without thought of reward."[4]

Luther's theology of justification grew out of his desire for certainty. He had belonged to a medieval church in which forgiveness of sin came by institutional declaration—the sinner confessed to a priest and was absolved—but the penances that the soul must do to earn this absolution were always changing, from sin to sin, from priest to priest, from parish to parish. Luther wanted a simple, foolproof method of knowing that forgiveness had been obtained, rather than a complex and baffling set of steps through which the sinner had to battle to reach freedom.

And yet, in searching for this simple assurance of forgiveness, Luther's Reformation magnified uncertainty tenfold because it removed from the individual sinner any possibility of external absolution. The Protestant sinner now had to look within his own soul and decide whether or not he met the criteria for forgiveness.

The criteria for forgiveness was genuine conversion: the possession of sincere faith in the justifying blood of Christ.[5] The reformer John Calvin broke from Luther in significant ways, but still affirmed that salvation came by faith alone. Faith, Calvin wrote, is "a firm and sure knowledge of the divine favor toward us, founded on the truth of a free promise in Christ, and revealed to our minds, and sealed on our hearts, by the Holy Spirit."[6] Calvin puts emphasis on God's unilateral action rather than human belief, because the complete corruption of original sin makes man helpless to act on his own behalf. The sinner is likewise incapable of producing true faith on his own. God, not man, brings about the sincere faith that arises in the believer's heart.[7]

This ought to be reassuring, but in fact isn't. Calvin's theology of original sin also leads him to assert that while some men are chosen before birth to be redeemed, others are chosen to be condemned. Sometimes the reprobates, those who are *not* genuinely called to redemption, may experience a "sense of divine love" that *feels* like the "proper knowledge of the divine will" that characterizes the truly redeemed. But this "sense" is temporary and evanescent. Only the passage of time can distinguish true faith from false security. The deceptive sense of divine love will eventually "wither away, though it may for several years not only put forth leaves and flowers" (in fact, God may even give some "slight knowledge of His Gospel" to those who are not elect, and afterward allow this knowledge to be extinguished). But the true "proper knowledge," even though it may be slight, endures to the end of life.[8] Practically speaking, this means that, at any given point, the Reformed believer is not sure whether he is a reprobate with a deceptive sense of divine love, or an elect believer with a proper knowledge of God's mercy.

Despite all Calvin's assurances, this is not a pleasant state of mind, and it proved a psychological torment for conscientious believers. Only one firm foothold appeared in the quicksand of uncertainty, one visible marker of redemption for sinners who had little else to reassure them. This was the moment of conversion: the point at which the sinner, like Paul on the road to Damascus, saw a blinding light and answered the call of God.

Although Luther himself experienced conversion as a sudden understanding of grace, a singular moment in time he could look back on to reassure himself of his salvation, he did not hold this up as the exclusive model. But in the hands of the English Puritans, the moment of conversion assumed a much greater importance. Luther's conversion story inspired John Bunyan's vivid description of Christian's justification in

Pilgrim's Progress. In a single blazing moment, the burden of sin falls from Christian's shoulders and rolls out of sight.

Compared to thrashing around in self-reflexive agonizing over one's own sureness of knowledge, the moment of conversion was a solid and visible signpost.[9] As long as the sinner could point back to that moment of conversion—the point at which he asserted his faith in God—he possessed a weapon against doubt. The moment of conversion acted, for the Protestant believer, like a priest's absolution for the Catholic: an external occurrence that guaranteed forgiveness and salvation.

It was best if this conversion took place in the sight of other believers; this provided an extra level of assurance that it had actually occurred. Should the conversion happen in private, though, the telling of the story of the conversion experience out loud, in front of others, fulfilled a double function. Public testifying provided the believer with witnesses who could attest to the conversion's reality. It also provided an extra level of reassurance that the believer's faith in Christ was genuine; the Gospels themselves record Jesus as saying, "Whoever acknowledges me before men, I will also acknowledge him before my Father in heaven."[10]

Conversion narratives were regularly offered by American Puritans as proof of living faith, a necessary prerequisite to church membership.[11] Patricia Caldwell points out that while it is impossible to know exactly when these conversion narratives became standard practice, they were certainly in use by the 1640s, and may have emerged under the guidance of John Cotton.[12] The New England narratives followed a regular pattern. A sinner comes to an understanding of just how great her sin is; she suffers under the bondage of evil, is struck with grief over her wrongdoing, and confesses her sin. Finally a sense of God's grace overcomes her, fills her with the assurance of God's forgiveness, and releases her from slavery.

Confession of sin was an essential element of the conversion narrative because it provided a clear contrast between the earlier, unredeemed life of the sinner and the sanctified behavior that followed salvation. But confession of sin did not remain merely an element of the conversion narrative. In the early American Puritan revivals, public confession of sin was undertaken both by believing individuals and by entire congregations as a way to regain God's favor. In essence, public confession of sin began to detach itself from the conversion narrative.

This detachment started with the very first Puritan revivals of the seventeenth century. David Hall quotes a sermon by John Davenport, the co-founder of New Haven, delivered less than twenty years after the colony's founding: "When people who have been formerly under the effects of Gods displeasure do turn unto Him with unfeigned Repentance, and Reformation of their former evil wayes, God will certainly turn unto them in mercy." This repentance and reassurance were intended for the regenerate colonists, who reacted to drought and other misfortunes by fasting, gaining "true sight of sin," repenting, and then rejoicing in a new sense of God's forgiveness and mercy.[13] American Puritan revivalism told a story of falling away: believers, already converted, had backslidden, and God's judgment was hovering above them. Public confession of sin, undertaken by the already-converted, was necessary before the community could return to God's favor.

The revivals of the eighteenth century, begun by the heirs of Puritanism, continued to emphasize the role of public confessions of sin, both by sinners converting to faith (as part of a conversion narrative) and by believers who had backslidden. In 1731, Jonathan Edwards preached his first published sermon, "God Glorified in the Work of Redemption." Sinners, he told his congregation, could prove that faith is real through confessing their sins:

> It is necessary in order to saving faith that man should be emptied of himself, be sensible that he is "wretched, and miserable, and poor, and blind, and naked". . . . It is the delight of a believing soul to abase itself and exalt God alone. . . . Hath any man hope that he is converted, and sanctified . . . that his sins are forgiven, and he received

into God's favour, and exalted to the honour and blessed-
ness of being his child, and an heir of eternal life? let him
give God all the glory; who alone makes him to differ
from the worst of men in this world, or the most misera-
ble of the damned in hell.[14]

Small wonder, then, that the 1734–1735 revival which broke
out under Edwards's preaching featured regular confession of
sin. The revival itself began in Northhampton, Massachussetts—
a city "not . . . much corrupted with vice," marked with "good
order . . . and purity in doctrine," thanks to the good pastoral
care its people had been receiving from Edwards's grandfather,
the redoubtable Solomon Stoddard. The citizens of Northhampton, Edwards explained in his own account of the revival,
were "noted for religion; and particularly remarkable for their
distinct knowledge of things that relate to heart religion, and
Christian experience, and their great regards thereto."[15]

Nevertheless, a number of them had "fallen away" and had
become less and less concerned with the things of God, so that
their more religious neighbours feared "that God was about to
withdraw from the land." During the 1734–1735 revival, hundreds were converted, but many backslidden believers also returned to the fold. Confession of sin, unconnected to the moment of conversion, was an essential element of this renewal.
Edwards himself offers a lengthy description of the already-
converted coming to the point of confession:

> [I]t is rare that any [who are converted] enjoy so full an
> assurance of their interest in Christ that self-examination
> should seem needless to them. . . . I think the main ground
> of the doubts and fears that persons after their conversion
> have been exercised with about their own state, has been,
> that they have found so much corruption remaining in
> their hearts. . . . When they . . . feel worldly dispositions
> working in them—pride, envy, stirrings of revenge, or
> some ill spirit towards some person that has injured them,
> as well as other workings of indwelling sin—their hearts

are almost sunk with the disappointment; and they are ready presently to think that they are mere hypocrites. They are ready to argue that, if God had indeed done such great things for them, as they hoped, such ingratitude would be inconsistent with it. They complain of the hardness and wickedness of their hearts; and say there is so much corruption, that it seems to them impossible there should be any goodness there. Many of them seem to be much more sensible how corrupt their hearts are, than before they were converted. . . . . They take more notice of what sin is there, which is now more burdensome to them; they strive more against it, and feel more of its strength. . . . . . They never realized it, that persons were wont to meet with such difficulties, after they were once converted . . . often, before the bestowment of any new remarkable comfort, especially after long continued deadness and ill frames, there are renewed humblings, in a great sense of their own exceeding vileness and unworthiness, as before their first comforts were bestowed.[16]

Edwards's uneasy Christians, continuing to confess their sins after they had received saving grace, were not unique. In 1740, the English Methodist George Whitefield and the New Jersey Presbyterian Gilbert Tennent began a preaching tour of New England that sparked a two-year revival. Whitefield's sermons continued to insist that willing confession of sin is vital, not just for the sinner approaching conversion, but for the already-converted. In "Marks of a True Conversion," Whitefield addresses those who already claimed Christ:

The Lord Jesus Christ knew . . . how desperately wicked and deceitful men's hearts were. . . . I think it is plain from many parts of Scripture, that these disciples, to whom our Lord addressed himself at this time, were in some degree converted before. . . . Our Lord means, that though they had already tasted the grace of God, yet there was so much of the old man, so much indwelling sin, and corruption, yet remaining in their hearts, that unless they were more converted than they were, unless a greater change past upon their souls, and sanctification was still carried on, they could give but very little evidence of their belonging to his kingdom. . . . I believe the words may be justly applied to saints and sinners; and as I suppose there are two sorts of people here, some who know Christ, and some of you that do not know him, some that are converted, and some that are strangers to conversion. . . . If ye confess your sins, and leave them, and lay hold on the Lord Jesus Christ, the Spirit of God shall be given you.[17]

Grover Cleveland, a lifelong Presbyterian, belonged not to the Catholic tradition of secret confession, but to this Protestant tradition, which encouraged saints to speak of their ongoing struggles with sin in the presence of other believers.

This sort of confession is exactly what the Reverend Kinsley Twining's intervention implied: when he announced with authority that Cleveland had behaved with honor, he was suggesting that a religious confession had already taken place. By inference, Cleveland's sin had been dealt with in the proper manner, in the presence of other believers. This impression was strengthened when the well-known Boston minister James Freeman Clarke met with Cleveland for a private conversation, and then threw his weight entirely behind Cleveland's candidacy.[18]

• • •

Although Cleveland's implied confession had not taken place in the full view of the general public, it had not been a strictly *private* confession. No Catholic priest, hearing the confession of a penitent, would report to the world that he had heard the case and absolved the sinner; the seal of the confessional prohibited even such an oblique revelation of what had been said inside.

But Protestant revivalism had done more than simply move confession to center stage of the sanctuary. By Cleveland's day, revivalist practice had also opened up the sanctuary to the gaze of the unconverted.

Strictly speaking, this had been the case since the eighteenth century. During the revivals of 1740–1742,[19] George Whitefield had departed from tradition by preaching outdoors. His ministry was carried on in open-sided tents and fields, literally within full public view. In an even more powerful sense, however, revivalists after Whitefield laid bare the mystical process of conversion, drawing away the veil of mystery from the sinner's rescue by God.

Whitefield's revivals, held outside the walls of local churches, channelled converts into the local pews; membership in the areas where Whitefield preached went up 400 percent during the years of his revivals. This dynamic held for the revivalist preachers who followed him. Revivals increased congregation size; this meant that the success of any particular revival could, theoretically, be *measured.*

In the half-century after Whitefield, the measurement of a revival's success tended to lie not only in the numbers converted, but also in the amount of religious sentiment on view. Whitefield's revivals were among the first to break the tradition of "respectful silence" in religious meetings, instead eliciting groans, sighs, and cries from his listeners; in his memoirs, Whitefield describes the "roarings, agonies, screamings, tremblings, dropping-down, ravings" of his listeners. "Thousands cried out, so that they almost drowned my voice," he wrote of a meeting in Pennsylvania."[20]

This was a style, as Mark Noll points out, that was easily transported to the frontier; and in fact revivalism moved west, breaking out at Cane Ridge in Kentucky. James McGready's Presbyterian congregation in Logan County had been praying for revival for three years; in 1800, a camp meeting at nearby Cane Ridge drew thousands. These meetings were noisy too, with listeners not only screaming and trembling, but also dancing, laughing, jerking, and barking.[21] The noisy, disruptive responses were themselves a public confession of sin, outward manifestations of the sinner's inward comprehension of his own guilt. "It is the will of God," revivalist James McGready asserted, "that the sinner should ... as a guilty condemned criminal, fall at the footstool of sovereign mercy, crying for pardon."[22]

The Cane Ridge response was hardly unique. Throughout the nineteenth century, attendees at camp meeting revivals continued to respond to the message of grace with unruly groans and sighs. Camp preacher Ezekiel Cooper, conducting revivals around the turn of the century, records that his listeners "in every part of the congregation" were "groaning for mercy" with "streaming eyes"; the architect Benjamin Henry Latrobe remarked (with some disapproval) on the "general groaning and shrieking" that accompanied a Virginia camp meeting in 1809.[23]

But as frontier areas were settled and towns became cities, the camp meetings became less ecstatic and more orderly. In Methodist hands, camp meetings developed their own set of rules for systematic proceedings, due in large part to Francis Asbury's insistence that "order, order, good order" characterize even the outpourings of the Spirit. By 1806, Methodist camp meetings were generally held from Friday afternoon until noon on Monday, and were advertised in advance. "Camp grounds" were set apart for the purpose of meetings. By the 1820s, an order of service was often prepared ahead of time and sometimes was printed and handed out. A regular 10 a.m. sermon became part of the day's work.[24]

As revivals were rationalized, the measure of their success increasingly shifted away from the volume of tears shed by the penitents toward a head count of the converted. In 1835, the Presbyterian-trained revivalist Charles Finney (who had been leading revivals in New York and Pennsylvania for the previous decade) published a handbook for revivalists. *Lectures on Revivals of Religion* laid out tried-and-true methods of drawing crowds and leading them to conversion; despite a perfunctory acknowledgment of the power of the Holy Spirit, the *Lectures* makes heavy use of the language of cause and effect.[25] A revival, Finney points out, is not a miracle; revival is not a "divine interference," but "a purely philosophical result of the right use of the constituted means." Revival should be judged "by the ordinary rules of cause and effect," and to treat it as a supernatural occurrence is "dangerous . . . to the prosperity of the church."[26] If a revival is planned and carried out in a rational manner, which includes providing comfortable seating ("If people do not sit easy, it is difficult to get or keep their attention"), preventing the meeting-house from becoming too warm ("the people, instead of listening to the truth, are fanning"), and properly advertising the meetings ("The object of our measures is to gain attention"), people will turn out and souls will be saved. Revivalists who pay no attention to the scientific laws of revival risk more than their livelihood: "And very often it is so," Finney warns, after covering air circulation, temperature, clean floors, and the necessity for people to leave dogs and noisy babies at home, "that if you drop a single link in the chain of argument, you lose the whole, and the people are damned, just because the careless church do not see to the proper regulation of these little matters."[27]

As revivals were regularized, so were the confessional responses of sinners; "order, order, good order" demanded that the confessions of sinners take place in a ritual space designated for this purpose. Finney was among the first revivalist preachers to marry together the revival-induced groans over sin and the conventions of the Puritan public profession of faith, producing—perhaps in its first widely-seen public incarnation—the ritual of coming forward to confess sin in response to Gospel preaching. Finney made use of an "anxious bench," borrowed from the Methodists, and encouraged those in his congregation who felt convicted of sin to come forward and wrestle in prayer on it, in full view of the rest of the attendees.[28] If Finney's convicted sinners needed to bark and faint, at least they had a special spot set aside for such activity. The ritual space for public confession had now become physically set off from the rest of the congregation.

In his classic study of Protestant revivals, William McLoughlin points out that, in the decades after Finney, revivalism completed the transition toward a business model. A revival, he concludes, was no longer held "to stir up pietistic fervor or millennial hope but to perform the routine function of maintaining a steady rate of church growth."[29]

The rationalization of revival reached a high point in the travelling campaigns of Dwight L. Moody, which began in the 1870s. Moody, a businessman by training, created "a complex division of labor with specialized roles and expertise to assure the smooth execution of every detail in the planning and execution of a revival."[30] "He looked like a businessman," the Reverend Lyman Abbott wrote approvingly, "he dressed like a businessman; he took the meeting in hand as a businessman would."[31] Moody advertised his revivals with handbills, posters, and newspaper ads, rather than waiting for the Holy Spirit to produce fervor: "It seems to me a good deal better to advertise and have a full house, than to preach to empty pews," he told his public. "This is the age of advertisement."[32]

Conversion was the goal of a Moody revival, as it had been for Finney and Whitefield. But in Moody's sermons the boundaries of public confession were broadened. Coming forward to the "anxious bench" was transformed into an "altar call"; the walk down to the front in order to demonstrate a change in life was still present, but Moody began to remove from it the embarrassment of admitting, publicly, to wrongdoing. In a Moody revival, the man or woman who responded to the altar call was a sinner—but that sinner walked forward, not to confess specific misdeeds, but to receive the love of Christ. The *form* of public confession of sin remained, and the confession took place within the same ritual space: a set-aside area at the front, in the sight of all present. But the "confession" itself was no longer merely one of sin. It was a "confession of faith," an admission of the willingness to receive what God would give. The walk forward, once an act of humiliation, was now merely an act of *humility*.

This was in line with Moody's pragmatic bent. He had no interest in defending theological positions that might drive sinners away; his goal was to get as many people converted as possible, by whatever means. His revivals *sold* the Gospel, offering sinners all the benefits of conversion while downplaying the possible drawbacks to coming forward. For this reason, he did not preach hellfire and damnation. "Christ's teaching was always constructive," he retorted to the revivalist R. A. Torrey, who had criticized him for failing to confront error directly. "His method of dealing with error was largely to ignore it, letting it melt away in the warm glow of the full intensity of truth expressed in love."[33]

As CEO of his own revival business, Moody became the center of a Gospel empire that encompassed a school for girls, another school for boys, a Bible training school, a summer conference site, and a publishing enterprise. It was a business, run by a businessman, making use of tried-and-true business techniques. Any member of the public who took the time to examine Moody's methods could understand his success; there was no need to be one of the elect to grasp how Moody won souls.

The Moody model was elaborated by his spiritual heir and successor, the Protestant baseball player-turned-evangelist Billy Sunday. Sunday, Grover Cleveland's contemporary, called his listeners to come forward without accusing them of moral blackness. "A man can be converted without any fuss," he insisted. "Multitudes of men live good, honest, upright, moral lives. They will not have much to change to become a Christian. . . . All God wants is for a man to be decent."[34] To walk forward in a Billy Sunday revival—to "hit the sawdust trail"—not only involved no humiliating confession, but did not even necessarily mean that you were being converted. Of Sunday's listeners who came forward and filled out a response card in answer to an altar call, between 50 and 80 percent checked "reconsecration." They had already been converted at some point in the past; they were coming down front to shake Billy Sunday's hand.[35] Sunday had expanded the forum of public confession yet again. It now encompassed not only confession of sin, but also the Moodyesque "confession of faith" and Sunday's own "confession of reconsecration."

Those response cards were important to Sunday. They served as the objective measure of a revival's success; afterward, he could provide local ministers with a head count of the people who had come forward and confessed. Theoretically, these confessing sinners would now seek out the pews of their local congregations. Sunday promised that this would benefit those ministers who supported his campaigns—a promise that William McLoughlin documents in his study of newspaper reports on Sunday's campaigns:

> Ministers whose church membership had increased as a result of a Sunday campaign wrote glowing reports of their newfound prosperity which were widely published in religious journals. One such minister claimed that Sunday's revival in his city "brought his church an addition of 305 members, . . . a beautiful $20,000 home, . . . increase of $600 in salary, . . . two weeks added to his vacation." Others told of new churches being erected, of enlarged Bible classes, and of old mortgages paid off, all because of the new zeal imparted by Sunday's preaching.[36]

Conversion was good business; confession brought benefit to more than the soul.

• • •

In Grover Cleveland's case, his implied confession—made before two different religious leaders who would testify on his behalf—brought him to the White House.

Here the double answer to the double riddle of Cleveland's success combines in a single explanation. As a confessing sinner, Cleveland admitted himself to be an ordinary man, as prone to struggle and fall as any member of the American public. The language of the Protestant confession had been levelling and egalitarian since the days of the Puritan revivals;[37] the sinner admitted himself to be, not holy and set apart, but a partaker in the common catastrophe of the Fall. "All have sinned and fallen short of the glory of God," the Epistle to the Romans decreed; "there is no one righteous; no, not one."[38] Luther's insight that *no one* could earn salvation through the ability to be good followed on the religious certainty that all were equally culpable in God's sight. Whether Cleveland ever actually made any sort of confession is beside the point. His implied confession satisfied the general public that his sins had been properly accounted for.

Grover Cleveland's scandal stands at a transitional moment in the history of public confession. Protestant revivalism had made the ritual of confession visible enough to be routine; thanks to this visibility, Cleveland could use the conventions of confession to reassure his public, while sidestepping a full public grovel. There were no rising and increasingly strident calls for him to make further public revelations about the exact nature of his involvement, which Cleveland attributed to his own skillful management of the affair. "I think the matter was arranged in the best possible way," he wrote to a friend, afterwards, "and that the policy of not cringing was not only necessary but the only possible way."[39] Cleveland was a competent politician, but in this he gave himself too much credit; in the 1880s, the practice of confession had not yet moved fully into public view.

A half-century later, another scandal would illuminate the next transitional moment in the history of confession. Aimee Semple McPherson, like Cleveland, avoided public confession. But as she did so, she used the new medium of radio to broadcast her alternate version of events, a decision which would help to bring public confession to the airwaves and into the limelight.

3

AIMEE SEMPLE MCPHERSON AND
THE DEVIL

I told the truth and walked in the light. I have nothing to confess.
—AIMEE SEMPLE MCPHERSON, 1927

AT 7:30 P.M. ON TUESDAY, MAY 18, 1926, the Angelus Temple in Los Angeles, California—a circular hall of concrete, topped with a dome and cross and flanked by radio towers—was filled with over seven thousand people who had come to see evangelist Aimee Semple McPherson's color slides of the Holy Land.

Less than four weeks before, McPherson had returned from a two-month journey that took her across Europe and into Jerusalem. In theory, the trip had been a vacation, forced upon the thirty-six-year-old evangelist by her mother and the staff of the Angelus Temple. McPherson was the linchpin of the entire Angelus Temple operation, which included not only regular services at the Temple that drew thousands, but also the publication of a regular magazine (*The Bridal Call*), a school for the education of future evangelists, regular radio broadcasts, over forty "satellite churches," and multiple campaigns, parades, and special events.[1]

Without McPherson, the whole ballooning operation might collapse, and McPherson had been preaching, broadcasting, travelling, and exhorting without pause. Her growing popularity had forced her to retreat on weekends to anonymous hotel rooms, where she could lock herself away from the public eye—a habit that had already caused journalists to prick up their ears. As early as August of the preceding year, McPherson's staff had been forced to explain this practice in words that suggest the possibility of scandal: "Sister McPherson always leaves the city after Friday evening services for her weekend rest," one official told the Los Angeles Times on August 30, 1925. "Nobody knows where she goes and . . . she seldom goes to the same place twice. Anyway, there's nothing to it."[2]

Now that McPherson had returned from her enforced "vacation" overseas, thousands had turned out to see color slides of the trip, an entertainment new to many of them. But when the May 18 service began, McPherson's mother Minnie Kennedy was standing on the platform to present the slides; McPherson herself was nowhere in sight.

When the slideshow ended, Minnie Kennedy announced calmly that McPherson had disappeared earlier in the day after setting out for a swim in the ocean. Her secretary, who had been with her, swore that she had watched McPherson swim into the ocean and disappear. "Sister is gone," Minnie Kennedy concluded. "We know she is with Jesus."[3]

Kennedy's immediate willingness to accept her daughter's death (only two days after the disappearance, she made the provisions of McPherson's will public) did not sit well with the Los Angeles authorities. Police divers continued to search along the ocean shore, while detectives hunted down reports that McPherson had been seen at a beach hotel or in a car after the supposed drowning. The New York Times speculated that McPherson had been kidnapped by "underworld characters" who resented her opposition to dance halls. A local doctor suggested that overwork had caused McPherson to snap, and that she was probably out "wandering demented in the wild Malibu hills."[4]

Meanwhile, reporters at the Los Angeles Times pointed out that McPherson's former radio engineer—a man named Kenneth Ormiston, whose close friendship with McPherson had caused so much gossip that McPherson had finally asked him to resign eighteen months earlier—had recently gone missing as well. In fact, Ormiston's wife had gone to the police and reported that "a certain prominent woman" was responsible for her husband's disappearance.

On June 20, a month after McPherson's disappearance, Minnie Kennedy held three memorial services for her daughter, complete with eulogies, memorial songs, flowers, and seventeen thousand weeping followers in attendance.[5] Three days later, Aimee Semple McPherson turned up at the police station at Douglas, Arizona, and was immediately taken to the local hospital.

From her bed, she told reporters her story. On May 18, she had been working on her sermons at the beach when a man and woman appeared, asking her to come to their car and pray for their dying baby. She agreed and walked with them to the car, where she was shoved into the back seat and chloroformed. Her kidnappers—a woman named Rosie, a man named Steve, and (in the words of the *Los Angeles Times*) a "huge ugly Mexican" named Felipe—took her to a "squalid little Mexican shack" and told her that they would hold her until a $500,000 ransom was paid; they also tied her hands and feet and tortured her with a cigar stub when she refused to cooperate. This went on until June 22, when McPherson's captors left her alone for the first time. "[A]lthough bound hand and foot," the *Times* reported, she "summoned all of her strength and rolled from the bed" in order to cut her bonds on the jagged edge of a tin can that lay on the floor. She then ran twenty miles through the desert, crossed over the U.S. border into Arizona, and collapsed.[6]

Despite the purple prose of the initial reports ("Mrs. McPherson wore a dainty pink silk dressing gown over a white silk nightgown," wrote *Los Angeles Times* reporter Read Kendall, "On her fingers were the marks of torture"), a note of skepticism rapidly appeared in newspaper coverage of McPherson's reappearance. By June 26, the *New York Times* was reporting that McPherson had "repeatedly failed" to identify any landmarks in Mexico along the route she had theoretically used in her escape. The next day, the paper trumpeted the news that a city official from Arizona had seen McPherson walking along a Tucson street during the weeks of her alleged captivity. The local sheriff pointed out that McPherson's clothing did not show signs of sweat or unusual wear. "I have no desire to cast any reflections on anyone," he wrote, delicately, "but my conclusions are that Mrs. McPherson's story is not borne out by the facts." Police from both Arizona and Mexico searched in vain for the "squalid Mexican shack."[7] Ormiston's reappearance did nothing to help McPherson's case; although he insisted he hadn't been with her, he had no proof of his whereabouts during the weeks in question.

McPherson's followers displayed no doubt in her story. On Saturday, June 26th, McPherson had arrived back in Los Angeles on the overnight train from Arizona. Over thirty thousand supporters greeted her train, cheering and throwing bouquets, and a band played hymns as she was carried on a flower-wreathed chair to her car.

But the Los Angeles district attorney, Asa Keyes (a personal friend of McPherson's), told reporters that he doubted that such a famous woman, "known almost all over the civilized world," could be "kidnapped in broad daylight from a crowded beach." On July 7, a grand jury was convened to hear McPherson's story, raising the possibility that she might be charged with filing a false police report. And the possibility of a more ominous charge arose when Keyes began to question McPherson and her mother about debts, including mortgages on the Angelus Temple itself. The *New York Times* reported that officials were particularly interested in "the alleged tampering with a letter . . . demanding half a million dollars for Mrs. McPherson's safe return." The *Times* added, "The ransom letter . . . was delivered to Angelus Temple prior to memorial services held there for the evangelist, during which a considerable sum of money is said to have been raised."[8]

McPherson refused to answer questions about the Angelus Temple finances, and lack of evidence that the letter had been generated by McPherson and her mother forced Keyes to drop this line of investigation. But his skepticism over the kidnapping tale was shared by the grand jury. Five days later, on July 20, the jury refused to issue any indictment against the unknown kidnappers.[9]

Encouraged by this public vote of no-confidence in McPherson's story, District Attorney Keyes spent the next six months gathering bits of evidence to prove that McPherson and Ormiston had spent the missing weeks together in a beach bungalow. Finally, the trickle of evidence pooled into a formal accusation. On September 17, the *New York Times* reported that Keyes had ordered the arrest of McPherson, Kennedy, Ormiston, and two others on charges of conspiracy to defeat justice. "It is with regret that I take action against a person so high in the religious esteem of many persons," Keyes told the *Times*, "but the community . . . would welcome a fair and open hearing of a situation which has become a national scandal." The *Times* speculated that Kenneth Ormiston had been granted immunity and would testify that he and McPherson had spent the weeks of her alleged captivity together.[10]

Barely two months later, Keyes was forced to ask that all charges be dismissed. His eyewitnesses had begun to change their stories, and bits of key evidence had mysteriously (and embarassingly) disappeared. Keyes insisted that the dropping of the charges did not prove McPherson's tale to be true. As far as he was concerned, McPherson had pulled a "disappearance hoax" and had managed to get away with it. McPherson's "so-called return from her so-called kidnapping," Keyes told the *New York Times*, would have to be "tried in the only court of her jurisdiction—the Court of Public Opinion."[11]

Neither the kidnappers nor the Mexican shack were ever found. The newspapers continued to suggest that McPherson had carried on a blatant affair with Ormiston and had lied to her congregation about it, after allowing them to believe she was dead. Yet the Court of Public Opinion declared McPherson innocent. She left California at once for an eighty-day national tour, and was greeted by throngs of cheering supporters at every stop. In New York, where the *Times* had provided unending hostile commentary on her ongoing legal troubles, she drew overflow crowds, despite a nor'easter that covered the city with snow. On her return to Los Angeles, she continued to preach to throngs at the Angelus Temple. Far from pushing her disappearance into the shadows, her followers celebrated its first anniversary by holding a party on the beach where she had allegedly been kidnapped.[12]

The year after the scandal, 1927, was McPherson's most successful year yet. Following her triumphant speaking tour, she incorporated the International Church of the Foursquare Gospel, founding a new Pentecostal denomination. In December of that year, reporter Sarah Comstock visited the Angelus Temple and wrote:

> [The worship of God] plays an important part in the drama, to be sure; but center stage is taken and held by Mrs. McPherson. It is in her praise that the band blares, that flowers are piled high, that applause splits the air. It is to see her and hear her that throngs travel, crushed in the aisles of electric cars, thrust, elbow, and bruise one another as they shove at the doors of her Temple. Ropes protect the several entrances; hundreds strain and struggle to be first when these are released. A whistle sounds, the ropes give way, a large detachment of the crowd surges through, as many as the ushers can handle. . . . Men and women stand against the wall, they sit upon the steps of the aisles, and still, when the final whistle blows, there are thousands turned away, thousands who stand for two, three, four hours on the street and in the nearby park, to listen to the concert and the inspired utterances as they scream themselves forth from the loud speaker outside the building.[13]

In the wake of a sexual scandal that should have destroyed her, Aimee Semple McPherson had become more popular than ever.

Some members of McPherson's own congregation did continue to question her story. One of her own temple administrators, Gladwyn Nichols, left the Angelus Temple ministry in July of 1927 (taking 280 congregants with him) and announced publicly that McPherson and her mother both had "a confession to make to the world" about the kidnapping. But McPherson retorted, "I told the truth and walked in the light. I have nothing to confess. I am not surprised at Mr. Nichols. . . . His [new] church needs advertising badly."[14] Nichols's demand remained the exception, not the rule, and McPherson never confessed any wrongdoing in connection with the disappearance—not even indirectly.

Even had McPherson wished to pursue the Cleveland strategy, it would have been exceedingly difficult for her to confess only to other believers within a protected sacred space. Her congregation was no longer a private place. The Angelus Temple was an auditorium where the business of revival was carried out, rather than a sanctuary where mysteries took place.

Likes Dwight Moody, McPherson had started out as a revival preacher, moving from city to city. She believed that she had been called to God's service during a 1915 camp meeting; seated in the congregation, she had gone forward to the front for the altar call, asked in tears "to be forgiven for wandering out of God's will," and recommitted herself to the service of Christ.[15] This was not a conversion, but the confession of a backslidden believer. McPherson had served with her first husband as a Pentecostal missionary in China for a brief period, but after his death in 1910 had returned to North America and remarried. Her sin, she believed, lay in her abandonment of full-time Christian ministry in favor of marriage and motherhood.

Now, re-energized by confession and forgiveness, she began to accept invitations to preach revival in small towns close to her childhood home. For the next eight years, she travelled from city to city, preaching in churches, auditoriums, outdoor arenas, and in her own canvas tents. As Lately Thomas would observe a half-century later,

> She was her own advance agent, business manager, and
> star of the show. She bossed the volunteer helpers who

were attracted to her in each town, arranged transportation, scattered handbills announcing her revivals, argued with unobliging police and fire inspectors, ordered the printing and paid the light bills[16]

Her revival meetings, unaffiliated with any local congregation, were often held in canvas "sanctuaries" that were (like George Whitefield's tents) literally open-sided.

Ground for McPherson's own sanctuary, the Angelus Temple, was broken in 1923, after nearly a decade of rootless revival preaching. The Temple, far from being a gathered congregation of visible saints, was a permanent camp-meeting; Blumhofer calls it "the hub of an evangelistic association rather than a typical independent church."[17] The Temple was not a sacred space within which McPherson could confess before other believers who were also self-admitted sinners, but an ongoing revival space, open and visible to all. The converted, the unconverted, the skeptics, the faithful, and (most of all) the reporters could all see directly into its center.

The visibility of the Temple services was magnified by McPherson's use of the relatively new medium of radio. McPherson had made her first steps into radio even before the Temple groundbreaking tok place. In April of 1922, she had been invited to preach her initial radio sermon on a San Francisco radio station. By the time she finished, the switchboard was lit up with phone calls—proving, as Edith Blumhofer notes, that "her invisible audience had indeed been large and far-ranging."[18]

McPherson seized at once on the possibility of communicating directly with that invisible and enormous army of followers. She preached several more times on a Los Angeles radio station before deciding that Angelus Temple needed a radio transmitter of its own. By 1923, she had begun a donation drive for the needed funds, using the Temple magazine *The Bridal Call* to reach her loyal followers. "These are the days . . . when the impossible has become possible!" she wrote in its pages. "Days more favorable than any that have ever been known for the preaching of the blessed Gospel of our Lord and Saviour, Jesus Christ! Now, the crowning blessing, the most golden opportunity, the most miraculous conveyance for the Message has come—The Radio!"

This chance to preach to the widest possible audience dovetailed with McPherson's Pentecostal beliefs. McPherson's particular style of revival preaching, indebted to the revivalist traditions of the eighteenth and nineteenth centuries, was also marked by the new theology of Pentecostalism.

The founding event of American Pentecostalism was the Asuza Street revival of 1906, which lasted for three years and drew crowds from all over the world.[19] The unique doctrine of Pentecostalism was the assertion that conversion was incomplete until it was followed by the baptism of the Holy Spirit, a supernatural experience of divine power that led the baptized to speak in tongues. Many Pentecostals had two different conversion narratives to tell. Pentecostals confessed their sins and were saved; then they confessed that they were cold believers, as McPherson had done in 1915, and they received the baptism of the Holy Spirit.[20]

This baptism was a symbol for the central belief of Pentecostalism: that the supernatural was real, present, powerful, and often even visible. Grant Wacker identifies several Pentecostal beliefs that demonstrate this: in the Pentecostal universe, demons and angels are "palpably real and always present"; miraculous healing shows the presence of Jesus Himself. For the Pentecostal believer, the present reality of the supernatural represented the imminent arrival of Christ on earth to set all things right, and the miracles that descend during Pentecostal worship are signs and wonders that prove the Second Coming is near at hand.[21] "Truly the Latter Rain had come," wrote one revivalist about the Asuza Street phenomenon, "and God was doing a new thing on the earth . . . The prophecy in Joel 2:28–32 was not all fulfilled at the first Pentecost, for we see . . . its ultimate fulfillment ushers in the return of the Lord."[22]

As a Pentecostal revivalist, Aimee Semple McPherson was not merely calling for the conversion of individuals. She was hoping to hasten the arrival of Christ. Pentecostal theology linked conversion and *parousia*: the "world-wide revival," announced the magazine of the Azusa mission, would act "to bring on Jesus."[23]

Thus the commitment to reach more sinners by radio was an active step in bringing Christ back. Radio's technological fit with the Pentecostal desire to hasten the millennial age by preaching the Gospel worldwide was so perfect that Pentecostals found it easy to identify the radio as a tool of the Spirit, "divinely inspired for the purposes of spreading the Christian message farther and faster, eclipsing time and transcending space, saving the heathen, bringing closer and making more probable the day of salvation."[24] Lest anyone doubt that radio was yet another tool for bringing in a new age, McPherson's call for donations to support the new radio ministry were accompanied by a drawing of the Angelus Temple, shining like the sun and bracketed by radio towers, with multitudes thronging toward it, as though pushing through the pearly gates into heaven itself.

The drive for contributions succeeded. By 1924, the Angelus Temple had its own broadcasting studio and its own station, KFSG. McPherson began regular broadcasts in February with a full program of music, readings, children's stories, and complete church services.[25] As far as McPherson was concerned, KFSG was a direct conduit for the voice of God Himself; when Herbert Hoover, then Secretary of Commerce, temporarily blocked McPherson's broadcasts in 1927 because she was wandering off her assigned wavelength, she sent him an indignant telegram:

PLEASE ORDER YOUR MINIONS OF SATAN TO
LEAVE MY STATION ALONE STOP YOU CANNOT
EXPECT THE ALMIGHTY TO ABIDE BY YOUR WAVE
LENGTH NONSENSE STOP

Help Convert *the* World *by* Radio

Greatest Opportunity to Spread Gospel World Has Ever Known

For Six Wonderful Months ANGELUS TEMPLE *has been scene of constant Holy Ghost Revival*

8000 Conversions.	Mighty Revival among the children.
1500 Baptized.	Watch Tower filled with intercessors night and day.
Hundreds Healed.	5000 voices lifted in Revival Song.
Hundreds filled with the Spirit.	Beautiful trained choir.
Almost 1000 young men and women uniting in crusade for souls.	30 piece orchestra.
	Great pipe organ.

Hundreds of Stirring Holy Ghost Sermons
By AIMEE SEMPLE McPHERSON, *Pastor-Evangelist*

All of These Meetings Might Have Been Broadcasted from Angelus Temple

Over a radius of 4800 miles, reaching hundreds of thousands in Canada, the United States, Mexico, Panama, Hawaii.

Think of the Prisons, Hospitals, Colleges, Steamships, Private Homes, Sick Rooms, Etc., now equipped with Radio receiving sets that await the message.

$25,000 Needed! :: *Donate Today!* :: *Share the Reward!*

Figure 3.1. The Angelus Temple

Ultimately, of course, McPherson's broadcasts *were* subject to Hoover's "wave-length nonsense." Radio was a two-way street. It brought McPherson into the homes of her listeners, but it also drew the entire listening audience back into the very core of McPherson's ministry. As a revivalist radio preacher, McPherson had no private area within the Angelus Temple; unlike Grover Cleveland, she was unable to confess in private and keep a dignified silence in public. She had to answer her critics directly, and in her own voice.

So, rather than confessing, McPherson chose to construct a story that would serve the same purpose. She knew it was essential for her to appear, not as a powerful leader who could use her popularity to raise money and do whatever she pleased, but as "one of them"—merely another Christian among Christians. Her story had to reassure not only her congregation but also her extended audience that she had not used her power to satisfy her own appetites.

The first facet of McPherson's strategy lay in her initial account of kidnapping. The account highlighted her essential vulnerability and weakness—largely by positioning her alongside the popular suffragists of the early twentieth century. In the 1920s, suffrage activists used their stories of brushes with the law and restraint by their enemies to demonstrate their heroism for the cause. Barbara Green describes how suffrage activists turned autobiographical accounts into suffrage speeches by publishing "testimonies of injuries suffered at the hands of anti-suffrage crowds or aggressive policemen. . . . [C]onfessions of the body in pain during hunger strikes and forcible feeding dominated the pages of . . . daily newspapers."[26] She calls this "spectacular feminism," and writes, "For feminists, the term [spectacle] was usually associated with the deliberate and sensational tactics used to draw public attention to the cause."[27]

McPherson's revival meetings themselves, with their pageantry and their appeal to listeners to "convert," or change their way of thinking, fit seamlessly into a suffrage movement

THE GOVERNMENT'S METHODS OF BARBARISM.

FORCIBLE FEEDING IN PRISON.

Figure 3.2. Suffrage Injuries: "The Government's Methods of Barbarism"

tactic that made heavy use of "street pageants" dramatizing the plight of women. McPherson's kidnapping tale extended this sense of identity. McPherson's reappearance in a hospital bed, dressed in white, and her account of being bound hand and foot by her male and female captors contain eerie echoes of contemporary suffrage cartoons. McPherson's opposition by the forces of law and order thus put her on the side of the angels; to be persecuted by the authorities was, for suffragettes, a badge of honor.

McPherson's exaggerated femininity also dovetailed with suffragette strategy, which strove to make "femininity visible." Green quotes Constance Lytton's *Prisons and Prisoners*: "There were no looking glasses anywhere in the prison except, so I heard it rumoured, in the doctor's room, but I never saw it when there. I did not attempt to dress my hair. . . . I had the greatest admiration for those prisoners who took a contrary view and who in the teeth of difficulties, such as no looking glass, an ever-diminishing supply of hair pins, and the brush and comb as described, yet managed to produce elaborately dressed heads of hair." Green herself argues that Lytton and other suffragettes "recontextualized female self-adornment" as an act of defiance.[28] In the same way, McPherson emphasized her own femininity when opposed by men: she wrapped herself in lace and silk, covered her chair and pulpit with flowers, and was frequently carried on a litter on the shoulders of four willing men. She could not be a liar or a sexual predator—not when she was so clearly identified with courageous victims and righteous martyrs. Like Cleveland, McPherson positioned herself as one of the "common people" in her flock, rather than a powerful leader.

And like Cleveland, McPherson managed to reverse the possible disadvantage of her gender. Cleveland had faced the possibility that he would be seen as a typical male exploiter, using his sexual prowess to victimize a helpless woman. As a female minister, McPherson had to face the possibility that she would be seen as a loose female, an Eve who had given in to temptation.

McPherson's own denomination viewed female ministers with suspicion. Due to its decentralized nature, Pentecostalism could not close its doors to women's leadership in the manner adopted by Protestant denominations.[29] But anecdotes of resistance to women's full participation in the shaping of Pentecostal theology abound. In 1905, an annual meeting of Pentecostal preachers passed a resolution to keep women out of "any pulpit within our bounds"; female evangelists were publicly rebuked during revival meetings; women's leadership was reckoned by many to be a sign of judgment, since Israel had been subject to female leadership as a punishment for moral decadence.[30]

Cleveland had managed to reverse the traditional seducer/seduced roles by implying that he had been the victim of a rapacious woman. Since the beginning of her ministry, McPherson had converted *her* gender into an advantage by linking herself to the promise of the Second Coming. In July 1922, she announced that the success of female preachers was indeed a "sign of the times," but a good sign: proof that the end times had come and the return of Christ was near at hand. "Women must preach to fulfill the Scriptures," she declared; and until Scripture was fulfilled, Christ would not come back to establish His kingdom on earth.[31] The "disadvantage" of her sex had been turned upside-down; her femininity was now the sign of her anointed power and her place in God's plan to restore the earth.

McPherson's story of her kidnapping used her femininity in exactly the same way. In a canny reversal of the Eve story, McPherson did not appear as a sexual predator giving in to the devil's temptation and then bringing down a righteous man, and so destroying Eden. Instead, she was an active agent of the new Eden, working hard to restore the new heaven and the new earth—and this had drawn the devil's wrath down upon her. Rather than confessing, McPherson placed herself on the front lines of a cosmic battle against the forces of evil. It was a strategy that meshed beautifully with her larger mission: to defeat Satan by bringing on the second coming of Christ.

As soon as the grand jury refused to affirm McPherson's kidnapping story, McPherson immediately made a statement, through her attorneys, welcoming their decision: "Mrs. McPherson's story . . . remains as firm and unshaken as the first time it was told," the attorneys declared. "The matter was taken before the grand jury . . . and has been thrashed out in a dignified manner. The vindication of Mrs. McPherson, who has withstood terrific attack of character assassination, has come at last. The official investigation not only bears her story out and proves it true, but reveals her to the world as a truthful, upright woman who has withstood the attacks in a religious, God-fearing manner."[32]

This startled onlookers who had thought the grand jury verdict proved exactly the opposite. But McPherson's strategy for dealing with her critics never varied from this point. According to her, the devil had attacked her reputation to prevent her from preaching the Gospel and destroying Satan's hold on this earth. But, with the help of God, she had triumphed. The Sunday after the grand jury issued its verdict, her sermon at the Angelus Temple began with the appearance of seven young actors, made up as demons, rising up out of painted craters and holding a meeting to discredit McPherson's character. McPherson, striding onto the stage, provided the dialogue:

> "Ah!" screamed the Devil, as he heard the pastor of Angelus Temple was only a poor little woman, "that makes it easier for all of us! All we have to do now is puncture the bubble of her reputation and she's gone! Go after her name, that's the way to wreck her!"

The sermon ended with two more actors, dressed as angels, floating down from the Temple dome; one brandished the sword of truth, while the other carried a chain to bind the devil and his lies.[33]

Blaming the devil was not only central to McPherson's defense, but also played into the most foundational longing of her hearers. Early Pentecostalism, writes Edith Blumhofer, was "most basically the expression of a yearning to recapture in the last moments of time the pristine purity . . . of personal Edenic perfection in this life."[34] In fact, the movement was itself a sign that the new heavens and the new earth—a recreated Eden—were just over the horizon. Pentecostals might locate their genesis at the Azusa Street Revival, but they knew that the first known "Spirit baptism" since the events recorded in Acts 2 had taken place on January 1, 1901, at Bethel College in Minnesota: the beginning of the new century, a date symbolizing the start of the new era of God's return.[35]

In this new era, every Pentecostal believer was a warrior with a "critical role to play in the defeat of Satan."[36] But the enemy was not human; and McPherson was careful to demonstrate that her opponents were not District Attorney Keyes and the

grand jury, or Robert Ormiston and his wife, or even her kidnappers. No: her enemy was the devil—and, unlike Eve,
McPherson had resisted his attacks. In all of her public statements about her kidnapping, McPherson reshaped the biblical
story of cosmic war so that she and Satan stood at the center of
it, nose to nose. Her position as a revivalist radio preacher
made the Angelus Temple an open-sided revival tent rather
than a protected "sanctuary," but rather than lament her lack
of privacy, McPherson expanded the story of her disappearance until it encompassed the entire universe and all of time,
and invited the world to look on as she returned and took up
her place on the side of holiness. "The local district attorney
has the newspapers on his side," H. L. Mencken commented in
December of 1926, just before Keyes was forced to drop the
charges against McPherson, "but Aimee herself has the radio,
and I believe that the radio will count most in the long run." [37]

In November of 1926, with her trial for perjury still loom-
ing, she announced that she would preach a sermon about
"the world's biggest liar." An expectant mob gathered, hoping
that she would finger an earthly culprit, but they were disappointed. "Contrary to general expectation," a reporter from
the *Los Angeles Times* wrote, "the unique figure is not a public
official nor a witness of record . . . [T]he world's greatest falsi-
fier, according to Mrs. McPherson, is none other than 'The
Devil—The Father of Lies.'"

A month later, McPherson staged a "Tableaux of Martyrs" at
the Angelus Temple, a seven-scene dramatic presentation that
began with the crucifixion of Christ, continued on with the
deaths of St. Stephen, St. Paul, and Joan of Arc, and ended
with a scene from the present day: a Bible "placed on a chair.
Lying beside it were a pair of scissors and a pile of mud." Right
after the charges were dropped, she had told a capacity crowd
in New York, "I can see [Satan] down in hell, hearing reports
from his captains. One came and said that he had bad news:
a great revival in Los Angeles, saving souls by the thousand.
The revivalist cannot be stopped. 'What, a woman!' exclaimed

Satan. 'That's easy, we'll prick her reputation and we'll destroy her like a bubble.' . . . They thought with me out of the way Angelus Temple would collapse, and it didn't . . . The 'Four-Square Gospel' carries on! Hallelujah!"[38]

McPherson kept hold of her following by positioning herself as a modern-day Stephen, an anti-Eve, a holy warrior, a woman who fought the devil and won. Less than ten years after the alleged kidnapping, a professor of rhetoric noted in the pages of a speech journal that McPherson's stories followed the well-known story patterns adopted by the penny papers of her day;[39] her story was one of a brave heroine wronged by the ultimate super-villain, a string-pulling Satan who made both kidnappers and law enforcement officials dance to his tune. This heroine would ultimately be vindicated and meet her Bridegroom to live forever in the ever-after of the new heaven and new earth.

Thus, deprived of the luxury of implied confession, McPherson had followed Grover Cleveland's lead and downplayed her personal power, emphasizing her solidarity with the weak and downtrodden, placing herself in opposition to the powerful political leaders of her day, and insisting on her own vulnerability. And she had added an extra element to the Cleveland strategy: she had placed herself on the side of good, in the cosmic battle between good and evil.

In the coming decades, politicians and preachers accused of wrongdoing would find themselves forced to adopt exactly the same posture. Unlike McPherson, though, they would not always be able to avoid full and open confession. Between McPherson's disappearance and a tragedy at Chappaquidick, confession itself would move to the center of the open space that the revivalists had unveiled.

4

CONFESSION GOES PUBLIC

*In God's design, the radio has been invented particularly for
the use of His Church and the upbuilding of His Kingdom.*
—EUGENE BERTERMANN, 1943

FORTY-THREE YEARS after McPherson's triumphant non-confession, Ted Kennedy's car plunged off the Dike Bridge and into the water below, drowning his passenger. Kennedy's chances of winning the White Houses may well have ended at the moment his car left the road. But his attempts to explain himself after the event extinguished any possibility that he might recover from the scandal.

As a lifelong Catholic, Kennedy found himself at cross purposes with the relatively new visibility of public confession. In Protestant hands, public confession had become detached from its moorings; no longer solely an element of the conversion narrative, it had taken its place as an element of public worship in its own right. Revivalists had already made the rite of repentance and renewal increasingly visible to the outside gaze. Between McPherson's rise to superstardom and the beginning of Edward Kennedy's political career, the ritual of public confession moved from the revival tent onto the airwaves, from the sanctuary into the therapist's office, and from sacred spaces to the center stage of secular American culture.

• • •

In McPherson's day, revivalists and evangelical preachers did not dominate the airwaves; in fact, they were blocked from most of the national radio networks. This embargo had resulted from a series of theological debates that began in the 1920s, dividing American Protestant Christianity into fundamentalists and modernists—two distinct branches of faith separated from each other by their view of Scripture, their take on modernism, and their understanding of how the Gospel should be spread.

Fundamentalists drew their name from *The Fundamentals,* a four-volume collection of essays published in 1909 under the direction of Moody disciple R. A. Torrey. According to these essays, which were welcomed by conservative Protestant ministers across the country, the five "fundamentals" of the Christian faith were the inerrancy of Scripture (which implied a literal reading of both the Old and New Testaments), the virgin birth of Christ, justification of sinners by the death of Christ, Christ's bodily resurrection, and the historical reality of miracles. As an adjunct to this, fundamentalists were convinced that America had fallen away from a previous shared Christian faith, and that personal evangelism leading to conversion was the only Biblical method of bringing the United States back to godliness.

George Marsden points out that by 1920, the "conservative evangelical community" (his term for those evangelicals who agreed with *The Fundamentals*) had by and large come to agree with the militant Presbyterian writer David S. Kennedy that although America was "born of moral progenitors and founded on an eternally moral foundation . . . purified by fire, and washed in blood," her Christian character was under assault. According to Kennedy, modern critical thought (for example, the historical-critical methods that viewed Scripture primarily as a product of man's creativity) was "poisoning and overthrowing" the biblical influences that made America great. The only way to avoid collapse was for America to "return to her standard of the word of God. She must believe, love and live her Bible . . . or else she might collapse."[1] This was the resurrection of the old Puritan revivalism, in which conversion of the individual could lead to the renewal of a nation. The fundamentalist call for individual renewal was also a call for the conversion of America—or, more accurately, the *re*-conversion.

Meanwhile, mainline Protestants welcomed many of the innovations of modernism, including the insights of biblical higher criticism, which encouraged much less dependence on literal readings of Scripture. As both George Marsden and Grant Wacker point out, the militant fundamentalism of the 1920s was a direct response to the spreading influence of "modernist thinking" which, in the hands of mainline Protestants, shaped a "New Theology." New Theology pastors were "persuaded that God is immanent in the process of modern culture" and were committed not only to Biblical higher criticism, but also to "a progressive view of history, and the notion that contemporary science and philosophy are in some sense normative for Christian theology."[2] Mainline ministers were much more likely to concentrate on social action and reform, rather than individual conversion, as the preferred way to make known the good news of Christ.

Essentially, mainline and fundamentalist methods of spreading the Gospel were grounded in two distinctly different views of human nature. Fundamentalist readings of the Old Testament yielded a picture of each individual soul as essentially fallen, self-serving and self-deceived. The evils of society were due to the evil nature of the individuals who made up society; therefore, the way to ameliorate social ills was to convert each individual man, one by one. Modernists, on the other hand, were willing to accept the new insights of social scientists who suggested that men were formed by their social surroundings, rather than vice versa. By tackling social ills directly, mainline thinkers were also attempting to redeem individual human souls—by removing the social evils that were seen as the source of individual wrongdoing.

This clash in Gospel-spreading methods lay at the center of a mainline/fundamentalist struggle over the right to use radio and television to preach the Protestant message. Mainline preachers, less suspicious of scientific advance than their fundamentalist brethren, seemed the natural beneficiaries of the new technologies. Yet a series of complex interactions between the two branches of Protestantism yielded ultimate control of the airwaves to the fundamentalists.

The approach of mainline Protestants to religious broadcasting was, in the early decades of the twentieth century, largely shaped by the desire of mainline ministers to distance themselves from preachers with revivalist ways—in other words, fundamentalists. In 1923, the mainline Protestant journal *The Christian Century* suggested that religious broadcasting was valuable because it could act as an "inconvenience to religious narrowness" (a code name for fundamentalism) and hasten the day of universal ecumenicism: "Vast congregations, without thought of name or creed, repeat the Lord's Prayer after the minister and hear his sermon, critically but intelligently," the *Christian Century* declared. "The new invention . . . is likely to work many a change in preaching style, in religious attitudes, and in the coming of a more catholic consciousness to the church of Christ." Mainline Protestant broadcasts should emphasize education, which might ameliorate social ills, over "gospel preaching," which emphasized individual conversion. The *Christian Century* even suggested that services without sermons (and their attendant altar calls) were most likely to meet this goal.[3]

The clash between mainline and fundamentalist styles was intensified by the limited amount of air time available for religious broadcasts. The national networks did not accept paid religious programming; instead they set aside a certain number of "public service" hours for religious broadcasts. In 1927, a committee of mainline ministers recommended to the new National Broadcasting Company (NBC) that five principles govern all public service religious broadcasting. The first three were designed to block evangelistic preaching: religious broadcasting should serve "national agencies of great religious faiths . . . as distinguished from . . . small group movements"; programs should be "nonsectarian and nondenominational"; and sermons should be "of the widest appeal" and deal only with "the broad claims of religion." In case a fundamentalist preacher should wiggle through the fence, however, the fifth principle would serve as an impenetrable wall: "National religious messages should only be broadcast by the recognized outstanding leaders of the several faiths as determined by the best counsel and advice available."[4]

The limited public service hours were promptly monopolized by the "recognized outstanding" Protestant leaders, who were all mainline preachers. Thus, the airtime allotted by the major networks for religious broadcasts was kept well out of the hands of their fundamentalist, conversion-preaching competitors— and was also off limits to Pentecostals, who certainly did not qualify as recognized outstanding leaders preaching nonsectarian messages. Harry Emerson Fosdick, minister of First Presbyterian Church in New York, put the fears of his mainline colleagues into words. "The air will be full of sermons in any case," he told a fellow minister. "The query is only whose sermons will be on the air. It is needless to name those representing a type of Christianity which you and I do not believe in. Ought we to leave the air to their monopoly? I do not believe we should."[5]

Neither Protestant fundamentalists nor their Pentecostal brethren were willing to give up the battle for airtime. Both groups of preachers believed that the conversion of sinners was central to the victory of the kingdom of heaven in the ongoing, invisible battle between good and evil. Thus the preaching of the Gospel to the entire world would hasten the defeat of Satan, and the enormous reach of radio made it the best possible weapon in the holy war. "We who are Christians," announced the evangelist Eugene Bertermann in 1947, "know that in God's design the radio has been invented particularly for the use of His Church and the upbuilding of His kingdom."[6]

Fundamentalist preachers, largely blocked from making use of the time set aside for religious broadcasting by the national networks (which sent their programming to local affiliates all over the country, thus guaranteeing national exposure), went directly to local stations. Each of these stations covered only a single geographical area—but unlike the national networks, they were willing to hand over large chunks of airtime in exchange for cash. Fundamentalist institutions such as the Bible

Institute of Los Angeles (BIOLA) and Moody Bible Institute even built their own stations. A *Sunday School Times* directory of conservative Protestant radio programs, published in 1932, lists over four hundred, all broadcasting on local stations.

Like fundamentalists, Pentecostal preachers also went directly to local stations. Aimee Semple McPherson's broadcasts from the Angelus Temple tower in the 1920s and 1930s were followed by scores of other Pentecostal broadcasts from other local stations; Pentecostal evangelists, such as William Branham and Kathryn Kuhlman, were able to vault to the same level of national exposure as Charles Fuller and other non-Pentecostal fundamentalists. A casual listener in the 1930s, flipping around the dial, was far more likely to come across a local fundamentalist or Pentecostal preacher calling for repentance than a genteel mainline message.

The arrival of television on the broadcast scene sharpened the competition between mainline and fundamentalist/Pentecostal programming. But religious programming on television was pioneered not by Protestants, but by a Catholic priest.

Catholic radio broadcasts had fallen into easy alignment with mainline Protestant programming, thanks to the willingness of mainline leaders to recognize Catholic priests as qualifying for the category of "recognized outstanding leaders of the several faiths," and thus eligible to broadcast "national religious messages." In return, Catholic programming was overwhelmingly oriented not towards conversion but towards education, making it compatible with mainline mores. Catholic priest Charles Coughlin began a regular national broadcast in 1926 and gained a huge audience.[7] In 1928, the Paulist Fathers sponsored a series of radio talks given by Fulton J. Sheen, an ordained priest who held two doctorates in philosophy and theology and taught at Catholic University. Two years later, Sheen's frequent appearances became a regular radio program, *The Catholic Hour.*[8] The programs, like those offered by mainline Protestants, were designed to educate listeners—and did not include any calls for conversion.

Sheen's radio presence shifted to television in 1952, when *Life Is Worth Living* became the first religious television program to airing regularly. Like his radio appearances, Sheen's television program was aimed at general religious education, not conversion. A typical sermon from *Life is Worth Living*, "How to Have a Good Time," begins with quotes from Seneca and Samuel Johnson. Sheen then presents his central thesis: "The truth of the matter is that the greatest pleasures and joys come when we are unconscious of time." He covers various false or neurotic ways of escaping time (opiates, surrounding oneself with noise) and finishes by explaining that three conditions are necessary for happiness: endless life, the possession of timeless truth, and timeless love. These are found only in the definition of God, and so "the possession of God is happiness." [9] When other Catholic priests criticized Sheen's failure to call sinners to repentance, he answered: "If the seed falls they have 52,000 branch offices of the Catholic Church where they can get instructions." [10]

Sheen's success was phenomenal. He was on the cover of *Time* magazine; he won an Emmy; and, in the ultimate proof of success, he was approached by secular American companies who offered to become commercial sponsors of his program. [11] Mainline Protestant use of the airwaves followed Sheen's lead. On television, as in radio, mainline Protestants involved themselves in educational programs with a wide intended audience: discussion shows, in which theologians talked about "religion in daily life"; religious drama; and Bible stories. [12]

The national television networks, like the national radio networks, did not accept payment for religious programming. Once again fundamentalist and Pentecostal preachers found themselves forced to buy time on local stations to get their messages out.

But the mainline strategy to block fundamentalism backfired in a spectacular fashion, leading to an almost total domination of the airwaves by fundamentalist and Pentecostal preachers. Mainline domination of the airwaves began to disintegrate when mainline leaders decided that it was inappropriate for them to buy airtime. Instead, they should continue to rely on the free time provided by the national networks.[13] In 1958, the National Council of Churchs formed a Study Commission on the Role of Radio, Television, and Films in Religion, which reached the conclusion that religious programming would be debased if it were sold to the highest bidder.

Meanwhile, fundamentalists and Pentecostals did not hesitate to ask for contributions from their listeners. The task of preaching the Gospel worldwide was too important to be held hostage by worries about what was or wasn't "debasing." By the early 1950s, scores of fundamentalist and Pentecostal preachers were raising funds and buying local television time in order to take their revivals and healing services directly to the American public. The Pentecostal revivalist Rex Humbard gave up his travelling campaigns and instead built a revival center especially designed for broadcasting his services on local television.[14] In Oklahoma, Pentecostal healer Oral Roberts began a radio broadcast in 1947 and a regular television program in 1954.[15] By 1958, the Roberts program was carried on 136 stations; Roberts grew so popular that *Life* magazine profiled him, along with another young evangelist named Billly Graham, as one of the "new revivalists" who were reviving the tradition of revival.[16]

With Oral Roberts, the *form* of public confession—walking down to the front in order to confess a need—reached a new height of national exposure. Roberts's services often involved two kinds of confession. The first was a traditional call to repentance and salvation, as described by a reporter who attended a Roberts service in person:

> Then he prays: "Dear God, grant me this miracle tonight. . . . Don't let [anyone] . . . who has heard me preach tonight, go to hell. . . . I want every man, every woman, every boy, and every girl here, who believes . . . that you may find the forgiveness of God for your many sins . . .

stand up on your feet! . . . You who are standing . . . come right now. Oh, thank God, they're coming down every aisle! Now, lift your heads, neighbors, and see what God is doing."

According to this report, quoted in Roberts's autobiography, as many as five thousand sometimes responded.[17]

After the call to confession and salvation, Roberts usually issued another call, this one for healing. Roberts himself describes a typical response: "When I gave the invitation, over three hundred came down the aisles to be saved. Following the altar call, we announced that I would pray for as many sick as were there. . . . More than a thousand people rose and came forward to be healed."[18] Roberts called this the "prayer line."

The prayer line was an orderly, ritualized procedure. The people in line filed in front of Roberts one at a time as he leaned down to place his hands on each one. While laying on hands, Roberts carried on a constant flow of conversation which emphasized the active, willing submission of the sick person to the power of God, and sometimes also addressed the sickness as an evil which needed to be recognized and cast out: "Brother! You got something. Go on and believe God . . . . Brother, take that home with you! . . . . Thou foul, tormenting TB, come out of this man! Come out of him! Come-on-out-of-him! Oh, glory! It's coming, Brother, did you feel that?"[19]

The Roberts prayer line, broadcast weekly for a number of years, was carried on a web of local stations that covered much of the midwest and a good part of the east. The prayer line took the elements of the classic Protestant public confession— the coming forward, the admission of weakness, the submission to the preached word of an evangelist—and placed them in an atmosphere where the sin became entirely externalized. To come forward in the prayer line was to come forward as a penitent, but not as one bearing blame; it was to come forward free of any admission of guilt. Sickness, unlike sin, did not imply that the penitent had yielded to temptation. In fact, since

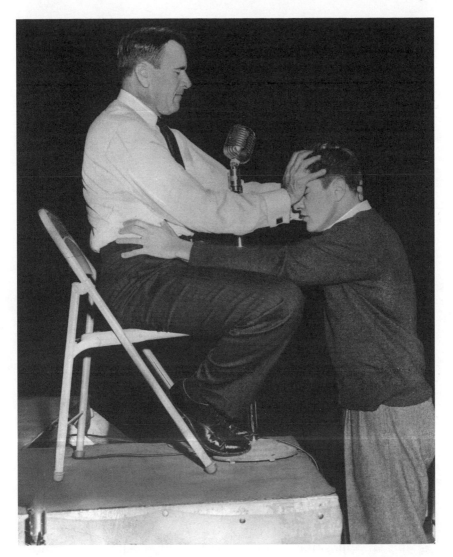

Figure 4.1. Oral Roberts's Prayer Line

Roberts often characterized sickness as caused by evil spirits, to admit to sickness was to *become* the battlefield between good and evil.

This kind of confession was even freer of embarrassment than the Moody altar calls of sixty years before. It implied no wrongdoing on the part of the "penitent." Rather, the person making the confession was coming forward to occupy the ritual space of the confession for two purposes. In the ritual space of confession, the "penitent" could *get* from God; in the early Roberts campaigns, the benefit for the penitent was primarily physical healing, but in his later campaigns, Roberts began to promise financial prosperity as well, a promise that became even more explicit in the sermons of later health-and-wealth evangelists.[20]

Roberts made an additional innovation in the practice of public confession; he used television to expand the response from the congregation. In his televised services, he would issue a call to his congregation to come forward to the ritual space at the front of the church, either for conversion or for healing. Then he would turn to the cameras and tell each watcher at home to symbolically join in this "altar call," either by placing a hand on the television and praying, or by placing "his hand on his heart and pray[ing] either for himself or for others who needed healing."[21] By widening the audience, television was extending the duty of response from the members of the Protestant congregation to a much wider segment of the population.[22]

A third group soon joined the Pentecostal-fundamentalist axis: neoevangelicals.[23] The militant fundamentalism of the 1920s had proved unsatisfying to many conservative Protestants. In its battle against theological liberalism, fundamentalism had also set itself against contemporary culture.[24] Billy Sunday's rhetoric, which places conversion and the social gospel in opposition, is typically fundamentalist: "You cannot bathe anybody into the kingdom of God," Sunday roared at his congregations.

[T]he road into the kingdom of God is not by the bath tub, the university, social service, or gymnasium, but by the blood-red road of the cross of Jesus Christ. . . . Take your scientific consolation into a room where a mother has lost her child. Try your doctrine of the survival of the fittest with that broken-hearted woman. Tell her that the child that died was not as fit to live as the one left alive. Where does that scientific junk lift the burden from her heart?[25]

As American popular culture absorbed more and more "scientific junk," fundamentalists were increasingly forced to isolate themselves from it, rejecting science-influenced educational trends and social movements; in the words of Mark Noll, fundamentalists had "lost the battles against evolution and the higher criticism of Scripture" and so "had angrily opted out of mainstream academic life." But a growing corps of younger, educated fundamentalists were increasingly discontent with the *de facto* exclusion of the fundamentalist viewpoint from mainstream America. Neoevangelicalism is characterized by this fusion of fundamentalist theology with a re-engaged perspective on American culture.[26]

Like fundamentalists, neoevangelicals affirmed the five fundamentals of the Christian faith. Like fundamentalists, neoevangelicals continued to insist on the centrality of individual conversion: "It is still the good pleasure of God to save by the foolishness of preaching them that believe."[27] Like fundamentalists, neoevangelicals believed that modernism was potentially destructive.

But unlike fundamentalists, neoevangelicals believed that modernism should be fought from the inside. They chose to participate *in* mainstream American culture, rather than completely rejecting it. In Douglas Sweeney's phrase, neoevangelicals hoped to *infuse* America with the Gospel, by taking part in education, politics, and even entertainment while operating from a conservative theological viewpoint.[28] The establishment of the magazine *Christianity Today* in 1956, in order to share "the depth and transforming power of the Gospel as it permeates all spheres of life," stands as a milestone in the self-identification of these re-engaged fundamentalists as neoevangelicals.[29] *Christianity Today's* first editor and co-founder, Carl F. H. Henry, had ten years earlier published one of the founding documents of neoevangelicalism, *The Uneasy Conscience of Modern Fundamentalism.*[30]

The other co-founder of *Christianity Today,* Billy Graham, became one of the most visible neoevangelicals. Thanks to his high profile, he played a pivotal role in bringing the practice of public confession onto the largest stage yet.

After graduating from college in 1943, Graham had conducted traditional revivals all around the country, drawing respectable but not large crowds. A 1948 campaign in Altoona, California, was so sparsely attended that Graham himself called it a "flop" and considered going back to school for a Ph.D. instead of staying on the revival trail. Several months later, ushers at a Los Angeles meeting were forced to space the congregation widely through the arena where he was preaching so that it would look less empty.[31]

Late in 1949, however, the newspaper publisher William Randolph Hearst heard good reports of Graham from one of his California editors and sent a telegram to all of his papers, telling them to "Puff Graham." Within weeks, Billy Graham's revivals had been headlined by fourteen Hearst papers. Stories in *Time, Life,* and *Newsweek* followed. The series of meetings Graham was in the middle of conducting in Los Angeles had to be extended five additional weeks, and Graham grew so desperate for sermon material that, in one of the last meetings, he read Jonathan Edwards's "Sinners in the Hands of an Angry God" word for word.[32]

Graham's choice of the Edwards sermon revealed his determination to call sinners to confession and redemption; his term for his evangelistic campaigns, "crusades," places him squarely within the "holy war" rhetoric used not only by McPherson but by scores of fundamentalist and Pentecostal preachers who followed her. In 1951, he too entered the broadcast fray by buying local television time for a program which he called *Hour of Decision* (actually a half-hour program), produced at KTTV in Los Angeles. But most of Graham's resources were spent on broadcasting his evangelistic crusades as special television events, using the airwaves as a massive revival tent.[33] In this way he gained a national reputation and a national audience. Huge numbers of TV-watchers tuned in; they heard Graham preach, but most of all, they saw crowds of people going forward on television, entering that ritual space of confession in floods. According to the evangelist's own records, in one ten-day campaign in California, around 384,000 people attended and 20,336 came down to the front and "made a decision" to be saved. And although the pentitents came forward not only to admit sin, but also to reaffirm their commitment to the Christian faith, the confession of sin remained central to Graham's rhetoric: "You have to be willing to repent of your sin and receive Christ into your heart," he preached in one of his many evangelistic sermons. "The Bible says, 'He that hardeneth his heart, being often reproved, shall suddenly be cut off, and that without remedy.' . . . [I]f you know you need Christ and you repent of your sin, then receive Him by faith . . . ."[34] Graham's words consistently re-connected the act of walking forward to the altar with an admission of sinfulness.

National networks often cancelled regular programming to cover the Graham crusades, which were special events viewed by as many Americans as had tuned in to Queen Elizabeth's coronation The sheer size of the televised confessing crowds (which increasingly took place in huge mainstream venues, such as stadiums, auditoriums, and even Madison Square Garden) brought Graham's campaigns right to the center of the American consciousness, and haloed his revivals with a mainstream acceptance that the local broadcasts of Oral Roberts and Rex Humbard would never achieve.

Clearly, revivalist preaching was capable of drawing a national audience, and fundamentalists, Pentecostals, and neo-evangelicals (henceforth, the "new evangelical alliance") grew increasingly irate over the mainline monopoly on free broadcast time.[35] *Christianity Today* pointed out that, going by the numbers, members of the new evangelical alliance constituted a bigger group than mainline Protestants and so deserved approximately

63 percent of the available public-service broadcast time; the conservative National Religious Broadcasters (formed in 1944 to combat new network policies that made it almost impossible for revivalist programming to gain significant air time) began to work more aggressively to change broadcast policies.[36]

And then the ground abruptly shifted. In 1960, the FCC ruled that networks could fulfill their responsibility to provide a certain amount of public service programming by *selling* air time. It was no longer necessary to make this time available free of charge.

Given that mainline denominations had come out strongly against on-air fundraising, this left mainline ministers without any good way to pay for the airtime which they had previously gotten for free. Fundamentalist, Pentecostal, and neoevangelical preachers, on the other hand, were accustomed paying their own way by raising funds from their listeners. By the end of the 1960s, religious programming coming from the new evangelical alliance had almost driven mainline programming from the airwaves.[37]

This programming was overwhelmingly conversion-oriented. "Christians are swept up in the third great revolution of human history," *Christianity Today* exulted in 1966, right before the World Congress on Evangelism, held in Berlin. This "revolution" in communication "offers worldwide information networks for presenting our Lord to a needy audience of billions." Television was equally promising; in 1968, *Christianity Today* called it "the most effective means of penetrating closed doors and closed minds that the Church has ever had. . . . If we fail, the world will never find the only solution to its desperate need." In that same year, just months after Chappaquiddick, the Pentecostal evangelist Jimmy Swaggart announced that he would spread the "old-fashioned Gospel to all nations on earth" through international television broadcasts.[38]

• • •

While religious confession was rising to higher and higher visibility, a secular form of confession was also developing in the

United States. It grew along a different trajectory than religious confession, but it too had strong connections with Protestant Christianity.

Until 1909, the care of the will and emotions had belonged to priests and pastors, who had the spiritual responsibility of dealing with the non-physical aspects of the person. In his history of psychotherapy in America, Eric Caplan points out that psychotherapy was "virtually nowhere to be found" as late as 1907. In that year, physician David Wells wrote that a doctor needed "courage and self-reliance to openly advocate and practice" therapeutic techniques which relied on mental, rather than physical, remedies. Medical training equipped doctors to deal with physical symptoms only. Insofar as physicians took notice of mental anguish, they were taught to view it as the outgrowth of some undiagnosed bodily condition.[39]

By the end of the decade, however, the first organized American attempt to bring psychotherapy under the umbrella of medicine had begun. The "Emmanuel movement" started in November of 1906, when the Emmanuel Church of Boston, a revered and socially respectable Episcopalian institution, sponsored a meeting for "neurasthenics" (patients who had been diagnosed with "nerve diseases" that resisted treatment) in which a physician and an Episcopalian minister both addressed the sufferers.

This public acknowledgment that not all diseases could be treated solely by somatic means gained an enthusiastic hearing. Similar meetings and classes sprang up all through the United States, and ministers from other Protestant denominations joined in.[40] Hundreds of patients attended.

The growing popularity of the joint spiritual-physical approach to neurasthenia drew increasing criticism from prominent physicians. But, as Caplan points out, this vocal opposition to the new "psychotherapy" reflects its every-increasing visibility in the public eye.[41] In the fall of 1908, the first issue of the journal *Psychotherapy: A Course of Readings in Sound Psychology, Sound Medicine, and Sound Religion* appeared, carrying articles from both physicians and clergymen. In 1909, Sigmund Freud spoke for the first time in the United States, giving a series of lectures in Massachusetts. The groundwork done by the Emmanuel movement guaranteed that his talks would be reported on by the popular press. Less than a decade later, the need to treat World War I veterans suffering from mental trauma added momentum to the gathering popularity of psychotherapy.[42]

From the earliest days of the Emmanuel movement, psychotherapy was frequently practiced in group settings. Much psychotherapy was based on the relatively new idea of the "social self"—a concept championed in the 1920s and 1930s by (among others) John Dewey, Charles Horton Cooley, and George Herbert Mead. This "new socio-psychological concept of identity . . . described the individual as inseparable from the greater whole."[43] Group therapy simply treated the individual within the context of that "greater whole." Psychotherapist L. Cody Marsh adopted as his slogan, "By the crowd they have been broken; by the crowd they shall be healed."

The notion that the human self was formed by society was antithetical to fundamentalists, since it reduced the doctrine of original sin to nonsense. It was also repugnant to Catholic theology; the privacy of the Catholic confessional acknowledged that the soul, as an individual creation of God, needed no community other than that of God and the (authoritative) priest to reach a true understanding of itself. But for psychotherapists who held to the ideas of Dewey, Cooley, and Mead, therapy in the presence of others made perfect sense.

This psychotherapeutic view of the self was anti-elitist; an individual whose personality has been molded by society can hardly claim superiority over its other members. Therapy groups were intended to function as ideal mini-societies, healing the rifts in personality caused by earlier social influences. Thus, therapy groups were theoretically egalitarian; in the words of therapist Trigant Burrow, one of the movement's founders, the group therapy model dictated "no one individual would hold an authoritative position in relation to others."[44] Later psychotherapy manuals compared the therapy group to a democracy, and warned therapists against intervening "too quickly or too zealously" in the natural evolution of relationships between group members. To do so would be "to move in the direction of an authoritarian system . . . with potentially stultifying and destructive implications for the human condition."[45]

However, the absolute democracy of the therapy group was an illusion. A therapist—a trained authority figure—was present, guiding and controlling the seemingly spontaneous conversation.

Although group psychotherapy deleveloped in theoretical independence from the norms of Protestant worship, the group therapy session shared several central elements with the religious public confession. The focus of the therapy session was the response of the members, but the session was controlled and guided by a single figure recognized by the group members to be the leader; in the religious service, confessions of sin were made by individual sinners, but in the setting of a meeting controlled and guided by the minister.

In addition, patients in therapeutic groups and members of Protestant congregations possessed (and still possess) the same kind of power. Within the Protestant congregation, the sinner is faced with a demand: confess and be saved. Yet, as a saved member of the congregation, the Protestant worshipper also holds power over his leader. He is a voluntary member of the congregation. Having brought him into the congregation through conversion, the minister has to *keep* him in the pew by satisfying his needs—whether those be for spiritual renewal, entertainment, intellectual stimulation, or regular social contact with other Christians. The convert has become a consumer of religious services, and since he can always take his membership (and his contributions) elsewhere, he has the power of a customer.

The patient in the therapy group is also faced with a demand: confess that your former way of life was unhealthy, accept the directions given by the group and the therapist, and get better. But as a patient who is paying the therapist's bills, the patient also has power. Like the Protestant worshipper, he can leave at any point if he is unsatisfied. The therapist, like the minister, has to meet the needs of his medical customer; the patient/consumer can always take his money (and his health insurance card) away.

In group therapy, patients were not the only members of the group forced into a confessional stance. The therapist, faced with the need to reassure the group that he was both their leader and their servant, also found himself confessing.

Each member of a therapy group knew the therapist's identity, and (in principle) accepted the therapist's leadership: in the words of Cohen et al., "authority derives from the consensual agreement among members in support of the therapist's responsibility . . . to take actions intended to move [the group] towards its goals."[46] Yet a therapist who acted with too much authority might well face a revolt from the group—a possibility addressed in dozens of training guides. This unstable dynamic illustrates that creeping discomfort which a democratically inclined people feels towards leaders drawn from their own ranks.

Both Cleveland and McPherson faced this discomfort and allayed it. Cleveland's behavior during the Halpin scandal successfully convinced a national constituency that he would not be inclined to lord it over them, should they choose to place him in office; McPherson, whose power over her congregation depended on their willingness to grant her leadership, cast herself as victim rather than predator. But both wielded significant power, even as they positioned themselves on the same level as their followers.

In the same way, the therapist who guided a group had to exercise leadership while positioning himself as one among equals: "The psychotherapist is the group's formal, designated leader," as one manual puts it, "[but] the operation of a psychotherapy group . . . permits, encourages, and requires of its individual participants that they too function as leaders."[47]

Given that, in the context of the group, the willingness of the members to reveal their shortcomings was a sign of increasing "healing," maturity, and mental balance, therapists were encouraged to confess their own psychological difficulties as a strategy to counter rising hostility from the group's members. Such confessions were intended to defuse rebellion against the therapist's authority by revealing the therapist to be "a positively valued, capable but earthbound person," rather than an "Olympian being" who must be resisted and overthrown.[48]

By the late 1960s, therapeutic groups were meeting across the country, listening to their leaders confess. Billy Graham's crusades and Pentecostal healing lines were playing on televisions all over the United States. Confessions of sin and confessions of sickness and need were clearly visible even to the secular eye.

Yet Kennedy, faced with the need to reassure his public, made no public confession.

5

TED KENNEDY MISREADS HIS PUBLIC

My conduct and conversations during the next several hours,
to the extent that I can remember them, make no sense to me at all.
—EDWARD KENNEDY, 1969

ON JULY 25, 1969, Edward M. Kennedy went on television to tell a national audience that he had been involved in the drowning death of a young woman.

This televised statement was Kennedy's second explanation; his first had been given to police a week earlier, the day after the crime occured. In that official statement, which had been published by the *New York Times* on July 19, Kennedy explained that he had been driving back to Martha's Vineyard from Chappaquiddick Island very late on the previous evening, when he lost his way and drove off the side of a narrow bridge:

> There was one passenger with me . . . a former secretary of my brother, Senator Robert Kennedy. The car turned over and sank into the water, and landed with roof resting on the bottom. I attempted to open the door and the window of the car, but had no recollection of how I got out of the car. I came to the surface and repeatedly dove down to the car in an attempt to see if the passenger was still in the car. I was unsuccessful in the attempt . . . I remember walking around for a period of time and then going back to my hotel room. When I fully realized what had happened this morning, I immediately contacted the police.[1]

Divers discovered the body of Kennedy's passenger, 28-year-old Mary Jo Kopechne, in the car's back seat. She had died with her face up against the last air pocket in the sunken vehicle.

Police immediately announced that Kennedy was not accused of "criminal negligence" in the death, but that a misdemeanor charge of "leaving the scene of an accident" would be filed the following Monday. In the week after the publication of the police statement, calls for Kennedy to make a fuller explanation grew louder. The *New York Times* reported that while Kennedy's lawyers challenged the police's right to prosecute him, a flood of telegrams and phone calls to the local police chief asked why the charges were not more serious.[2] Kennedy's conduct suggested to many that his relationship with Kopechne was less than innocent—and that he had intentionally left her to drown, in order to avoid making her presence in his car public knowledge.

Realizing that his police statement would not satisfy the questioners, Kennedy arranged to give a televised explanation.

On the morning of July 25, Kennedy spent nine minutes in an Edgartown, Massachusetts courtroom, where he pleaded guilty to leaving the scene of an accident.[3] That same evening, cameramen came into his father's home to film his statement to the American people. Kennedy sat behind a desk, in front of an elegant bookcase filled with leather-bound volumes, reading from a prepared script. "This morning," he announced, "I entered a plea of guilty to the charge of leaving the scene of an accident."[4]

According to Kennedy, he had lost his way while driving, which led his car to go off "a narrow bridge which had no guard rails and was built on a left angle to the road." Kennedy continued:

> I remember thinking as the cold water rushed in around my head that I was for certain drowning. Then water entered my lungs and I actual felt the sensation of drowning. But somehow I struggled to the surface alive.
>
> I made immediate and repeated efforts to save Mary Jo by diving into strong and murky current, but succeeded only in increasing my state of utter exhaustion and alarm. My conduct and conversations during the next several hours, to the extent that I can remember them, make no

sense to me at all. . . . Instead of looking directly for a
telephone after lying exhausted in the grass for an undetermined time, I walked back to the cottage where the
party was being held and requested the help of two
friends, my cousin, Joseph Gargan and Phil Markham,
and directed them to return immediately to the scene
with me—this was sometime after midnight—in order to
undertake a new effort to dive down and locate Miss Kopechne. Their strenuous efforts, undertaken at some risk
to their own lives, also proved futile.

Instructing Gargan and Markham not to alarm Mary
Jo's friends that night, I had them take me to the ferry
crossing. The ferry having shut down for the night, I suddenly jumped into the water and impulsively swam across,
nearly drowning once again in the effort, and returned to
my hotel about 2 a.m. and collapsed in my room. . . . In
the morning [of Saturday, July 19], with my mind somewhat more lucid, I made an effort to call a family legal
advisor, Burke Marshall, from a public telephone on the
Chappaquiddick side of the ferry and belatedly reported
the accident to the Martha's Vineyard police.

Today, as I mentioned, I felt morally obligated to plead
guilty to the charge of leaving the scene of an accident.

This was not a confession; it was an explanation. It contained
only one admission—Kennedy "confessed" to concussion (hardly
a moral failing). His statement that he "felt morally obligated to
plead guilty" utilizes a phrase commonly applied to situations in
which there is no moral fault.[5] He repeated again and again that
he was not in complete command of his decision-making facul-
ties, while insisting that he was nevertheless not making excuses
for himself: "My conduct and conversations during the next several hours, to the extent that I can remember them, make no
sense to me at all," he told his television audience.

Although my doctors informed me that I suffered a cerebral concussion, as well as shock, I do not seek to escape

responsibility. . . . All kinds of scrambled thoughts—all of them confused, some of them irrational, many of them which I cannot recall, and some of which I would not have seriously entertained under normal circumstances— went through my mind during this period. They were reflected in the various inexplicable, inconsistent, and inconclusive things I said and did. . . . I was overcome, I'm frank to say, by a jumble of emotions, grief, fear, doubt, exhaustion, panic, confusion and shock.

None of these admissions contained a *confession*. Kennedy claimed that his failure to report the accident was due to his concussion (and was remedied the next morning when, "with my mind somewhat more lucid," he called his lawyer and asked his legal counsel to contact police). "There is no truth, no truth whatever, to the widely circulated suspicions of immoral conduct that have been leveled at my behavior and hers regarding that evening," he insisted. "Nor was I driving under the influence of liquor."

Early reaction to Kennedy's televised explanation was largely, although not universally, positive. A roundup of newspaper editorials appearing the day after the apology shows a willingness to accept Kennedy's version of events: "The speech cleared up many of the mysteries surrounding Miss Kopechne's death," said the *New York Daily News*. The Springfield, Massachusetts, *Daily News* protested that the "mistake was not so terrible . . . that it should completely erase his past and future value." The *Chicago Daily News* marvelled, "His extraordinary report to the people surely earned him high marks for courage as well as stage presence."[6]

Almost every one of the papers which approved of Kennedy's performance also pointed out that the week-long gap between Kopechne's death and Kennedy's speech remained the most troubling aspect of the incident. But in the face of an event that could conceivably have led to accusations of manslaughter, this was a mild criticism. An August 4 Louis Harris poll suggested that "Americans are taking a forgiving view of Senator Edward M. Kennedy," while a Gallup Poll reported that while "Kennedy's popularity had fallen sharply since the accident . . . his standing as a potential Presidential candidate was unchanged . . . . Generally favorable opinions of the Senator outweighed negative feelings by 3 to 1."[7]

But this day-after judgment did not stand. Almost at once, calls for Kennedy to make a fuller explanation began. Kennedy ran into ongoing opposition in the Senate, where Republican Senators opposed his agendas. In December 1969, his tax reform project was defeated on the Senate floor, as were several other bills and amendments that he had sponsored. Legal proceedings in the Kopechne case dragged on; a further inquest was conducted in January of 1970, and although authorities decided that no new charges would result, the inquest drew plenty of newspaper attention.

Before long, it became clear that Kennedy's chances of becoming President had dwindled away. Kennedy had been the obvious choice for the 1972 Democratic presidential nomination. Jack Olsen's 1970 study of Kennedy takes his eventual candidacy for granted: "EMK in '72 . . . buttons were all over the place," he writes, "and one could also see placards—HAPPINESS IS TED KENNEDY IN 72—in many a Washington office."[8]

But before 1970 was over, Kennedy had gone on the *Today* show and announced that he would definitely not run for President in 1972. He did run for re-election to the Senate, a race that he won by a half-million votes; this was a respectable margin of victory, but significantly smaller than his previous triumphs in Massachusetts. In any case, it only assured him of the loyalty of Massachusetts residents and said nothing about the temper of the rest of the country.[9]

The following year, he lost his job of Minority Whip in an embarrassing defeat.[10] He began to mention the possibility of running for president in 1976, but questions about his part in Kopechne's death continued to circulate; a *National Lampoon* cartoon published in July 1972 shows a skeletal Kopechne

Figure 5.1. The Delegate from Chappaquiddick

crashing a Democratic nominating convention that boasts a huge "Teddy for President" banner.

In 1973, another *National Lampoon* cartoon caused so much furor that the *Lampoon* finally withdrew the issue in which it appeared, in order to avoid a lawsuit; a takeoff on a popular series of Volkswagen ads, it showed a VW Bug floating in water, with copy that read, "If Ted Kennedy drove a Volkswagen, he'd

If Ted Kennedy drove a Volkswagen, he'd be President today.

It floats.

The way our body is built, we'd be surprised if it didn't.

The sheet of flat steel that goes underneath every Volkswagen keeps out water, as well as dirt and salt and other nasty things that can eat away at the underside of a car. So it's watertight at the bottom.

And everybody knows it's easier to shut the door on a Volkswagen after you've rolled down the window a little. That proves it's practically airtight on top.

If it was a boat, we could call it the Water Bug.

But it's not a boat, it's a car.

And, like Mary Jo Kopechne, it's only

99 and 44/100 percent pure.

So it won't stay afloat forever. Just long enough.

Poor Teddy.

If he'd been smart enough to buy a Volkswagen, he never would have gotten into hot water.

Figure 5.2. Floating Volkswagen

be President today. It floats. . . . Poor Teddy. If he'd been smart enough to buy a Volkswagen, he never would have gotten into hot water." But the threat of a lawsuit came from Volkswagen, not from the Kennedys. The company had no wish to be identified with Edward Kennedy even in satire.

A year later, Kennedy again announced that he would not run for president. This, he insisted, was to keep his family from the pressures of a campaign, but his aides told reporters that Chappaquidick would have "made things much tougher" on both Kennedy and his family.[11]

He entered the primaries once more in 1980. But an early interview with Roger Mudd on CBS showed that Chappaquiddick was still haunting Kennedy. Mudd pointed out that the judge who presided over Kennedy's confession had said that he believed Kennedy was lying, and suggested that no one would "ever fully believe" Kennedy's explanation.[12]

Defeated by Democratic incumbent Jimmy Carter in primary after primary, Kennedy withdrew from the race for the Democratic nomination on August 11, 1980. He never campaigned for the presidency again.

Kennedy had failed to understand the growing public expectation that confession should be part of the storytelling that surrounded scandal. More deeply, he had no comprehension of his need to reassure his followers that he had no intention of wielding inappropriate power over them—a need that full public confession could have helped satisfy.

Unlike Cleveland or McPherson, Kennedy faced repeated calls to confess. Both Democrats and Republicans in the Senate, speaking on condition of anonymity, urged Kennedy to give a much clearer account of the evening; one Democratic senator said that, in Kennedy's shoes, he would "try to answer every question, whether it hurts or not"; and another said, "The longer the delay, the worse it looks."[13] "One hopes that Senator Edward M. Kennedy will hesitate no longer to clear up the details of the tragic accident at Chappaquiddick," the *Times* editorialized. "[H]is story leaves serious gaps. . . . Too many questions remained unanswered. . . . There is much that needs explaining."[14]

This call for a full confession remained unanswered, but the need to hear it remained. Ten years later, the *New York Daily News* could still editorialize on the subject: "What was required here was an old-fashioned Catholic confession, 'Bless me, Father, for I have sinned,'" wrote columnist Jimmy Breslin; "You don't say the sins were committed by some guy standing on the side someplace; you were there and you did it, so tell what you did and how you feel."[15]

It is perfectly possibly that Kennedy did ever make an old-fashioned Catholic confession, but if he did, Breslin (and the rest of the voting public) would never know. Confession of sin was a profoundly *private* act for the Catholic sinner, an act in which the forgiveness of other men and women had almost no part.

• • •

The Catholic practice of confession was rooted in the the fourth-century thought of Augustine, who envisioned regular confession as necessary for the *internal* health of the *individual* soul.[16] This idea was in contrast to classical thought; before Augustine, confession was most often compelled by an outside force.[17] A sinner confessed to wrongdoing not primarily because of some sense of personal guilt, but in response to the authority of the law. Confession was an act to which individuals had to be brought as a last resort: "No one speaks against himself unless something drives him to do it," wrote the Roman orator known as Pseudo-Quintilian. To confess to a wrongdoing, except under interrogation, was to be either drunk or "impelled by madness."[18]

Augustine pictured both law and confession differently. His *Confessions* portrayed man not merely as a subject under the pressure of external earthly power, but also as a created being with a duty owed solely to his Creator. Augustine relocates that external power of the sovereign so that it lies *within*, the God-within-man part of the the human soul.[19] No longer does the will of a sovereign struggle with the will of a subject. Rather, the conflict between law and subject becomes a conflict between the light and dark sides of a single self. The sovereign now lives within the self, but another part of the self is in constant revolt against it.

Augustine's years with the Manicheans, who saw all of existence as a battleground for the cosmic war between the two powers of good and evil, left him with a lifelong habit of dividing the world into two factions in every conceivable way—spirit and matter, Israel and Egypt, the eternal and the temporal, the unchanging and the mutable, city of God and city of man.[20] This philosophical habit was reinforced by political realities. It is no coincidence that Augustine lived in a post-classical African world where the Roman emperor was far away and the Roman governor was not always loyal. In grasping for a new sense of responsibility, Augustine was attempting to understand authority in a world where it was no longer single-voiced, but divided and ambiguous.

Augustine's sense of doubleness not only reflected the reality of his world, but also allowed him the psychological luxury of confession. Confession no longer demanded that the self capitulate to a separate, hostile will. Since there are two selves in Augustine, he can easily ascribe blame to one, in the confidence that the other remains blameless. "What I used to think was true, I now think is wrong," he said easily in 392, in a debate with a Manichean priest; it is the sort of statement only possible for a man who believes that some part of him was right all along.[21]

In order to confess sin, a man must identify the part of himself that reflects truth, and separate it from the part of the self that resists God's sovereignty. In other words, the self must consider *itself*. This act of contemplation, to which the philosopher Charles Taylor has given the useful name "radical reflexivity," allows the self to consider itself, and to confess only to the God that lives inside it. Radical reflexivity allows confession to take place with no reference to outside law. Radical reflexivity makes private confession possible.[22]

For the privately confessing self, the nature of wrongdoing has also changed. In the classical world, to confess was to own up to an external act that broke the laws imposed by the sovereign. But Augustine goes so far as to suggest that "no decisive criterion exists for judging external acts on their own terms." Rather, what determines evil is is the interior motivation. That is evil which is done with an evil disposition.[23] For Augustine, what is actually *done* is secondary to what is *thought*. Confession becomes an exploration of motives, a place where the self considers the reasons for its own decisions.

In the post-Augustine world, the act of confession was one in which a sinner found evil motivation within himself, held that evil up against the reflection of God in his own soul, told the story of how this evil motivation led him into action, and then begged for God's grace. It was an act that took place again and again in order to assure the health of the soul.

Private confession took place when this set of steps was carried out in the presence of a priest who heard the story from the sinner's own lips. The priest had unquestioned access to the most personal and private details of individual lives: the frequency of married sex during Lent, the mixing of small pieces of iron into bundles in order to sell the whole, jealousy of a business rival—all of these appear in thirteenth-century accounts as commonplace topics for confession.[24] The official teaching of the "seal of confession," which prohibited the priest from speaking of any of these private matters that might be confessed to him by a penitent, was first set down in 1151 in Gratian's compiled Edicts of the Church, and was affirmed by the Lateran Council in 1215. But both of these written formulations probably grant the force of church law to a long-standing custom.[25]

As the Church moved through and then past the years of the Fourth Lateran Council, the priest's private interaction with the sinner rose in importance. Confession consisted of three parts: the sinner's account, the priest's diagnosis and recommendation, and the performance of the appropriate penance. F. J. Heggen argues that in the centuries immediately after Augustine, the Church's emphasis lay on the performance of penance as the prime atoning element of the confessional process. But by the thirteenth century, emphasis had shifted to the sinner's account; the act of confession itself was now central.[26] Heggen claims that, during the eleventh and twelfth centuries, a trend toward confessing venial sins (sins that do not fatally breach the relationship between man and God, and so do not require confession) appears, because the very action of confessing sins (even the unimportant ones) was the key that opened the door to atonement.[27]

In the years before the Protestant Reformation, a third element became central to confession: the sincerity of repentance, the motivation of the sinner's heart as he told the story of his sin.[28] Late medieval handbooks encouraged priests to inquire closely into the circumstances of each confessed sin and to extract the story of the offense even from sinners who did not volunteer a narrative. The fourteenth-century confessor's guide known as the *Astesana* suggests that priests use the easily remembered verse:

> *Quis, quid, ubi, per quos, quotiens, cur, quomodo, quando,*
> *Quilibet obseruet, animae medicamina dando.*

which is translated in a sixteenth-century English handbook as:

> Who, what, and where, by what helpe and by whose;
> Why, how, and when, doe many things disclose.[29]

Furthermore, the intensifying focus on the motivations and intentions of the sinner's heart developed a newly vertical emphasis in confession.

Peter Biller points out that before 1400 confessional manuals tended to attach much severer penalties to those sins that affect the community (such as short-changing customers or using inaccurate weights), rather than to those that might corrupt the soul (such as doubt). Even the penances for sexual sins are weighted heavily toward those that damage others. After 1400, however, manuals shift toward increasingly strict penances for sins of thought and motivation—sins that do not affect others.[30] John Bossy argues that the years around 1400 saw confessional interrogation move away from the Seven Deadly Sins, which tended to focus on the horizontal relationship between a sinner and his neighbors, and toward the Ten Commandments, which emphasized a greater responsibility toward God. Christians were thus shifted toward a "moral code," Bossy concludes, that was "stronger on obligations towards God," and "somewhat narrower" on obligations toward one's neighbor.[31]

This concentration on the attitude of the heart only made the act of confession more vertical—and thus more private. In confessing his sins, the penitent increasingly was directed to concentrate on those sins of the heart that had affected his relationship with God. Less on display was any effect that his sin might have had on family or friends.[32] Healing for this damage in the soul consisted of private diagnosis, private penance, and private forgiveness. Apart from the priest, who acted as soul-doctor, other Christian believers were given no opportunity to offer forgiveness. Sin, which existed as a block between the sinner and God, was resolved between the sinner and God. No one else needed to have any part in the ritual.

Despite minor shifts in emphasis throughout the following centuries, private confession that centered on the the motivations of the heart continued to be *de rigeur* for practicing Catholics.[33] Kennedy's private confession, if there was one, remains invisible to us. But his rhetoric suggests that he had in fact engaged in exactly the sort of self-analysis that private confession required.

Kennedy's statement at his court hearing, made through his attorney, makes abundantly clear that since he had no *intention* of harming Kopechne, he did not class his own actions as immoral, merely as illegal—a conclusion with which the judge apparently agreed. Asked whether there were any mitigating circumstances that he wished to bring out before sentencing, Kennedy's attorney Richard J. McCarron answered, "The defendant is adamant in this matter, your Honor, that he wishes to plead guilty to the offense of operating a motor vehicle and going away. . . . I believe [the defendant's] character is well known to the world. We would therefore ask that any sentence that the court may impose be suspended." The judge answered that Kennedy had "already been and will continue to be punished far beyond anything this court can impose. The ends of justice would be satisfied by the imposition of the minimum jail sentence and the suspension of that sentence"[34] That decision by the judge was based not on the outcome of Kennedy's actions, but on his motivations.

Kennedy's explanations continued to show that he did not truly consider his actions to be immoral. As an educated Catholic, Kennedy was undoubtedly aware that a serious transgression of moral law—a "mortal sin"—required three elements: the breach of an *important* (and not trivial) law; full mental knowledge of the sin's gravity ("we must *know* and *recollect* its gravity at the time of acting," in the words of Alfred Wilson's 1947 classic, *Pardon and Peace*); and full consent of the will to the act of sin itself.[35]

Leaving the scene of the accident was clearly an act that had grave consequences. Nevertheless, leaving the scene was not essentially a grave sin (as reflected by its legal classification as a misdemeanor). As an act that was in itself trivial, it could only become a grave sin if done with malice and evil will.

According to Kennedy's lights, all that was necessary for him to prove his lack of culpability was to prove that he had no malice or evil will—something that explains his willingness to accept legal responsibility, while still repeating again and again that his concussion had impaired his full consent to his actions. Rather than admitting to moral blame, Edward Kennedy gave his listeners an argument—a set of reasons why he had acted as he did.

Augustine would have found this profoundly inadequate. Augustine, after all, was well aware that verbal fluency could turn explanation into excuse. He gave up teaching rhetoric for this reason, saying in the *Confessions* that he could no longer act as "a salesman of words in the markets of rhetoric."[36] His students were learning from him how to talk their way out of reliance on God's grace; lawyerly rhetoric gave the illusion that the penitent could explain and justify, without divine aid, all of his actions. [37]

Most of Kennedy's listeners found his verbal fluency equally inadequate. The immediately favorable response to his televised explanation was due, at least in part, to his appeal at the end of his speech ("And so I ask you tonight, the people of Massachusetts, to think this through with me. In facing this decision, I seek your advice and opinion"). The words led to a flood of phone calls and telegrams, two to one in favor of Kennedy remaining in office.[38]

In this, Kennedy showed some awareness of the growing influence of Protestant public confession on the American public. Whereas his own Catholic tradition gave no role to the larger community in the forgiveness of sin, the Protestant public confession, by its nature, demanded that the hearers affirm and respond to the ritual of confession. And there were many, many hearers. Kennedy's television address was broadcast by all three national networks at prime time. More viewers saw his confession than watched Neil Armstrong walk on the moon.[39]

Yet Kennedy seems to have taken the initial responsiveness of those hearers as proof that no more needed to be said on the matter. In fact, his explanation—which had centered entirely around his reasons for making his guilty plea—had been only the first phase of the needed confession. The public had heard Kennedy's confession of legal fault. Now, the voters wanted to hear Kennedy admit that his actions had been immoral.

Kennedy remained unwilling to do so. He insisted he had not been having an affair with Kopechne, but although gossip about their relationship continued, this was not the primary immorality that needed confession. Kennedy's desertion of Kopechne in the car was the greater offense, the larger transgression of moral law.

It was also a stark illustration of the abuse of power. Kennedy, the powerful elected politician, had taken advantage of Kopechne's weakness in the most literal manner possible: he had swum away and summoned his lawyers as she drowned. His failure to admit moral responsibility demonstrated that he had almost no understanding of *why* his public needed to hear his confession. His constituency needed to see that Kennedy, whose political power was intensified by his position as senior member of a powerful political dynasty, would not use that power to oppress. Kennedy needed, like Cleveland a century before, to show that he was on the side of the common man.

This he proved unable to do.

Kennedy's initial explanation shows him (and his speechwriters) grasping instinctively for some kind of identification with the oppressed and downtrodden. He references all of the Kennedy tragedies: Kopechne was identified as "one of the most devoted members of the staff of Senator Robert Kennedy," immediately bringing Bobby's tragic murder into view; Kennedy, describing his "scrambled thoughts" after his concussion, said that he wondered (while Kopechne was drowning) "whether some awful curse did actually hang over all the Kennedys." He references his assassinated brother, John F. Kennedy, twice—once when asking whether he should resign ("The people of this State, the State which sent . . . John Kennedy to the United States Senate, are entitled to representation in that body by men who inspire their utmost confidence"), and again when reminding his listeners that the choice to resign was his alone ("The stories of the past courage cannot supply courage itself. For this, each man must look into his own soul. I pray that I can have the courage to make the right decision").

But this attempt to align himself with the other tragic Kennedys backfired. Instead of placing him in the company of heroes-attacked-by-ill-fortune, the speech simply emphasized that Kennedy's political career had followed on the heels of his brothers' accomplishments.

Reinforcing these images of a powerful family cabal were Kennedy's references to his family traditions and even to his friends. "On the weekend of July 18," he began, "I was on Martha's Vineyard Island participating . . . as for thirty years my family has participated, in the annual Edgartown Sailing Regatta." The attempt to place himself in a warm, loyal family setting also happened to remind his listeners that the family had been sailing boats off the privileged coast of Martha's Vineyard for almost as long as Kennedy had been alive.

Kennedy explained that he had asked both his cousin Joseph Gargan and his friend Phil Markham to help him find Kopechne; their heroic efforts to dive down to the car aside, both these men were lawyers, members of the professional elite who were expert at protecting their clients (and both knew perfectly well that the police should have been summoned).

Figure 5.3. Kennedy's Television Appearance

As Kennedy biographer Adam Clymer points out, neither one had had a concussion. Rather, "[t]heir instinct, and perhaps Kennedy's too, appears to have been to prevent disclosure of his having been in the car with a pretty young woman under circumstances that invited suspicion."[40] Every mention Kennedy made of a friend or relation (as well as his revealing remark that he had called his lawyer, not the police, to report the crime) strengthened the sense of a man surrounded and assisted by powerful, ruthless allies. Even his choice of backgrounds for broadcast emphasized his privileged, educated, protected world: he gave his address from his father's home, sitting at a desk with rows and rows of expensive, leatherbound, legal tomes behind him.

Not only did Kennedy fail to align himself with his listeners, but his silence about Kopechne allowed his opponents to portray him as a sexual predator (exactly the fate that McPherson and Cleveland had both escaped). Kennedy already had a reputation as a womanizer; Joan Kennedy later claimed that, during the Chappaquiddick crisis, he had called his then-girlfriend Helga to break the news before coming to talk to Joan herself. Kopechne's presence in the car suggested that he had been attempting to corrupt a good Catholic girl, pictures of whom suggested total, blonde innocence. And since he had undoubtedly played a part in her death, he was at best a seducer— and at worst a destroyer.

Like clerical leaders, elected officials wield a peculiar kind of authority over their followers: they have power to command, but this power is given to them only by the consent of the governed. Like clerical leaders, elected officials are admitted to have a certain kind of superiority: they are peculiarly fitted, by character and ability, to rule over others. Kennedy's confession suggested in multiple ways that his superiority was an illusion— not based on character and ability, but instead on family position and power. Rather than avoiding a backlash reaction to his authority as Cleveland had, Kennedy fueled one with his continual references (both verbal and symbolic) to his wealth and elite status. His involvement with Kopechne aroused fears that this family-based authority would be used, not for the good of his consituency, but for personal gain.

When Kennedy re-entered the presidential primaries in 1980, he had still not realized the need to confess *publicly*. Roger Mudd asked him, during an interview on CBS, whether "anybody will ever fully believe your explanation of Chappaquiddick." Kennedy gave a rambling answer that once again hid from view any moral failing:

Oh, there's, the problem is, from that night, I, I found the conduct, the behavior almost beyond belief myself. I mean that's why it's been, but I think that's the way it was. Now, I find that as I have stated that I have found the conduct that in, in that evening and in, in the, as a result

of the accident of the, and the sense of loss, the sense of
hope, and the, and the sense of tragedy, and the whole
set of circumstances, that the behavior was inexplicable.
So I find that those, those, types of questions as they apply
to that, questions of my own soul, as well. But that happens to be the way it was.[41]

More than a decade later, Kennedy still did not understand
that his insistence on privately thrashing out his moral issues,
rather than publicly confessing his moral failings, stood in the
way of his election.

The Protestant-style public confession, which might have
saved Kennedy, was foreign to his own religious training. But
the reaction to Kennedy's scandal suggests that it had become
very familiar indeed to millions of American voters. The American public had begun to develop the expectation that public
wrongdoing would be followed by a full, neoevangelical-style
grovel—even when the wrongdoing took place well outside of
the neoevangelical sphere. Kennedy never understood this expectation; nor did he show the willingness to hand over power
to his followers, or the patience to wait until they handed it
back.

And although his political opponent Jimmy Carter did seem
to have a grasp of both ideas, Carter's 1976 campaign revealed
that even a neoevangelical-style grovel could fail disastrously.

PART II

The Age of Public Confession

6

JIMMY CARTER, TRAITOR TO THE CAUSE

I've looked on a lot of women with lust.
I've committed adultery in my heart many times.
—JIMMY CARTER, 1976

IN JULY 1976, at the Democratic National Convention in New York City, Jimmy Carter was nominated as the Democratic candidate for president. Right after the convention, Carter agreed to meet with Robert Scheer, a reporter from *Playboy*, for a series of interviews. The decision to grant *Playboy* an interview was part of a carefully considered strategy. Both Carter and his campaign manager hoped that the *Playboy* interview would show that Carter was a "regular guy,"[1] rather than a religious fanatic.

Carter, an outspoken Christian, had grown up within fundamentalism, and now stood squarely in the camp of the neoevangelicals—a stance that seems to have made Robert Scheer nervous. In four different sessions, Scheer asked Carter dozens of questions, but continually circled back to the question of how Carter's religious beliefs would affect his actions as President—particularly his positions on legislation. Scheer wanted to know whether Carter would appoint judges who would enforce laws on drug use, adultery, sodomy, homosexuality, and other "private" behaviors: "What we're getting at," he told Carter, "is how much you'd tolerate behavior that your religion considers wrong."[2]

After Scheer returned to this subject again and again, Carter grew frustrated. "I think we've pursued this conversation long enough," he told Scheer, to which Scheer answered, "We're being so persistent because of this matter of self-righteousness, because of the moral certainty of so many of your statements."

In the final moments of the last interview, Scheer—standing at the door, ready to leave, said casually, "Do you feel you've reassured people with this interview, people who are uneasy about your religious beliefs, who wonder if you're going to make a rigid, unbending President?" Carter, clearly still troubled by his failure to break through Scheer's suspicion, made one last effort to explain exactly how his faith shaped his thinking:

> What Christ taught about most was pride, that one person should never think he was better than anybody else. . . . The thing that's drummed into us all the time is not to be proud, not to be better than anyone else, not to look down on people but to make ourselves acceptable in God's eyes through our own actions and recognize the simple truth that we're saved by grace. . . . I try not to commit a deliberate sin. I recognize that I'm going to do it anyhow, because I'm human and I'm tempted. And Christ set some almost impossible standards for us. Christ said, "I tell you that anyone who looks on a woman with lust has in his heart already committed adultery."
>
> I've looked on a lot of women with lust. I've committed adultery in my heart many times. This is something that God recognizes I will do—and I have done it—and God forgives me for it. But that doesn't mean that I condemn someone who not only looks on a woman with lust but who leaves his wife and shacks up with somebody out of wedlock.
>
> Christ says, Don't consider yourself better than someone else because one guy screws a whole bunch of women while the other guy is loyal to his wife. The guy who's loyal to his wife ought not to be condescending or proud because of the relative degree of sinfulness. . . .
>
> I don't inject these beliefs in my answers to your secular questions.
>
> But I don't think I would *ever* take on the same frame of mind that Nixon or Johnson did—lying, cheating, and

distorting the truth. Not taking into consideration my hope for my strength of character, I think that my religious beliefs alone would prevent that from happening to me.[3]

On September 11, Robert Scheer and *Playboy* editor Barry Golson appeared on the *Today* show to talk about the interview. On the same day, they sent a copy to Carter's headquarters. Journalists covering the Carter campaign also received copies. Although the interview was not due to come out until October 14, *Playboy* released Carter's remarks to the Associated Press and NBC *Nightly News* on September 20, a decision that allowed newspapers time to pick and choose their quotes. The *Los Angeles Times* quoted his interview extensively, headlining it "Carter Admits to 'Adultery in my Heart.'" The *New York Times* called the confession of lust and mental adultery "unusually candid for a Presidential aspirant."[4] On September 23, Lee Dembart of the *Times* pointed out that the full interview was "much less stunning than the few excerpted quotations imply."[5] However, those three or four sentences from the multipart, nine-page interview continued to be quoted and requoted for the next three weeks. By the time the full interview was published in *Playboy*, the entire four-part, nine-page article had been labelled "The 'Lust in his Heart' Confession."

The results of the interview, according to the chairman of the Georgia Democratic Party, were "Bad, bad, bad . . . uniformly negative."[6] The numbers bore him out. As a reward for his willing confession of moral fault, Carter lost 15 percentage points in national polls.[7] His lead—the "largest ever recorded in a presidential race"—was wiped out.[8]

Unlike Kennedy, Carter was concealing nothing. Unlike Kennedy, Carter was placing himself in the shoes of his followers. Unlike Kennedy, Carter was admitting that he was essentially flawed and fallen, without trying to explain his way out of moral responsibility for his actions. And if any might have been sympathetic to Carter's desire to confess the sins of his heart, it should have been his Protestant Christian supporters.

In the Baptist churches where Carter grew up, a believer who admitted to a sinful heart was simply revealing his reliance on God's grace and his need for forgiveness. By this measure, Carter's confession was thoroughly orthodox: "God forgives me for [lust]," he told Scheer (a remark that was not widely quoted in newspaper accounts).

But conservative Protestants of all shades announced themselves appalled. The Reverend W. A. Criswell, pastor of the largest Baptist church in America, declared, "I am highly offended by this. I think he's mixed up in his moral values, and I think the entire church membership will feel the same way. The whole thing is highly distasteful."[9] Vice-President Rockefeller's comment to campaign crowds in Ohio was typical: "I never thought I'd see the day when Christ's teachings were discussed in *Playboy*," he told Ford-Dole supporters, "and I'm a Baptist, ladies and gentlemen!"[10]

Rockefeller was clearly making political hay out of Carter's misstep, but the larger question remains: *Why* was it so widely viewed as a misstep rather than an act of pious humility? Why did conservatives ignore the fact that Carter's affirmation of faith in *Playboy* was not so very different than the Gospel accounts of Jesus attending parties with "taxpayers and sinners"?[11] Why wasn't it a *good* thing to see Christ's teachings in *Playboy*, since the readers of *Playboy* undoubtedly needed to hear them?

Why was the reaction bad, bad, and uniformly bad?

• • •

Carter's words fell into a highly polarized political climate. Although the power of evangelical voters would not peak until the 1980s, the concept of holy war was already gaining currency, and was increasingly married to political rhetoric. Fundamentalists and neoevangelicals had begun to draw battle lines, both politically and theologically, that separated them from their enemies.

In the decades leading up to Carter's confession, three political issues, each one involving authority and submission, had become inextricably entwined with the worldview of the new evangelical alliance. The four-way braid that resulted brought strands of religious practice into the secular political arena, where they remain to this day. This polarization produced a very specific need in public confessions: politicians who served in the secular realm would nevertheless need, as Aimee Semple McPherson had, to bring language of the holy war into the realm of politics.

It was a language that Jimmy Carter had not mastered.

In the world of the new evangelical alliance, holy-war language was nothing new. In American Protestantism, this type of rhetoric—used so effectively by McPherson in her fight to save her reputation—had been employed by revivalists for at least two centuries: The battle to win sinners to Christ was not only a fight for individual souls, but also a strategy in the larger war against Satan. This religious rhetoric had grown more intense during the fundamentalist-modernist controversies of the 1920s. Reading the book of Revelation literally, and making use of martial rhetoric inherited from the years of World War I, fundamentalist preachers declared that their theological battles were earthly manifestations of the ongoing battle between God and Satan. World War II provided preachers with a plethora of military metaphors. Charles Fuller opened his radio broadcasts with a choir singing the hymn "Jesus Saves" ("Sing above the battle strife, / Jesus saves! Jesus saves!") and compared Americans to "soldiers in a foxhole," waiting for the rescue of the Gospel. "Because of conditions in this war-weary and sin-sick old world," he wrote in 1942, "people are thinking more than ever of eternal things, and in the hearts of the unsaved there is . . . a greater openness to the Gospel than I have ever seen before. . . . Oh, friends, what a doubly rich opportunity God has given us—to reach by radio . . . that great army of those who need the comfort of Scripture in those days."[12]

In 1952, the election of Dwight Eisenhower gave conservative Protestants direct access to the White House. They spoke of the war between God and Satan; they spoke of the intersection between secular political issues and the necessity to fight for God's kingdom. Their loudest speeches railed against Communism, the post–World War threat with the highest political profile.

Communism had been associated with a threat to Christian America before. Aimee Semple McPherson had preached against the triple menace of atheism, Communism, and evolution, all "threatening to undermine the country's foundation" unless revival brought America back to God.[13] As far back as 1920, the fundamentalist Presbyterian minister David S. Kennedy had exhorted his brothers-at-arms to counteract "that German destructive criticism which has found its way into the religious and moral thought of our people as the conception and propaganda of the *Reds* have found their way with poisoning and overthrowing influence into their civil and industrial life."[14]

But for David Kennedy the two threats were parallel and separate; and, as Matthew Avery Sutton has pointed out, McPherson's preaching was unusual in its linkage of religious revival and political reform.[15] The Republicans' return to power in the 1950s provided a chance to unite the spiritual and political dangers into one enemy. Like McPherson, the neoevangelical preacher Billy Graham used the rhetoric of holy war to describe a political threat; Communism, Graham warned, was "inspired, directed, and motivated by the Devil himself."[16]

Communism was particularly repugnant to neoevangelicals and fundamentalists because it claimed an authority that rivaled the authority of God's Word. Marx and Engels had accounted for the ills of mankind by substituting class struggle for original sin; religion, far from being the only lens that gave a clear view world of the world, was yet another form of class antagonism.[17] Meanwhile, the fundamentalist struggle of the 1920s had asserted that the will of God, as revealed *only* through literal interpretation of the Bible, was the sole source of authority for man. This principle continued to be central to both fundamentalism and neoevangelicalism throughout and beyond the 1950s. Neoevangelical theologian J. I. Packer, writing in 1958, argued that the "foundation principle" that divided theological liberals from conservatives was "disagreement as to the principle of authority. . . . [T]here can be no stable agreement on anything between those who disagree here. . . . [I]t is the heart of the controversy, and it is here that our discussion must centre."[18] The very name *Christian* was at stake:

> . . . the essential step in sound theologizing is to bring all views—one's own as well as those of others—to the touchstone of Scripture. . . . Our first task must be to test all the words of men by the authoritative Word of God, to receive only what Scripture endorses, and to reject all that is contrary to it. . . . [T]he Evangelical asks his critics to come and join him in submitting the methods and conclusions of their respective theologies to the judgment of the written Word of God. . . . Jesus Christ constituted Christianity a religion of biblical authority. . . . Anything short of unconditional submission to Scripture, therefore, is a kind of impenitence; any views that subject the written word of God to the opinions and pronouncements of men involve unbelief and disloyalty towards Christ.[19]

Communism was not merely another political system; it was an act of rebellion against the authority of God.

By the end of the 1950s, the battle lines that would divide God's friends from His enemies were being carved through secular wargrounds. God's friends were those who submitted to His authority; God's enemies were those who rebelled by choosing man's wisdom instead.

In the two decades after Eisenhower, the new evangelical alliance took up arms against two more enemies: anti-Zionism and secular humanism. Both of these foes had political faces; both threatened to put human wisdom above God's revelation.

In the 1960s and 1970s, fundamentalists and neoevangelicals increasingly supported the cause of the new state of Israel and accused supporters of the Palestinian cause of allying themselves with the forces of evil. This Christian Zionism resulted from the overlap of fundamentalism with *dispensationalism*, the nineteenth-century theological system that held that God's dealings with humanity fell into distinct stages ("dispensations"). During each dispensation, God's method of working out His plan in history appeared to change, but His central purposes remained the same.[20]

Reading the prophecies of the Old Testament, dispensationalists discovered that God's favor on Israel was eternal: "Thine house and thy kingdom shall be established forever," in the words of II Samuel 7:16. "Forever" meant, quite clearly, *forever.* It was not figurative, or metaphorical. Therefore, it seemed obvious that the Jews were divinely ordained to regain their homeland. When the dispensationalist preacher Charles Scofield published his hugely influential reference Bible in 1909, his summary on the subject "Israel" read, "According to the prophets, Israel, regathered from all nations, restored to her own land and converted, is yet to have her greatest earthly exaltation and glory."[21] The promise that Abraham's descendents would become a great nation was unconditional; as popular neoevangelical preacher Donald Grey Barnhouse wrote in 1965, "This promise . . . must be fulfilled, or the Lord is found false."[22]

Literal readings of the prophets and the book of Revelation also suggested that Israel's nationhood was a sign of the end times. Barnhouse's 1965 book *The Invisible War: The Panorama of the Continuing Conflict Between Good and Evil* tracked the holy war between God and Satan from its beginnings in the book of Genesis all the way through God's final, predicted victory in the time yet to come. "When the Lord Jesus Christ begins the work of His return," Barnhouse concluded, "He will do something for the Jews simultaneously." In Barnhouse's schema, the political state of Israel would reach its zenith after the return of Christ: the Jews would recognize Jesus as the awaited Messiah and then, in the "final scene" of history, "Israel shall be brought to the place of government of all the world as the colonial administrators of God."[23]

Israel's victory in the Six-Day War of 1967 convinced many Christian Zionists that the triumph of God was very close at hand. Fundamentalist theologian Hal Lindsey wrote in 1970 that the "paramount prophetic sign" showing that the prophecies of the Bible were about to be literally fulfilled was the return of Israel, as a nation, to "the land of its forefathers . . . shortly before the events which will culminate with the personal, visible return of the Messiah, Jesus Christ, to set up an everlasting Kingdom."[24]

The Late Great Planet Earth was a smash hit; Zondervan, the evangelical publishing house that had put the book out, ordered 26 hardcover printings between 1970 and 1973, and the paperback edition went through an additional 18 printings before 1976. By associating the return of Christ with the Six-Day War, Lindsey had established an earthly, political time-line for the spiritual war that McPherson had spoken of in timeless terms. "Within forty years or so," Lindsey concluded, ". . . all these things could take place."[25] Acceptance of this historical scheme and commitment to the support of political Israel as a sign of faithfulness to God's Word was also widespread among Pentecostals. In 1967, Pentecostal preacher Pat Robertson broke ground for his new television studio on the first day of the Six-Day War, a coincidence he saw as divinely ordained.[26] As Israel fought for its political survival, Robertson was waging his own battle against Satan on the airwaves. The two battles were part of a single war.[27]

Communism and anti-Zionism both set a rational standard for truth that bypassed Scripture. Israel's place in history was laid out in the Bible; it could be seen only by those who were willing to accept the Bible as the final authority on the unfolding of history; thus, support for Israel was a sign of obedience."[28] In Christian Zionism, the political and theological messages had become indistinguishable, and both required submission to God's authority.

The final enemy, secular humanism, was a philosophy that by the early 1970s was increasingly viewed as the greatest modern threat to Biblical authority. "Humanism" as an articulated, self-aware philosophy had been around at least since 1933, when the first Humanist Manifesto proposed that mankind should adopt the "vital, fearless and frank religion" of humanism because, unlike traditional religions, humanism could face the problems of the twentieth century with some hope of success. The "religious forms and ideas of our fathers [are] no longer adequate," the manifesto insisted, because "Man . . . alone is responsible for the realization of the world of his dreams."[29]

In 1973, a Second Humanist Manifesto was issued by Paul Kurtz and Edwin H. Wilson, who made clear their attitude toward divine authority in the preface:

> As in 1933, humanists still believe that traditional theism, especially faith in the prayer-hearing God, assumed to live and care for persons, to hear and understand their prayers, and to be able to do something about them, is an unproved and outmoded faith. Salvationism . . . still appears as harmful, diverting people with false hopes of heaven hereafter. Reasonable minds look to other means for survival.[30]

Drawing on this outspoken hostility, neoevangelicals and their comrades-in-arms turned to identify humanism as a spiritual and political enemy of God's people. They used as ammunition not only the words of the manifesto, but also a 1961 Supreme Court decision that characterized "secular humanism" as a religion, along with Buddhism and Taoism.[31]

Throughout the 1970s, the threat of secular humanism occupied a central place in the political rhetoric of the new evangelical alliance. Humanism affected the soul: neoevangelical pastor and psychologist Tim LaHaye's 1974 bestseller *How To Win Over Depression* even chalks up mental illness to secular humanism. "One of the great tragedies of our times," he insists, "is that atheistic humanists have so brainwashed our culture . . . that most people possess few spiritual reserves upon which to draw in times of mental, emotional, or physical distress." Anyone who wants to triumph over depression must first confess his sins and accept the pardon of God; only then, as a child of God, will he have "the capacity for living a depressed-free life."[32] Humanism threatened America's schools: in 1976, educator Onalee McGraw wrote the hugely popular *Secular Humanism and the Schools: The Issue Whose Time Has Come.* Humanism, McGraw warned, rejected Christian principles in favor of teaching "materialistic values found only in man's nature," and was infiltrating the teaching of public schools.[33] McGraw's work provided a rallying point for private Christian schools, which positioned themselves as fighting the good fight by removing children from the corrupt influence of humanistic classrooms.

In 1980, Tim LaHaye published what may have been the most influential neoevangelical rallying cry against secular humanism, *The Battle for the Mind.* "Most of the evils in the world today can be traced to humanism," he wrote, "which has taken over our government, the U.N., education, TV and most of the other influential things in life."[34] What Christianity needed was "an army of moral activists" to combat this threat.[35]

In 1981, neoevangelical theologian Francis Schaeffer responded to the Humanist Manifesto with *A Christian Manifesto.* Schaeffer, widely respected as an honest Christian intellectual, used the same rhetoric of war as LaHaye: "The humanist view has infiltrated every level of society," he wrote. "If we are going to join the battle . . . we must do battle on the entire front." Combined with this language was a call for a national revival in the good old-fashioned Puritan sense. America had been taken prisoner by secular humanism, Schaeffer concluded, because "the church has forsaken its duty to be the salt of our culture."[36] Repentance and revival must follow before the enemy can be defeated; LaHaye's "army of moral activists" must first examine their own hearts.

• • •

Had it taken place in another venue, Jimmy Carter's confession might have reassured neoevangelicals and their allies. Confession of sin generally signifies that the sinner is aligning himself with the will of God; in fact, throughout the 1970s, calls to repentance and confession were interwoven with the battle cry against God's political enemies. "The political goal of religious humanism is a one-world government controlled by man, not God," declared Christian evangelist and educator Bill Gothard, who throughout the decade held huge week-long training sessions for Christian families in arenas and auditoriums all across the United States. "God has allowed humanism to rise in power in order to motivate Christians to . . . acknowledge transgressions, ours and our forefathers', and turn from them. . . . The time is come that judgment must begin at the house of God."[37] In the materials handed out to thousands of seminar attendees, Gothard laid out a detailed four-step procedure for confessing sins and asking forgiveness from those have been offended. Unless Christians are willing to ask forgiveness not only from God but from each other, Gothard warns, they will never gain a clear conscience, and their effectiveness in fighting for the kingdom of God will be hindered.[38]

Confession of sin was one of the strongest possible ways to demonstrate submission to God. To confess was, essentially, an anti-rational act. Pseudo-Quintilian had articulated this even before Augustine, when he insisted that only drunks and madmen made willing confessions of wrong.[39] Kevin Crotty points out the act of confession is "deeply and pervasively critical . . . it criticizes first and most fundamentally the very idea of self. It then provides the basis for a searching critique of the social structures that entrench the idea of self."[40] In the neoevangelical context, confession is an anti-Enlightenment act; it is the formal acceptance of a moral code thought to originate outside man, a willing submission to an authority that is beyond man's understanding.

Just as, in the political realm, confession levels leaders and followers, so in the religious realm, confession "levels" believers, setting not only their wills but their intellects firmly *beneath* the authority of God. Marx and Engels believed that the battle between man's mind and God's Word was over ("Christian ideas succumbed in the eighteenth century to rationalist ideas," the *Communist Manifesto* blithely states[41]), but the fight against rationality as the ultimate standard of truth still raged.

Unfortunately, Jimmy Carter's confession nevertheless backfired.

Carter, an outspoken Christian, was clearly attempting to show his submission to God's will. He had first been baptised at the age of eleven, after a revival service. He then had a second conversion in 1966, in which he described himself as being "born again." Afterward, Carter traced the beginnings of his "real" Christian life back to the 1966 conversion; before that, he claimed, "I never had really committed myself totally to God—my Christian beliefs were superficial. . . . I formed a much more intimate relationship with Christ. And since then, I've had just about like a new life."[42] In that same year, Carter agreed to host showings of Billy Graham's evangelistic films in the small town of Americus, Georgia; he himself gave the altar call at the end of each evening.[43] The ritual of public confession was not only familiar to Carter, but central to his own religious experience.

Thanks to Carter's neoevangelical background, he saw his personal moral rectitude as vitally important to his task as a political leader. Biographer Kenneth Morris points out that Carter, like any good revivalist, thought society would be renewed as individuals were converted: "He did not believe that government could be good," Morris writes, ". . . he merely believed that through politics an individual Christian might augment his capacity for service. . . . Carter remained a faithful proponent of evangelicalism's social logic throughout his career." His focus was primarily on his own role as a Christian who happened to be president, and who thus had an unusually powerful voice to speak for those who were "poor, disadvantaged, rural, illiterate, without influence."[44]

Carter's own words show a man convinced, in true neoevangelical fashion, that his personal redemption could spread and influence society. In a May 16, 1976, interview with Bill Moyers, broadcast on public television in Washington, DC, and in New York city and published in transcript in the *Los Angeles Times*, Carter answered Moyer's question, "Do you think this is a just society?" with:

> No, no, I don't. I think one of the major responsibilities I have as a leader and as a potential leader is to try to establish justice. And that applies to a broad gamut of things—international affairs, peace, equality, elimination of injustice in racial discrimination, elimination of injustice in tax programs, elimination of injustice in our criminal justice system and so forth. And it's not a crusade. It's just common sense. . . . There's only one person that can set a standard of ethics and morality and excellence and greatness . . . and that's the President.[45]

This was the very moral stance that gave Robert Scheer pause.

Scheer saw Carter's faith as a source for possibly rigid top-down legislation, and he was asking Carter for the same reassurance that Kennedy's public had needed—the assurance that he would not use power granted to him by the voters for his own gain. In Scheer's case, the "gain" in question was legislation based on Carter's Baptist principles. Scheer's questions reflected the democratic fear that an elected official might wield power for personal gain (in this case, religious dominance); Carter's insistence on his sinful heart was an attempt to reassure Scheer that this abuse would never happen. Unlike Kennedy, Carter sensed that a confession of moral fault would achieve the purpose of showing voters that he was "one of them," rather than a man who would use an inborn superiority—in this case, a moral superiority—to support autocratic legislation.

This was all well and good, but Carter completely failed to realize the symbolic effect of his testifying to all of this in the pages of *Playboy*, a magazine that promoted every one of the self-oriented "humanistic" principles evangelicals condemned. As a Christian, Carter had not only to repent and confess, but to demonstrate that he stood solidly in the ranks of holy warriors.

Neoevangelicals who preached cultural engagement and the need to bring the Gospel to the unredeemed might easily have rejoiced over seeing a Christian point of view infiltrating one of the country's most self-oriented publications—but *Playboy* was too far behind enemy lines. Any holy warrior skulking around the *Playboy* tent had obviously gone over to the other side.

Conservative disgust over Carter's attempt to explain himself in the pages of *Playboy* reveals one of the ongoing dilemmas of neoevangelicals. Infiltrating mainstream society was all very well, but a Christian who infiltrated rather than separated was much more likely to be infiltrated, in return, by less-than-Christian philosophies. The writings of LaHaye, Schaeffer, McGraw, and (slightly later) James Dobson are filled with warnings about the power of evil philosophies—particularly secular humanism—to pull Christians away from God without their noticing. Paradoxically, the more a neoevangelical was dedicated to the task of evangelizing from *within*, the more vigilant he needed to be in policing his own heart.

In this context, Carter's use of the very mild vulgarity "screw" pushed him even further into the enemy camp. Not only was he *in* the pages of *Playboy*, talking about lust, but he was using the enemy's terms—a sure indication that *he* was being infiltrated in turn. The *New York Times* quoted a Louisiana lawyer (who had certainly heard worse) as saying that Carter's language had changed his vote: "I certainly can't [vote for him] now."[46] The editor of the *Augusta Chronicle* condemned Carter for "the way he expressed himself, especially through the use of words and phrases that could be construed as 'gutter language.'"[47] William Safire complained that Carter was "making friends by talking dirty. . . . Mr. Carter . . . hoped to win the heart of the *Playboy* audience by the use of a [mild] obscenity."[48]

When Carter ran for re-election in 1980, the *Playboy* confession was still reverberating in neoevangelical Protestant ears. Right-wing politician Homer Duncan wrote in his 1979 book *Secular Humanism: The Most Dangerous Religion in America,* "Personally, I would rather elect a man not committed to biblical morality than one who loudly proclaims that he is a born-again Christian but refuses to define his moral position. For example, we have witnessed the presidency of a self-acknowledged, born-again leader who surrounded himself with amoral or immoral promoters during his campaign."[49] Aimee Semple McPherson had managed to portray herself as under attack by Satan, fighting on the side of the kingdom of heaven; Carter inadvertently put himself on the wrong side of the war, a transgression made more offensive by his claim to be a Christian.

Carter's confession, off-putting to religious conservatives, also alienated his secular supporters. Robert Scheer and his editors may have worried about puritanical legislation and a possible neoevangelical takeover, but other concerns dominated the wider political landscape. In 1976, neoevangelicals were only beginning their ascent to political influence; Carter's claim to be "born again" was one of the earliest uses of neoevangelical rhetoric by a politician. In contrast, the politics of feminism were front and center.

In the early 1970s, legal advances for women had been frequent, but opposition to feminist reforms was also vocal. The Equal Rights Amendment, proposed in 1972, had been ratified by a number of states in 1972 and 1973, but between 1973 and 1975 only four more states had ratified the ERA, and in 1976 it had not passed a single state legislature. The *Roe v. Wade* decision, issued by the Supreme Court in 1973, had affirmed the right to abortion, but prolife action groups such as the Pro-Family Forum were forming to fight against it; the first annual protest "March for Life" was held in 1974, and Carter, a supporter of *Roe v. Wade*, had been mobbed by anti-abortion demonstraters at a rally just two days before the *Playboy* interview became public.

Carter had been strongly supported by women voters, thanks to a combination of factors: his wife Rosalynn was energetically involved with his campaign; he came out early in support of abortion rights (he had written the foreword to *Women in Need*, a book calling for continued access to abortion services);

he had expressed his approval of the Equal Rights Amendment; and both Betty Friedan and Bella Abzug had met with him and supported his candidacy.[50] But confession of adultery (of any kind) appearing in the pages of *Playboy*, a magazine dedicated to the exploitation of female sexuality for male ends, symbolized the exact opposite of all that he had promised women.

Carter's remarks themselves were neither anti-woman nor exploitative. But his words on the page were seen side by side with the *Playboy* logo; every quote drawn from the interview was referenced as "from the *Playboy* interview." His words about lust and adultery were always heard with the hedonistic, exploitative world of *Playboy* shaping them.

Grover Cleveland had successfully positioned himself as a friend of the poor and hungry; Aimee Semple McPherson had symbolically aligned herself with suffragettes and sufferers. But Carter's appearance in *Playboy* managed to position him as a member of an oppressive class: white men who see women primarily as sexual objects. "A woman in southern Missouri said that Mr. Carter had expressed a 'typical masculine attitude,'" wrote Lee Dembert in the *New York Times*, and this was no compliment.[51]

Women's disgust over the interview's appearance in *Playboy* was not soothed after the full interview was published. In it, although he affirmed the Supreme Court legalization of abortion, he added "I think abortion is wrong" (Peter Bourne points out that he had drawn criticism from Roman Catholics on his earlier outspoken support of abortion rights). Scheer also quizzed Carter about the "relatively few women in important staff positions" in his campaign. Carter insisted that women had been in charge of his campaign in a number of areas, but admitted that his top staff members were (in Scheer's words) "white males."[52] At the same time, female reporters were often treated as unimportant by Carter's campaign aides, and the women who worked in his campaign offices were shut out of meetings by the male staff. One of these women finally complained to the *Wall Street*

Journal, leading to a news article about the gap between Carter's outspoken commitment to women's rights and the way women were actually treated by his political organization.[53]

The *Playboy* interview tended to confirm suspicions that Carter's pro-woman rhetoric was hypocritical. While attempting to soothe fears that he would use the authority of the presidency to take advantage of his constituency, Carter confessed to sexual desire in the pages of a magazine dedicated to the sexual subjugation of women. The contradiction did not go unnoticed; Carter had symbolically (and in all likelihood unintentionally) allied himself with Hugh Hefner.

Edward Kennedy had demonstrated that legal confession was not enough. A leader suspected of using his position for personal advantage had to confess to moral failings as well; by 1969, Grover Cleveland's strategy of dignified silence was no longer an option. Jimmy Carter's experience showed that confession to moral failings was also inadequate, unless the confession used appropriate symbols and rhetoric to place the leader on the right side of the battle of good against evil, justice against oppression.

7

JIM BAKKER SHOOTS HIS ALLIES

I sorrowfully acknowledge that seven years ago, in an isolated incident,
I was wickedly manipulated by treacherous former friends and then
colleagues who victimized me with the aid of a female confederate.

—JIM BAKKER, 1987

IN THE TEN YEARS after 1976, the "Year of the Evangelical," the voices of the new evangelical alliance grew more and more audible to secular America. But the born-again were due for an embarrassment. On Friday, March 20, 1987, the *Charlotte Observer* broke the story of TV preacher Jim Bakker's adultery.

Bakker had risen from humble beginnings as a puppetmaster on a children's show (on Jimmy Swaggart's Christian Broadcasting Network) to superstar status in the world of Christian programming. He owned and controlled the PTL ("Praise the Lord" or "People that Love") network, which by 1987 was syndicated across the United States and in a number of foreign countries. With funds raised through appeals on his signature chat show, the *PTL Club*, Bakker built a theme park, Heritage Village, and a complex of residences, including condominiums and the Heritage Grand Hotel, to surround it. The whole resort, which sprawled across 2,300 acres, was known as Heritage USA. By the mid-1980s, six million people visited Heritage USA each year, and PTL programming was streaming to at least 1,400 TV stations worldwide.[1]

Now Bakker was accused of meeting a woman in a hotel room for sex in December of 1980, seven years earlier. The *Charlotte Observer* had first learned about this story a month before, when the woman—Jessica Hahn, a church secretary from Oklahoma—decided to sue PTL, claiming that PTL leadership had paid her off to keep silent. Hahn's representative sent a copy of the lawsuit to the *Observer*, which asked Bakker for comment.

According to the newspaper, Bakker then confessed the adultery in a telephoned statement made to the *Observer* on Thursday, March 19, 1987. With "his voice trembling," the paper claimed, he announced that he was resigning as president of his multimillion-dollar organization, PTL, "for the good of my family, the church, and of all of our related ministries."[2]

The *Observer* printed only a selection of Bakker's actual words, given below:

> [I have resigned] for the good of my family, the church and of all of our related ministries. . . . I sorrowfully acknowledge that seven years ago in an isolated incident I was wickedly manipulated by treacherous former friends and then colleagues who victimized me with the aid of a female confederate. They conspired to betray me into a sexual encounter at a time of great stress in my marital life. Vulnerable as I was at the time, I was set up as part of a scheme to co-opt me and obtain some advantage for themselves over me in connection with their hope for position in the ministry. . . . [Then I] succumbed to blackmail to protect and spare the ministry and my family. Unfortunately, money was paid in order to avoid further suffering or hurt to anyone to appease these persons who were determined to destroy this ministry. I now, in hindsight, realize payment should have been resisted and we ought to have exposed the blackmailers to the penalties of the law. . . . I am not able to muster the resources needed to combat a new wave of attack that I have learned is about to be launched against us by the *Charlotte Observer*, which has attacked us incessantly for the past 12 years. . . . My and Tammy's physical and emotional resources have been so overwhelmed that we are presently under full-time therapy at a treatment center in California. Tammy Faye

and I and our ministries have been subjected to constant harassment and pressures by various groups and forces whose objective has been to undermine and to destroy us. I cannot deny that the personal toll that these pressures have exerted on me and my wife and family have been more than we can bear. . . . I categorically deny that I've ever sexually assaulted or harassed anyone. . . . Anyone who knows Jim Bakker knows that I never physically assaulted anyone in my life.[3]

Like Edward Kennedy twenty years before, Bakker was determined to admit to a kind of fault, while avoiding any admission of moral transgression ("I paid in order to . . . appease these persons who were determined to destroy this ministry"). Like Kennedy, he showed no understanding of the role of public confession in reassuring his followers that he would not take advantage of them. And, like Carter, Bakker failed to align himself with his followers on the battlefield of holy war. It was a disastrous non-apology.

Public confession of wrongdoing was more necessary than ever—particularly for Bakker. In the decade since Carter's interview the practice of confession had entwined itself ever more firmly into radio and television programming, and Bakker's primary outreach was through a television format that was, in its essence, confessional. The language of holy war, which Bakker had spoken for years, also made it essential that he reassure his followers he was still fighting for God's causes despite his flirtation with the dark side.

Yet throughout the next months, Bakker made excuses, refused to make use of the platform of his own confessional program, and opened fire on his allies.

• • •

By 1987, Jim and Tammy Faye Bakker had spent thirteen years hosting their daily television talk show, sitting on a set which grew increasingly more elaborate, encouraging guests to reveal more and more about their private lives, their sins and shortcomings, and their stories of redemption. *The PTL Club* was a confessional program not primarily because of the Bakkers' religious bent, but because the talk shows of the 1980s were fundamentally confessional.

The groundwork for confessional programming on radio and TV was laid in the 1940s, when New York deejay Barry Gray began to experiment with the format of a radio call-in show. Call-in programs, which tried to engage a previously passive audience, gained popularity throughout the fifties, leading to the debut of all-talk radio stations in the early 1960s.

These early programs were not yet confessional in nature. But therapists had in the meantime been experimenting with the airwaves. Group therapy and broadcast technology had begun a journey toward intersection in the 1940s, when the National Association for Mental Health began to produce a national radio drama series called *Hi, Neighbor!* In these radio dramas, "NAMH psychiatrists demonstrated . . . how families and communities could safe-guard mental health by importing therapeutics into schools and recreation centers."[4] By 1950, the episodes had been broadcast over 10,000 times in 450 cities. In 1954, the *International Journal of Group Psychotherapy* carried an article on "The Use of Radio as a Medium for Mental Health." In 1958, psychologist Joyce Brothers hosted the first therapy-based programming on television. Viewers of the *Dr. Joyce Brothers Show*, which ran on NBC in the afternoons, sent in letters detailing their personal problems; Brothers, treating the letters as if they were patients, analyzed them and suggested solutions. In just a few months, Brothers was receiving over a thousand letters a week.[5] Radio and television had the potential to provide psychotherapists with the ultimate tool for reaching large groups with their message of mental health—just as they had provided the new evangelical alliance with the ultimate tool for evangelism.

In 1975, clinical psychologist Toni Grant hosted the earliest syndicated radio therapy program, which married the call-in format to the therapeutic model; on her show, on Los Angeles's

KFI, she encouraged listeners to phone in and describe their problems to all of Los Angeles. In 1980, a second prominent psychotherapist began a similiar call-in show, also in Los Angeles (this one on KABC): David Viscott, a psychiatrist with an M.D. from Tufts University, concentrated on pressuring his listeners into confessing their shortcomings. "Dr. Viscott," wrote a *New York Times* reporter, in a story on the immense popularity of call-in therapy, ". . . does not tread very gently. . . . [H]e often seems to shove people verbally into self-reckonings."[6] The broadcast programs of these two co-founders of the practice of "radio therapy," were joined in the 1980s by a host of other call-in psychotherapy shows.

In essence, radio therapy invited callers to include a vast radio audience in a massive group therapy session. However, because the technical limitations of radio meant that the "group" itself was invisible and, for the most part, silent, interaction between individual callers and therapists occupied most of the broadcasts. Television, which was evolving a more participatory format, proved a more natural home for group therapy. While radio hosts were popularizing the call-in format, television hosts were experimenting with the television talk show.

The earliest talk shows were late-night entertainment, conversational and celebrity-focused: a host chatted with movie stars, musicians, and occasionally politicians, while the audience listened. This format was merely an entertainment-focused version of a newscast, with the host playing the part of reporter. The earliest late-night talk show to become a national hit was the *Tonight Show*, which began in 1954 and was hosted by Steve Allen and Jack Paar.[7]

In 1967, Phil Donahue (who had previously hosted a radio talk show) pioneered a new format: a television talk show, structured like the late-night entertainment show with conversation between host and guests as an audience watched, but drawing on the principles of group therapy, interwoven with elements of the religious meeting. The name of the show, *Donahue*, demonstrated the host's leadership and control. Phil

Donahue, who held the microphone, occupied a place more analagous to that of a preacher like Oral Roberts than that of a group therapy leader. His leadership was not at all muted. Audience participation, which had been passive and muted in the late-night talk show format, was modelled on the group therapy session: the audience of *Donahue* was encouraged to react to the revelations of the guests, to ask questions of guest experts, and to raise problems of their own. As in the therapy session, the talk show was carefully controlled, despite the necessity of appearing spontaneous and heartfelt. Bernard M. Timberg documents the ahead-of-time preparation of 80 percent of the average talk show content, with scripting and production values defining a rigid space within which the guest and host could exercise a small amount of freedom.[8]

The success of *Donahue* spawned an entire genre of television talk, with its heyday in the 1980s. *Maury Povich* and *Geraldo* used the same format with an even stronger emphasis on uncovering secrets and eliciting confessions, inviting troubled "guests" to air their difficulties in front of a studio audience, with the host acting as lay psychotherapist. Geraldo Rivera was Hispanic; the format widened its racial and gender appeal when Oprah Winfrey, Sally Jessy Raphael, and Montel Williams hosted their own wildly popular shows.[9]

While these television talk shows drew their inspiration from group psychotherapy, their titles revealed that they shared an underlying assumption with fundamentalist Protestantism. Overwhelmingly, the guests who aired their problems were representative of wider social problems: "When Mothers Sell Babies for Drugs," or "Ministers Who Seduce Ladies."[10] The guests on these shows were given labels that placed them in a larger social context: " a woman who wants to give away a violent child," on one *Oprah* show, "a woman who plotted her husband's death" on another.[11]

In some cases, the solutions suggested by the audience and invited experts in response to the confessions of the guests were intended to change the individuals on stage, but the hosts continually drew on the experts into applying those same solutions to related national issues. The implication was clear: conversion of these individual wrongdoers from sin to upright-ness would begin to bring the entire country back to the nar-row path of nighteousness. In other cases, the guests them-selves were confessing in order to "evangelize" the listeners. "I thought it was actually a real gift to be given the opportunity to be able to reach millions of people and perhaps change some consciousness around lesbianism," one *Donahue* guest told researcher Patricia Priest. Another guest, a woman who had been tricked by con artists, agreed. Her appearance on the show, she said, was a chance to warn others, "just kind of spreading the gospel." Priest concludes that the talk show guests she interviewed were, "like religious evangelicals, . . . ar-dent believers in the critical importance of their message as a way to foster understanding and thereby effect personal and political transformation."[12] The confessions—the "voluntary disclosures"— of the guests were central to this purpose.

In a third intersection with Protestantism and group therapy, talk shows shared with both an emphasis on the democratic relationship between leader and followers. In 1985, Oprah Winfrey revealed her understanding of this dynamic by partak-ing in confession herself. While interviewing a woman who had been sexually abused as a child, she revealed that she, too, had been molested at age nine.[13] The host had joined the guest; the leader had shown oneness with the penitent.

This was only the first of Oprah Winfrey's personal confes-sions, in which she showed that despite her celebrity she was like the members of her largely female audience. Her confes-sions about her troubles with food and weight earned her the undying loyalty of women who also struggled with the ideal of thinness. Her more spectacular confessions, such as her later admission (1995) that she had been addicted to cocaine, helped her maintain this double identity: she was a celebrity (with access to drugs and money), but also flawed and human in her weakness. "Such 'personal' disclosures [were] part of a skillful balancing act," writes television scholar Jane Shattuc, "creating an aura of spontaneity and truth while also maintaining a highly managed image at the heart of a \$50-million enterprise."[14] Winfrey also included her audience in her confessions, asking them continually to respond to her in the "call and response" patterns of southern black church services: "Winfrey's show drew forth antiphonal confessions of empathy from a largely female audience of 'sisters,'. . . who had themselves experienced victimization and powerlessness," concludes Bernard Timberg.[15]

Oprah had grasped the central dynamic between patient/ worshipper/talk-show audience and therapist/minister/celebrity host: The patient or worshipper *wanted* to remain within the group, but needed the therapist or minister to acknowledge his/her power as a consumer. Confession of flaws allowed this power to become visible: the patient/worshipper generously extended forgiveness, and the talk-show audience reached out in empathy and acceptance to the celebrity host. Oprah's confessional style is still visible on her program, which remains the most popular (and long-lasting) television talk show of all time.

Public confession had moved from church to airwaves, and then, sideways, from sacred airwaves to secular programming. By the 1990s, the essential weirdness of laying out one's personal psychiatric troubles in front of an entire nation had been so blunted by exposure that the television show *Frasier*, centered around a psychiatrist who practices his calling on the air, took its place alongside *Friends* (set in a New York apartment), *Cheers* (set in a Boston bar), and *NewsRadio* (set in a radio station) as simply another sitcom.

The *PTL Club*, a cross between *Oprah* and *The Tonight Show*, featured musical performances, celebrity interviewees—and long, intimate discussions about the shortcomings, sins, and needs of the guests who sat across from the Bakkers. Jim Bakker even uncovered the personal lives of guests who were *not* on the show, announcing that he was praying for the spiritual and physical needs of viewers whom he had glimpsed through supernatural knowledge. Like Oprah Winfrey, he and Tammy Faye confessed their own difficulties, describing everything from their weight problems to struggles in their marriage. First aired on the *PTL Club* set, these confessions then often served as material for confessional self-help books (such as the co-authored *How We Lost Weight and Kept It Off*), tapes, and even retreats. "Not only did the Bakkers air their problems on television," writes Peter S. Hawkins, ". . . but they developed weekend 'marriage workshops' . . . [that] combined group therapy with 'trained counselors' [and] 'couples' prayer.'"[16]

Fund-raising for the work of God was wound together with the confessions of the Bakkers and their guests. Bakker, insisting that God's work required more money, exhorted listeners to send gifts. As he appealed for funds, both he and Tammy Faye often wept. Like the weeping over sin that accompanied revivalist confessions of sin, these tears revealed the weakness of the two hosts, their inability to raise money on their own, and their reliance on God. Weeping inevitably boosted contributions from listeners, who saw this expression of humility as a levelling confession, a bridge-building emotion that connected glittering TV leader and living-room bound watcher.[17] A faithful *PTL Club* listener, interviewed by journalist Larry Martz after Bakker's fall, reveals the connection between democratic confession and weeping: "Every time Tammy cried, I cried and grabbed my 'ol checkbook," she said. "Millions of people did the same thing."[18] The confessional tears had made the Bakkers appear "one of the flock."

And it was absolutely necessary for the Bakkers' survival that their listeners feel empathy and oneness with them and their purposes. The televangelist (like the Protestant minister who can be dismissed by the vote of his congregation) cannot afford to alienate too many viewers. The format of such popular programs as The *PTL Club,* The *700 Club,* and Oral Roberts's regular broadcasts reveals the extent to which the "worshipper" had become a customer. In return for contributions, listeners were promised renewal, a better marriage, a slimmer figure, a better life. They were also offered books, tapes, and other products; just as on the Home Shopping Network, books and videos were displayed, discussed, and then offered for bargain prices to anyone who would call in with a credit card number. Purchasers could also pray with the operator who answered the phone, adding a spiritual dimension to the pseudo-therapeutic nature of the purchase. Spiritual and emotional needs could now be met through purchase.[19]

Bakker hosted his confessional talk show from 1974 to 1987, thirteen years during which the holy war for America's soul grew more and more intense. Christian television was central to the fight; during the 1970s, Baptist minister Jerry Falwell and his colleague Elmer Towns called for "saturation" of radio and television airwaves so that the Gospel could be heard by "every available person at every available time by every available means. . . . The church will stand accountable at the judgment seat of Christ for its failure to utilize every means available to us to reach every creature."[20] Toward the end of the decade, the possibility of saturation took a leap forward when Pat Robertson's Christian Broadcasting Network (based in Virginia Beach, Virginia) spun off two new Christian networks. The Trinity Broadcasting Network, or TBN, was founded by Paul and Jan Crouch and Jim and Tammy Faye Bakker in 1973; the PTL network was then started by the Bakkers after they had a falling out with the Crouches and left TBN.[21]

Ben Armstrong, founder and executive director of the National Religious Broadcasters, wrote in his 1979 book *The Electric Church* that television and radio had practically returned the church to the apostolic age: "Radio and television have broken through the walls of tradition we have built up around the church, and have restored conditions remarkably similar to the early church." Jumping ahead a few centuries, Armstrong also compared religious broadcasting to the Protestant Reformation: it would bring about "revolution as dramatic as the revolution that began when Martin Luther nailed his ninety-five theses to the cathedral door at Wittenberg."[22] The title of Falwell's *Old Time Gospel Hour* is merely one example of this mingling of nostalgia for a shining Christian past with the technology of the corrupt present.

By 1987, returning to this mythical Christian past had become one of the main goals of the American holy war. Shifting social conditions in the late 1970s and early 1980s, particularly changing gender roles and sexual norms, encouraged neoevangelicals and fundamentalists to look back with longing to the earlier decades of the twentieth century, ignoring the fact that those decades had been a time of fundamentalist fomenting against modernism.[23] A *Focus on the Family* magazine cover from 1995 reveals the persistence of this new anti-modernism; it shows the Cleaver family (of the 1950s television show, *Leave It to Beaver*) smiling into the camera, with the large headline "June & Ward Were Right."[24] The battle for the faith was also a battle to restore the past.

The Second Coming did not disappear from the evangelical horizon, but the battle for the past was more immediate, more tangible, and more likely to succeed. Converting sinners was a long, uncertain, arduous process that could take years, centuries, or millennia; the New Testament was very clear in warning that no one could predict the time of the parousia.[25] Evangelism was a spiritual labor without a visible ending point.

The battle for the past, on the other hand, was a fight with easily quantifiable goals, and with the election of Ronald Reagan in 1980, victory seemed more likely than ever. Carter's breach with neoevangelicals had never fully healed, and neoevangelical opposition to Carter helped bring Ronald Reagan into office in 1980. Pollster Louis Harris credited the Moral Majority, Jerry Falwell's brand-new political organization, and the followers of other televangelists with providing the victory margin.[26]

Falwell's consitutency was largely Baptist, but Pentecostals were quick to leap onto the bandwagon of political activism. *Christian Voice*, established in 1979, with an "anti-gay and anti-pornography" agenda, drew much of its membership from

Figure 7.1. Nostalgia at Heritage USA

Assemblies of God congregations.[27] While declaring that Christ would return once the Gospel had been preached to the world, Swaggart also published a 1982 book, *The Rape of America*, which lamented America's slide from her historical commitment to God.[28] His sermons in 1984 repeat this theme: he hoped to "redirect a nation to the paths of righteousness," not merely to enable the coming of Christ in judgment on it.

Bakker's own "Heritage Village," although showing a typically Pentecostal disregard for chronology, reflected the neo-evangelical preoccupation with America's "Christian past." The ground for Heritage Village was broken on Independence Day (July 4, 1978), a date that became the village's anniversary. The village contained a reconstruction of the Upper Room, site of the Last Supper; a replica of the town center of ancient Jerusalem; Revolutionary-era split-rail fences surrounding a recreated nineteenth-century-American settlement; a Victorian-themed shopping mall; and Billy Graham's childhood home (removed from its original location, board by board, and carefully rebuilt). "It's like you come into a whole different world . . . an oasis," one visitor remarked. The oasis did not point forward to the restored heavens and earth; instead, it offered a cozy, idealized, mostly American past.[29]

Throughout the 1980s, neoevangelicals and Pentecostals alike continued to be preoccupied with a mythical Christian heritage, a preoccupation that led to increasing calls for confession and repentance. Like the first Puritan communities, America had declined from its previous spiritual heights, and revival was needed. In 1986, Jerry Falwell preached that spiritual awakening would begin with "deep national conviction because of our sins." Confession and repentance would produce "divine healing in America and a spiritual awakening that would glorify Christ and promote holiness and change the national lifestyle. And it isn't revival if it doesn't change the national lifestyle. That is why I say you cannot separate the sacred from the secular."[30] Pentecostal minister Jimmy Swaggart linked his own broadcasts to both evangelism and a return to past national standards: "When I realize that nearly forty million people in forty countries will tune in this week to our telecast," he told his listeners in 1984, "the immensity of the audience is almost beyond my human comprehension. And parallel with this unprecedented ability to appear before people is the opportunity to influence them: We can redirect a nation to the paths of righteousness; we can introduce (often for the first time) masses to the Gospel of Jesus Christ."[31]

These calls for national confession and recommitment—phrased as "We as a nation have fallen away from Your will"—allowed the Christian right to connect itself to an idealized Christian past, as well as to a political past. This assertion implied that there *had* once been a Christian America. Jeremiads about the decline of American Christianity placed neoevangelicals and Pentecostals in the same pulpit as Edward Taylor and John Cotton.

Even more importantly, the calls to national repentance reveal the extent to which the members of the new evangelical alliance were now conflating their identity as Americans with their identity as citizens of the kingdom of heaven. After all, the faithful who sat and listened to these sermons did *not* consider that *they* had fallen away. They were confessing the sins of the rest of the nation, particularly the Democrats. In these jeremiads, the responsibility of the congregation expanded; no longer simply affirming and witnessing the confessions of others, the hearers were using the collective identity of "We, the people" to confess *on behalf* of others.

Critics of televangelists accused them of "mixing politics and religion," as though the two were separate. But the rhetoric of confession and conversion so central to the new evangelical alliance had always carried with it an intrinsic political message. Neoevangelicals and their allies had opposed the social gospel of the mainline denominations by arguing that society could be changed only one sinner at a time; social renewal must arise from a swelling mass of converted grassroots disciples—not from top-down regulation. To convert sinners is to bring them out of the kingdom of darkness into the kingdom of light, but it is also to expect that this journey will have visible effects here and now, in the society in which we live. In a democracy, the Christian morality of a mass of converts must eventually seep up into the elected leadership. This emphasis on bottom-to-top, rather than top-to-bottom, change explains why the new evangelical alliance found the Republican party's rhetoric of less government regulation so appealing.[32]

Public confessions, whether connected to conversion or to spiritual recommitment, were organically related to the project of social renewal. To confess and repent, whether for yourself or for other sinners, was to demonstrate your loyalty to those past, picture-perfect days of faith. Repentance and confession was a powerful step in the political renewal of America. The repentance of individual sinners was the dynamic that the new evangelical alliance longed to see in the nation as a whole.

For the neoevangelicals and Pentecostals of the 1980s, fighting against what they saw as a rising tide of secular humanism exalting the reason and judgment of men, confession was an act of resistance to the mainstream culture of America. Confession of sin (particularly sins of lust and greed) was a rejection of those values neoevangelicals ascribed to secular American culture—a focus on self and on the fulfillment of personal desires and ambitions, even at the expense of others.

By the 1980s, Protestants were confessing more than ever, more publicly than ever, to a wider audience than ever before. In America, wrote *Time* magazine reporter Ezra Bowen in 1987, "compulsions to repent and punish sin remain just beneath the skin, erupting like fever blisters in times of stress."[33]

Yet Jim Bakker, who desperately needed to situate himself on the right side of the holy war, and who had spent over a decade confessing on television, continued to avoid the need for open confession of his sins. In fact, he even avoided addressing the issue on his own television talk show, where he might have spoken directly to his supporters.

Instead, Bakker gave his explanation through the *Charlotte Observer*—which surrounded his actual words with their own critical commentary. The italics below are the *Observer*'s text into which Bakker's confession was set:

> *PTL President Jim Bakker . . . resigned Thursday from PTL* for the good of my family, the church, and of all of our related ministries. . . . I sorrowfully acknowledge that seven years ago in an isolated incident I was wickedly manipulated by treacherous former friends and then colleagues who victimized me with the aid of a female confederate. They conspired to betray me into a sexual encounter at a time of great stress in my marital life. *He did not identify those people.* Vulnerable as I was at the time, I was set up as part of a scheme to co-opt me and obtain some advantage for themselves over me in connection with their hope for position in the ministry. . . . *Then, Bakker said, he* succumbed to blackmail to protect and spare the ministry and my family. Unfortunately, money was paid in order to avoid further suffering or hurt to anyone to appease these persons who were determined to destroy this ministry. I now, in hindsight, realize payment should have been resisted and we ought to have exposed the blackmailers to the penalties of the law. *Bakker made the comments as The Observer was investigating allegations that a New York woman*

and her representatives received $115,000 in 1985 after she told PTL she had sexual relations with Bakker in a Florida hotel room. . . . I am not able to muster the resources needed to combat a new wave of attack that I have learned is about to be launched against us by *the Charlotte Observer*, which has attacked us incessantly for the past 12 years. *Rich Oppel, editor of the* Observer, *responded in a statement: "We were investigating allegations about PTL's Jim Bakker at the time of his resignation. . . . No article would have been published unless we were convinced of the accuracy and fairness of the information, which did involve allegations of a sexual encounter and subsequent payments. Mr. Bakker often has questioned our motives in pursuing coverage of PTL's activities. The accuracy of our coverage has never been successfully challenged." . . . The developments open a new chapter for PTL, which reported $129 million in revenues in 1986. . . . [Bakker] used his personality and gift for TV to raise hundreds of millions of dollars from viewers. The weekday broadcast once known as the "PTL Club," for Praise The Lord or People That Love, was renamed after Bakker and his wife. . . . Denomination officials told the* Observer *in the past week that they had begun formally investigating allegations against PTL, including the charge of sexual misconduct by Bakker. The investigation will continue, despite the resignations, church officials said Thursday. Bakker disclosed that* my and Tammy's physical and emotional resources have been so overwhelmed that we are presently under full-time therapy at a treatment center in California. Tammy Faye and I and our ministries have been subjected to constant harassment and pressures by various groups and forces whose objective has been to undermine and to destroy us. I cannot deny that the personal toll that these pressures have exerted on me and my wife and family have been more than we can bear, *he said. On March 6, in a videotape shown to PTL viewers, Bakker and his wife of 26 years disclosed that Tammy Bakker was being treated for drug dependence. . . . The entire board of directors at PTL, which Bakker had chaired,* *resigned. At least two of eight members of the board had resigned in recent weeks. . . . Thursday's events have their roots on a sunny, breezy Saturday afternoon in Clearwater Beach, Fla., six years ago. Bakker, then 40, was in Florida Dec. 6, 1980, to appear on a broadcast for a nearby Christian TV station. . . . Also at Bakker's hotel in Clearwater Beach was a 21-year-old church secretary from New York named Jessica Hahn. Fletcher had arranged for her to fly to Florida to meet Bakker and see the broadcast, according to Fletcher and Hahn. She said she was emotionally troubled by the encounter, which she said she did not expect. . . . In his statement Thursday, Bakker said:* I categorically deny that I've ever sexually assaulted or harassed anyone. . . . Anyone who knows Jim Bakker knows that I never physically assaulted anyone in my life. *Oppel, the* Observer *editor, said the newspaper's investigation didn't involve allegations of sexual assault or harassment.*

Bakker was in control of a cable network that, according to *Time* magazine, reached "13.5 million households over 171 stations."[34] Yet he never used this network to speak directly to his supporters. Not until March 24, four days after the story broke, did he go on television, and then only on a local station, not on the PTL network. Perhaps the confessional nature of the program struck him as too dangerous.

By the time two months had passed, Bakker had apparently decided to hold to his strategy of avoiding any true confession. He held his first press conference on May 1, 1987. "In that informal, 30-minute session with reporters," the *Charlotte Observer* recorded two days later, "Bakker said he would issue a complete statement and answer questions this week. But seven hours later, about 7:15 p.m. (PDT), Bakker's aides announced he would not hold a news conference. 'Jim and Tammy have decided to make no further statements,' said associate April Espinoza."[35] The offer of complete revelation, followed by its almost immediate withdrawal, was more damaging than previous partial revelations had been.

Bakker's refusal to address honestly and openly his sexual misdeeds led to a serious backlash. His attempts to portray himself as a victim of a scheming woman were universally unsuccessful, thanks in large part to the *Observer* commentary. Bakker claimed that he had been taken advantage of by a "female confederate"; the *Observer* pointed out that Hahn was a "21-year-old church secretary." The "treacherous former friend" in Bakker's statement was revealed by the *Observer* to be "Oklahoma City evangelist John Wesley Fletcher, then a friend of Bakker's and a regular guest on PTL broadcasts." In the *Observer* story, Fletcher, who admits to arranging the meeting between Bakker and Hahn, appears as a weak, unthreatening figure:

> Fletcher could not be reached Thursday. In a Feb. 24 interview, Fletcher told the *Observer* that Bakker was depressed by his marital troubles: "Anything that I did for Jim, I did, honest to God, because I thought I was helping him. I believed it," Fletcher said. Fletcher, crying during portions of the interview, said he regrets his actions.

In an exact reversal of Grover Cleveland's strategy for dealing with Maria Halpin, Bakker grew to look more and more like a sexual predator.

Bakker's refusal to confess (or even to give the appearance of open confession) acted to focus attention more and more acutely on his financial standing. Revelation of one type of predatory behavior compounded attention on the second; the sexual led to the financial. As the scandal continued to unfold, Bakker's opulent lifestyle was consistently portrayed against the backdrop of the hundreds of thousands of ordinary working people who had sent him contributions. Bakker showed absolutely no comprehension of his need to reassure his followers that he was simply "one of them." Rather, while PTL was going through bankruptcy hearings (attended, according to *Time*, by "anxious crowds" of donors), the Bakkers were staying on the "105-ft. ocean-going yacht" of their new lawyer, Melvin Belli; while staying in San Francisco on the yacht, they were "taken to parties, dinners, and exclusives stores, by Belli's wife Lia. Tammy enjoyed a makeover at Lia's favorite hair salon. . . . A week earlier Jim and Tammy [Faye] Bakker had been supervising $300,000 worth of renovations to their Gatlinburg, Tenn., home," where Bakker greeted *Time* reporters with "hammer in hand."[36] Bakker did nothing to defuse the fears that he might be using his moral authority for personal gain. His opulent lifestyle showed him to be a financial predator as well as a sexual predator.

At numerous points, Bakker could have admitted that his finances had been mismanaged; he could have apologized, pledged to take a smaller salary, promised to do his best to pay back any misused money—all without actually admitting to financial *wrongdoing*. Instead, he insisted that his wealth was deserved, and that he should continue to draw his full salary, keep his homes, and even retain the services of a full-time secretary and housekeeper.

Bakker's refusal even to appear in a confessional *stance* when it came to his finances stemmed from a cross-current of Pentecostal confession, one with a much shorter pedigree. In the 1980s, another kind of confession had arisen on religious broadcasts: the "confession" of health and wealth. Health-and-wealth preachers such as Robert Tilton gained their followings by telling largely working-class Pentecostals that they too deserved to share in the wealth of the decade. Tilton's tracts demonstrate a weaving together of the act of confession and positive thinking with the idea of holy war. According to Tilton's 1988 booklet *The Power to Create Wealth*, belief in Christ gives the believer the power to "harness our mind—to control and restrain the thoughts which try to enter and hurt you. . . . The natural man's mind is uncontrolled. However, the born-again believer is spiritually minded." If a believer "confesses with his mouth" that he deserves wealth, God will give it to him—and will "take the wealth out of" the hands of "sinners."

Positive confession is a tool not only against sinners, but against Satan: "The devil wants to keep the church in darkness,"

Tilton writes, "because when she comes out of the dark ages, she is going to be doing something. . . . The church won't ever get her job done as long as the devil keeps her blinded to the truth. The more we find out about the way it is in Heaven, the more we're going to release that into the earth. The more we release into the earth, the less territory there is for the devil to operate in." At the end of his booklet, Tilton lists five "case studies"—stories of people who were in debt who watched his television program *Success-N-Life*, made public "vows of faith" by confessing (in letters to the Tilton headquarters) that they had not trusted God before but now intended to, and were then rewarded with money, cars, houses, and a heavy-duty washing machine.[37]

This confession of wealth is linked to the confession of sin; the two are subsequent steps in the war against Satan. "[I]f you will confess your sins," Tilton writes in another booklet, called *How to Kick the Devil Out of your Life*, "the Bible says God is faithful to forgive you and to cleanse you of all unrighteousness. . . . No longer will Satan have dominion over you. . . . Jesus said that whatever you demand, whatever you speak to in His name . . . He would see it done. . . . Speak the Word of God in the Name of Jesus and DEMAND that [Satan] leave!"[38]

The audiences who accepted Tilton's assertions and "confessed" that they deserved wealth were, like neoevangelicals confessing sin, setting themselves apart from mainstream American culture. Their claim to wealth was based on their position as children of God, "Sons of the King," who deserved to share in the "King's riches." While rejecting American sexual values, the health-and-wealth confessions accepted another facet of American mainstream culture: the right to material prosperity.

Bakker himself had indulged in a fair amount of this sort of preaching. "As a child of God, you ought to live in victory," he told his followers in the 1983 pamphlet, *You Can Make It*. "Christianity is a winning way of life. God intends for you to be successful in every part of living."[39] Both Jim and Tammy Faye repeatedly claimed their wealth was a sign of God's blessing on their lives, a reward for their commitment to the ministry. Heritage USA itself, in all its luxury, represented the sort of life that Christians could have if they would only "confess" their right to it: "Our lodging accomodations, restaurants, shops and recreational facilities offer all the enjoyment to which our guests and congregations are *entitled*," PTL promotional literature boasted.[40]

Many of Bakker's Pentecostal followers found the doctrine of prosperity immensely satisfying. As Edith Blumhofer points out:

> Having gone unnoticed for many years, they took pride in and lavished funds on those who gave them visibility and reshaped their public image. Like Bakker and Swaggart, many of them recalled years of deprivation. They seemed inclined to revel in possessions and to find appealing emphases that emanated from independent Pentecostal centers urging the reasonableness of health and wealth for believers.[41]

Confession of *wrongdoing* warred against this contrary sort of confession. For Bakker to confess financial misdealings—even though it might well have served to pacify the loyalists among his following—was to speak against the prosperity that he was supposed to "confess" with his mouth. "Talk negatively and you will have a negative life," he had preached to his followers. "As soon as we speak in faith God starts the wheels turning in our life. We move ahead victoriously. . . . Don't camp at your problem. When you are negative, your life is going to be like a mudhole. You stay stuck in it."[42]

Refusing to confess either sexual sins or financial missteps, Bakker failed to create a sense of oneness with his followers. He also failed to place himself on the right side of the holy war. Worse, his explanations blurred the distinction between his allies and his enemies. Bakker did not, as Carter had, inadvertently place himself on the wrong side of the battle lines;

he actively engaged in rubbing out the lines so no one could tell where they were.

At first, Bakker accused the *Charlotte Observer* itself of leading an evil campaign to "destroy" the ministry of the gospel—at the same time he was using the newspaper as his vehicle for confession. Bakker's attitude towards the *Observer* was not unusual. Conservative Protestants generally saw the "secular media" as firmly on the wrong side of the battle against evil, and dominated by editors and reporters who were actively hostile to Christianity. Unfortunately, since Bakker was also using the *Observer* as his vehicle for confession, his accusations were accompanied by the newspaper's own defense of itself.[43]

Next, Bakker turned around and accused other Christians of treachery. In his initial statement, Bakker placed himself, his wife, the Baptist minister Jerry Falwell (who had been asked to take over temporary leadership of PTL), and PTL Executive Director Richard Dortch on the righteous side of a battle to destroy his ministry; on the other side of the line were the forces of evil, including Jessica Hahn and John Wesley Fletcher (both self-proclaimed neoevangelicals).

On March 24, Bakker bought broadcast time on a local cable channel and expanded on his accusations. He told viewers that the scandal had been arranged by "well-known individuals," as part of a "plot of the downfall of PTL," and claimed that the plot had been stalled by the involvement of "honest ministers," such as Jerry Falwell.[44] The following day, his lawyer accused Pentecostal minister Jimmy Swaggart of being the moving force behind this plot.

Far from being a battle of good against evil, this was now one of Pentecostal versus Pentecostal, which made Bakker's claim to be oppressed by evildoers even less believable. Swaggart denied the charge, and even within the Bakker camp, reaction to this accusation was mixed; Falwell, now identified as one of the "honest ministers," also said that Swaggart was not involved.[45]

Bakker responded by upping his rhetoric. The alleged scheme now became a "diabolical plot," with Swaggart cast as agent of Satan. (Swaggart, in turn, remarked, "I think I'm more of a victim than anything else.")[46] To complicate the issue, the battle sides, now drawn up with Swaggart on one side, Bakker on the other, and Falwell standing on the line, contained a ringer: over on Bakker's "righteous" side was his new lawyer, Norman Roy Grutman, who had represented *Penthouse* magazine in the lawsuit Falwell had brought against it to prevent it from publishing an interview with Falwell.[47]

Then, Bakker also put himself in opposition to his own Pentecostal denomination, the Assemblies of God. Bakker had resigned from the Assemblies, a standard gesture by an embattled minister, but Assemblies officials had already warned that this might not be the end of the matter. The day after Bakker's *Observer* confession, Assemblies assistant general superintendent Everett Stenhouse told the *New York Times* that "the scandal had hurt the church," and that "church leaders could reject Mr. Bakker's resignation and instead strip him of his ministries."[48]

At this point, Pentecostal faith-healer Oral Roberts further confused the issue by condemning both the Assemblies of God *and* the *Charlotte Observer* at the same time. At the end of March, Roberts said on his television program that he had been given a word from God. The word was this:

> Flee, my brother, the Lord is saying to those people in the headquarters of that denomination [the Assemblies of God], where Jim out of graciousness turned in his ordination papers because they wanted him to, and you've not accepted it. You've said, "No, we're gonna strip him. We're gonna crush him." The Word of the Lord is coming to you from Oral Roberts' mouth today: if you strip Jim Bakker, you've touched God's anointed, you've harmed God's prophet. And the Word of the Lord says, "Touch not my anointed, do no harm to my prophets." I beg you, headquarters of a great denomination, one that we respect and love, desist, move back, and treat Jim Bakker as what

he is, an anointed man, a prophet of God. And the hand of the Lord will not fall upon you. But the Lord will bless you. And to the great newspaper [*Charlotte Observer*]. You seem so immune to what our God can do. You've come into an unholy alliance with these others in the name of religion and morality. You've set yourself up to be a standard of morality, when you're not. The Word of the Lord comes unto you from my mouth. And the Lord says that He'll create a great dissension in your ranks. You'll have such dissension in your ranks. You'll have such dissension that it'll spread across the news media of America and you will not know what you're doing.[49]

By May 25, a mere two months after the original confession, Bakker himself was held up widely as an example of a man who was dishonoring and blocking the Gospel. Jerry Falwell remarked that Bakker's problems were creating a "backwash that could hurt every Gospel ministry in America, if not the world," while Swaggart famously called Bakker a "cancer on the body of Christ."[50] *Time* ran a special issue about the decline of ethics in America; in its major story, "Looking to Its Roots," Jim Bakker was identified as one of the causes of moral decline in America. *Time* reporter Ezra Bowen quoted a raft of academics lamenting America's "widespread sense of moral disarray" and warning of a national loss of "moral landmarks." In this bleak picture of America's moral collapse, Jim Bakker is cited as a "manifestation of the personhood cult," an American "obsession with self and image" that puts personal fulfillment ahead of all duty and responsibility.[51]

Bakker made one more attempt to cross back over to the side of the light. On Ted Koppel's *Nightline* broadcast of May 26, 1987, he tried to cast *Falwell* as the villain: "I did not choose Jerry Falwell to take over my ministry," he told Koppel. Falwell, not Swaggart, was now the moving force behind the attempt to "steal" PTL.

But Falwell, at the head of PTL, shoved Bakker firmly back into the enemy camp. "I don't see any repentance there," he said to the *Augusta Chronicle*, two days after the *Nightline* broadcast. "I see greed, the self-centeredness, the avarice that brought them down." Falwell added that it would be a "disservice to God and to the church at large" if Bakker were allowed to take PTL back: "I love Richard Nixon; a lot of people loved him, but I don't think anybody in American would ask Mr. Nixon to come back to the presidency," Falwell told the *Augusta Chronicle*.[52] The juxtaposition of Nixon and Bakker immediately placed Bakker in the category of wrongdoers who refuse to confess their sin.

Falwell also made another, even more damaging accusation: Bakker, he insisted, had been engaging in homosexual behavior for years, and Falwell himself had "'sat at the table' across from men who described homosexual advances made to them by Bakker."[53] This was canny positioning, which again put not only Bakker but also the men who had drawn his (theoretical) homosexual gaze on the other side of a physical barrier separating Falwell, the protector of righteousness, from agents of moral decline. In the rhetoric of the new evangelical alliance, homosexuality was much more than a sexual orientation. It was a sign of the decadence of modern American culture. Public acceptance of homosexuality represented the relinquishing of absolute moral standards. Homosexuality was not a condition; it was a choice, and homosexuals were active agents in the destruction of America's Christian faith.

Bakker responded to Falwell's *Augusta Chronicle* remarks of May 28 by telling the *Desert Sun* that he and Tammy Faye wanted "to go back and preach the Gospel of Jesus Christ to hurting people"; in yet another reorganization of the battle lines, he now claimed that he had spoken to Jimmy Swaggart about collaborating with him, and that "good things are happening."[54] (Swaggart, no fool, immediately denied ever speaking about this to Bakker.)

On June 8, Bakker tried to make a graceful retreat from the front lines: "If this be a holy war, I am declaring a cease-fire

Figure 7.2. Decay at Heritage USA

and a truce," he said. "I'm just going to step out of the arena. I made a mistake by ever stepping out and trying to tell our side of the story."[55]

But Bakker's mistake had been in *failing* to step out and confess. Falwell showed a much more acute understanding of the remedy needed when he told the *Augusta Chronicle*, "Bakker needs to ask Ms. Hahn for forgiveness, acknowledge the homosexual allegations and return the 'millions' taken from PTL coffers." In other words, he needed to confess his sin, get himself on the right side of the holy war through repentance, and symbolically place himself on the side of the thousands of watchers who had sent in money.

Bakker did none of these things. In the end, he lost control of PTL, which was reorganized by a new board in order to avoid bankruptcy. After the reorganization, most of the Heritage USA complex sat untended, decayed, and vandalized. Bakker himself went to jail for five years after being convicted of defrauding PTL supporters out of $158 million.

When Bakker emerged in 1994, he announced that he wanted to return to the pulpit. But he had still not offered a satisfying confession. The *Charlotte Observer* remarked on the day of his release, "To this day, he has yet to publicly talk in depth about what he did."[56]

For two years, Bakker was unable to interest his followers in finding his return to television. Finally he published his autobiography; titled *I Was Wrong*, it might have provided a convincing confession that would have allowed him to return to television. But instead Bakker repeated the conspiracy stories, added judges and lawyers to his list of victimizers ("My lawyers did little to defend me against the government's charges"), and blamed his wife's coldness and lack of spirituality for his decision to go into Jessica Hahn's hotel room ("I felt I had a vision and a commission from God to build PTL ... [but] Tammy Faye ... loved being on television. ... To Tammy, life was supposed to be fun, fun, fun, not work, work, work. ... Tammy Faye was seeing another man.") He also insisted that he had not confessed at the time of the incident (1980, seven years before the March 1987 revelation to the *Observer*) because "my friends ... were counting on me" to go on fundraising, and because confessing to the Assemblies of God leadership would have thrown his whole staff out of work.[57]

Rather than admitting fault and asking for forgiveness, each "I was wrong" statement in the autobiography pointed a finger at someone else. They included:

Bakker thought that his advisors were handling Hahn's "false accusations" properly; he was wrong.

Bakker trusted his doctor to give him anti-anxiety drugs; he was wrong (the drugs made him irrational instead).

Bakker trusted his wife to stick by him during his prison sentence; he was wrong.

Bakker allowed people to be on the PTL programs and staff "who were living with willful sin in their lives. I knew it, and I winked at it because of their spiritual gifts. ... I allowed individuals to sin flagrantly and repeatedly, without calling them on it. ... I was wrong."[58]

This reconstruction of the events so that Bakker was wronged, rather than sinning, did not reassure his former followers. Although Bakker preached to local congregations over the next few years, his attempts to raise money for another "television ministry" failed, and the watchdog organization Trinity Foundation publicly announced its skepticism over Bakker's return to ministry, citing Bakker's refusal to "admit to any crime."[59]

Even more damaging was a coincidence in timing: Bakker's attempts to get back on national TV were juxtaposed with the settlement of a class action suit against PTL in a North Carolina court. The settlement, covered widely in national papers, gave 165,000 people who had invested $1000 each in Heritage USA a payment of $6.45 each.[60] Once again Bakker appeared in the papers as a financial predator, an exploiter, and a traitor in the holy war.

Years later, struggling to appear on TV whenever possible, Bakker was still refusing to confess, and his sense of elite entitlement was more powerful than ever. In January 2007, as a guest on a Christian talk show affiliated with the Assemblies of God, Bakker again broke down in tears, shouting, "I don't understand mean Christians! . . . I don't get it! No one, no one, I used to walk with presidents, and I could get no one to hear me!"[61] Refusing to confess, unable to show his one-ness with his followers, confusing the battle lines of holy war, Bakker remains unable to return to ministry.

But Bakker's flaming spiral downward provided a vivid illustration of the need for confession. Less than a year after Bakker's fall, Jimmy Swaggart put the lesson to use.

8

JIMMY SWAGGART'S MODEL CONFESSION

I take the responsibility. I take the blame. I take the fault.
—JIMMY SWAGGART, 1988

ON FEBRUARY 21, 1988—a little less than a year after Bakker's "confession" to the *Charlotte Observer*—Jimmy Swaggart stepped behind the pulpit of his church, the Family Worship Center in Baton Rouge, Louisiana, and confessed that he had sinned.

First, he addressed his wife Frances: "I have sinned against you," he told her, "and I beg your forgiveness." Then he turned to his son and daughter-in-law and said, "Donnie and Debbie, I have sinned against you and I beg you to forgive me." Next was the Assemblies of God: "To its thousands and thousands of pastors that are godly," Swaggart said, "that uphold its standard of righteousness, its evangelists that are heralds and criers of redemption, its missionaries on the front lines, holding back the path of hell—I have sinned against you and I have brought disgrace and humiliation and embarrassment upon you. I beg your forgiveness." He then told his church, ministry, and Bible college, "I have sinned against you. I have brought shame and embarrassment to you. I beg your forgiveness."

Nor was that all. He asked forgiveness from "my fellow television ministers and evangelists," and then from "the hundreds of millions that I have stood before in over a hundred countries of the world." And then finally he addressed "my Lord and my Savior, my Redeemer, the One whom I have served and I love and I worship. . . . I have sinned against You, my Lord. And I would ask that Your precious blood would wash and cleanse every stain, until it is in the seas of God's forgetfulness, never to be remembered against me anymore."[1]

Swaggart's congregation already knew that something was wrong. Three days earlier, a private investigator had taken pictures of Swaggart going into a Travel Inn motel with a prostitute.[2] The story broke on ABC's *Nightline* on February 19; the next day, the *New York Times*, CBS News, and the *Washington Post* also carried reports. An Assemblies of God spokesman insisted that the photos were "open to interpretation," but that Swaggart was "under investigation" for "allegations of sexual misconduct."[3]

Unlike Bakker, Swaggart immediately made an open and willing confession.

This was a kind of rhetoric very familiar to him. His career as a preacher had begun with an emotional, public confession of sin. At the age of seventeen, he had responded to an altar call by going down to the front of the church. There, "he knelt and sincerely, passionately begged God's forgiveness for his four years of rebellion." Swaggart's first sermon was preached when he was eighteen, from a flatbed truck. He would be a preacher as long as people gathered to hear him: they were his congregation and also his authorization.

On the day that the story of Swaggart's misdeeds broke, he responded to newspaper and television requests for a comment with silence, and even refused to say whether or not he would appear at church on the following day; his spokeswoman and his lawyer also refused to comment.[4] Instead, he made his confession directly to his congregation. He invited an Assemblies of God official to address the congregation right before his sermon; this official assured the audience that Swaggart had made a full confession to his spiritual leaders and to his family, and that this confession had been sincere and humble. The confession itself took place at the front of the church, in the ritual space set aside for confessions—not in the pages of a hostile newspaper, or surrounded by images of barely-dressed Playboy bunnies.

Swaggart did not engage in any blameshifting. He again and again took blame, repeating "I have sinned" again and again without ever excusing himself. His brief sermon contained no less than nine clear statements of fault, and eight pleas for forgiveness. Perhaps profiting once again by Bakker's fall, Swaggart began his confession by refusing to blame anyone for it: "I do not lay the fault or the blame of the charge at anyone else's feet," he said. This unequivocal acceptance of blame struck the media so forcefully that Swaggart's words became the Feb. 22 "Quotation of the Day" on page A1 of the *New York Times*: "I do not plan in any way to whitewash my sin. I do not call it a mistake, a mendacity. I call it a sin."

Furthermore, as far as his congregation was concerned, Swaggart's sin was victimless. There was no breath of financial scandal. His sin involved, not a vulnerable church secretary, but a paid prostitute; later reports said that Swaggart had not had sex with the prostitute, but had paid her to pose for him. There was no sense here that he had taken advantage of a vulnerable woman dazzled by his prominence. The prostitute herself, Debra Murphee, showed up in West Palm Beach and told reporters that she had met with Swaggart in a "yearlong series of motel meetings," but that "no intercourse had occurred . . . she customarily posed naked for him." The *Washington Post* then cited various uncredited sources as saying that Swaggart often picked up prostitutes, but no proof of this ever emerged.[5]

In the days after the initial confession, Swaggart was faced with the challenge of continuing to portray himself as a man who was a sinner, but not a predator. He had to make a difficult decision almost at once. Ten days after stepping down from his pulpit and handing his ministry over to the Assemblies of God, Swaggart was told by the local Assemblies of God leadership that he would be barred from preaching for three months and assigned to a two-year "rehabilitation program" that included counseling. The national Assemblies of God officials suggested that the Louisiana leadership reconsider and impose a year-long absence from preaching instead, but the Louisiana leaders remained firm on their three-month sanction.

A three-week argument between the two associations ended on March 30, when the national leadership overrode the more lenient local recommendations, barred Swaggart from preaching for a year, and also imposed two years of counseling. He was also barred from distributing any videotaped sermons.[6]

The next day, Swaggart announced that he would hold to the three-month suspension only, and would defy the national leadership's year-long ban.

Although this could have cast doubt on Swaggart's original confession, in which he announced that he would be subject to the Assemblies of God, Swaggart's lawyer told reporters from the *Augusta Chronicle* that the issue was really one of local versus national government. "He is willing to submit himself to the Louisiana District," the lawyer insisted, but disagreed that the national organization could overrule the state Assemblies leadership.[7] In the South, with its local pride and its suspicion of national government, this insistence put Swaggart on the side of small local government against "big regulation." Again, Swaggart was cannily allying himself with the congregation which supported him and gave him his authority, showing that he shared their own preoccupations and worries.

Swaggart resumed preaching on May 22, after three months of suspension. On April 8, he was defrocked by the national Assemblies of God organization, which cited his refusal to accept church terms. Swaggart himself announced that "to stay out of the public for a year would totally destroy the television ministry and greatly adversely affect the college." He still refused to chastise the national organization, however, announcing that "I must regretfully withdraw from the Assemblies of God, understanding that they will have no choice except to dismiss me from the fellowship." The Assemblies spokesman confirmed that Swaggart had withdrawn with a "gracious" letter, and that Swaggart would remain in the "sincere prayers" of the Assembly of God leadership.[8]

In this, Swaggart showed a clear understanding of the need to appear on the right side of the ongoing holy war between the forces of evil and the kingdom of God. He praised his denomination and his fellow ministers for their part in the holy war, and then placed himself in their camp with a clever portrayal of the state of holy war. "The Assemblies of God," he announced, " . . . helped bring the gospel to my little beleaguered town when my family was lost without Jesus . . . [it] has been more instrumental in taking this gospel through the night of darkness to the far-flung hundreds of millions . . . to its thousands and thousands of pastors . . . its evangelists that are heralds and criers of redemption, its missionaries on the front lines. . . . holding back the path of hell—I have sinned against you . . . I beg your forgiveness."

Swaggart had clearly seen Bakker's self-defeating battle with other Christians as a strategy to be avoided. His decision to bring a spokesman of the Assemblies of God to church with him on the day of his confession was a right turn away from Bakker's mistakes. Before Swaggart himself took the pulpit, this official told the congregation, "He has shown true humility and repentance and has not tried to blame anyone else for his failure."[9] Even in the moment of his confession of moral failure, Swaggart was able to portray himself as an equal part of his Christian community, a Christian among other Christians rather than a leader grasping for power over his flock. His attempts were successful, as the *New York Times* report of the congregational reaction showed:

> Hundreds in the congregation got to their feet and went to the altar to gather around him at the end of the Sunday morning service that had become a sobbing pastoral confession. They fell to their knees and appeared to grant his wish. As he spoke, many sobbed openly, called the name of Jesus, and began a ululating prayer in an unknown tongue, held by Pentecostals to be a manifestation of possession by the Holy Spirit. It spread through the congregation for perhaps a minute as the evangelist said, finally, that he had also sinned against God and asked for his forgiveness.[10]

Swaggart's refusal to set himself at odds with the Christian community was reflected in his symbolic enfolding by his own congregation, which came forward to join him in the place of the altar call/public confession of sin. The manifestation of glossolalia showed that they had also allied themselves with God in offering forgiveness. Swaggart was definitely on the side of the angels—no mean feat for a man who had been photographed with a prostitute just days before.

Swaggart had, as a background to his confession, years of claiming that his ministry was one of a struggle not against earthly powers, but against Satan himself. A week after the confession, the *New York Times* quoted Swaggart's tale of having a nightmare in which "a hideous beast with the body of a bear and the face of a man" tried to attack Swaggart in "a windowless, bare room suffused with a palpable sense of evil." Swaggart was only able to vanquish the creature, a demon threatening his soul, by saying, "In the name of Jesus" several times.[11]

In his return to the pulpit on May 23, Swaggart immediately served notice that he was returning to battle: "I am serving notice on demons and devils and Hell!"[12] he told his congregation at the Family Worship Center, and then put his finger for the first time on the earthly agents of Satan:

> There are . . . a lot of people . . . in this country . . . very determined to destroy this preacher, using any method at their disposal to do so The pornographers are one of them.

In the words of rhetorician Michael J. Giuliano, Swaggart pointed out that "the blame should be laid at the feet of Satan [and] the pornography industry."[13] In this way, he managed to admit indirectly the nature of his own sin while simultaneously implicating that he had been right all along: America's obsession with sex was destroying the country.

In his comeback sermon, Swaggart then went on to tell about a prophetic dream that he had had: he was trapped in an empty church, fighting a huge serpent with a "sword or club," while a mysterious man watched "without comment as I fought this thing." After Swaggart killed the serpent, he walked outside and found himself facing an even huger serpent. "I know what it meant," he told his congregation. The serpent was Satan, and the battle represented Satan's infiltration of Swaggart's own will: "I could not overcome him within myself," Swaggart said, "but Jesus Christ overcame him for me. . . .[God] spoke to my heart, and said, 'Your struggles could never have defeated this enemy. But all I had to do was say, 'Satan I rebuke thee and he is defeated.'"[14] The forces of evil had attacked Swaggart, but with the help of God he would still triumph.

This highly dramatic story of fighting off the serpent once again reassured Swaggart's congregation that his moral authority would be used to combat evil, rather than to take advantage of his flock. It also replaced any attempt to tell a story about the wrongdoing itself. Swaggart continued to avoid disturbing details which might cast doubt on his victim-hood, while at the same time avoiding accusations of not owning up to his actual sin.

Later revelations by the *Washington Post* quoted an unnamed source as saying that Swaggart "paid the prostitute to perform pornographic acts," while *Time* reported that Swaggart "had battled an obsession with pornography since his youth," and had asked the prostitute to disrobe. But Swaggart never confirmed any of this.[15] On March 6, he told his TV viewers in a taped message that "someday" he would tell them about the "unspecified sin . . . when the time was right."[16]

Instead, Swaggart aligned himself with a Biblical story: David's sin with Bathsheba. He referenced David's sin at least three different times in the course of his confession. Near the beginning of his speech, he announced, "God said to David 3,000 years ago, you have done this thing in secret, but I will do what I do openly before all of Israel. My sin was done in secret and God has said to me, 'I will do what I do before the whole world.' Blessed be the name of the Lord." In his appeal to God for forgiveness, in the middle of the confession, he quoted indirectly from David's words in Psalm 51: "I have sinned against You, My Lord . . . wash and cleanse every stain." And he concluded with the whole of Psalm 51, first saying, "I close this today with the words of another man that lived 3,000 years ago—and I started to say who committed sin that was worse than mine, but I take that back." The implication was not that Swaggart's sin was equivalent to the adultery and judicial murder practiced by David. Rather, Swaggart was pointing out that God had forgiven David of an equally severe offense.

After the initial confession, donations to Swaggart's ministry had dropped, and both of the national religious networks which had carried his programs cancelled his air time. But at the time of his comeback sermon, five thousand people still sat in the Family Worship Center. They had been reassured by his confession; he was their leader and wielded authority over them, but his confession had reassured them that he was nevertheless, just like them, a sinner fighting off the evil American culture that was attempting to destroy them all.

One year later, Swaggart's television ministry had not recovered all of its broadcast time. But his church was full. His donations were up to $60 million for the year. His program was reaching 800,000 households, instead of the 2.2 million it had reached at Swaggart's height, but the numbers were still impressive.[17]

The confession had succeeded. He had shown his followers that he was like them, a sinner among sinners; he had allied himself with the forces of good against evil; he had managed to appear more victim than victimizer; he had asked them to respond with forgiveness. When Swaggart laid his power down, his congregation picked it up and handed it back.

. . .

Three years later, on Oct. 15, 1991, Swaggart again left his pulpit after being arrested for a traffic violation with a known prostitute in his car.[18]

This time, Swaggart did not confess. The very next day, he announced to his congregation that God had told him to return to preaching, and that "the Lord told me it's flat none of your business."[19] He refused to admit to any fault or to ask forgiveness. In stark contrast to the loyalty of his earlier congregation, his 1991 congregation began to seep away.

By 1998, when Randall Balmer visited the Family Life Center in order to write an article for *Christianity Today*, only a small part of the space was necessary for Swaggart's shrunken congregation: "The entire wraparound balcony of the octagonal building was closed, shrouded in darkness," Balmer wrote afterwards, "and huge sections of the main floor had been cordoned off."[20] Only forty-five students attended the Jimmy Swaggart Bible College. The campus of the Worship Center was disintegrating.

Balmer's interview with Swaggart demonstrated that Swaggart had lost both his initial ability to portray himself as simply one Christian among many, and his determination to stay on the right side of the holy war. Swaggart told Balmer that *Christianity Today* had said "some pretty hurtful things about me. . . . I don't want anything to do with that magazine. In fact . . . I don't even want anything *good* about me going into the magazine. . . . I'm sorry. If you were writing for the *Washington Post* that might be a different matter."[21] He had retained his unwillingness to condemn the secular media, but, like Bakker, Swaggart had now cast other Christians as his enemy.

Swaggart's first confession managed to remind his congregation that he was fighting with them, on the right side of the holy war against Satan; it had been so effective that, in the next decade, the President of the United States would copy the Swaggart strategy to save himself. Swaggart's refusal to follow the same path, in the face of his second scandal, brought his ministry to a low point from which it never recovered.

9

CLINTON AND THE THREE
PUBLIC CONFESSIONS

I don't think there is a fancy way to say that I have sinned.
—BILL CLINTON, 1998

IN 1998, the President of the United States was accused of adultery and perjury and began a nine-month journey towards confession.

The confession was too long in coming, but when his words finally reached the American public, Bill Clinton pulled out every repentant stop. In two explicit acts of contrition, one broadcast directly to the American public and a second filtered through media reports of a Prayer Breakfast meeting, he managed to portray himself as an American among Americans, align himself with the poor and oppressed, avoid the appearance of being a predator, and place himself on the right side of a holy war. Every strategy of Cleveland, McPherson, and Swaggart was pressed into service—while the mistakes of Carter and Bakker were studiously avoided.

On the night of January 20, 1998, the *Washington Post* reported in its late edition that independent counsel Kenneth W. Starr, who had been investigating Clinton's involvement in the Whitewater real estate development for nearly four years, was now looking into Clinton's relationship with Monica Lewinsky.

Lewinsky, a twenty-four-year-old White House intern who had worked in the Oval Office, denied any sexual relationship with Clinton. She had even made out an affidavit confirming this on January 12, less than two weeks before the *Post*'s revelations.

But the affidavit did not kill the story.[1] ABC News ran a radio report at 12:45 on the morning of the 21st; the *Los Angeles Times* ran the story in its morning edition; a little later that same day, CNN, MSNBC, Fox News, and ABC all broadcast reports from the White House daily briefing.

At 3:32 p.m. on the 21st, Clinton made his first statement in response to the accusation, to Jim Lehrer of PBS's *Newshour.* Lehrer began the conversation him by saying, "Kenneth Starr, independent counsel, is investigating allegations that you suborned perjury by encouraging a 24-year-old woman, former White House intern, to lie under oath in a civil deposition about her having had an affair with you. Mr. President, is that true?"

Clinton answered, "That is not true. That is not true. I did not ask anyone to tell anything other than the truth. There is no improper relationship. . . . [T]hat is not true."

Asked to define "improper relationship," Clinton said, "It means that there is not a sexual relationship, an improper sexual relationship, or any other kind of improper relationship. . . . There is not a sexual relationship; that is accurate." Again asked for clarification, he said, "There is no improper relationship. The allegations I have read are not true. . . . I have got to get back to the work of the country. I was up past midnight with Prime Minister Netanyahu last night. I've got Mr. Arafat coming in. We've got action all over the world and a State of the Union to do. I'll do my best to cooperate with this, just as I have through every other issue that's come up over the last several years, but I have got to get back to work." Impatient with the continued questioning, he then snapped, "[H]ardly anyone has ever been subject to the level of attack I have. You know, it made a lot of people mad when I got elected president. And the better the country does, it seems like the madder some of them get."[2]

A little later on the same day, Clinton repeated the same sequence of statements to NPR reporters Mara Liasson and Robert Siegel. "I think it's more important for me to tell the

American people that there wasn't improper relations," he told them, "I didn't ask anybody to lie, and I intend to cooperate. And I think that's all I should say right now so I can get back to the work of the country."[3] He also made a similar statement to the congressional newspaper *Roll Call:* "I made it very clear that the allegations are not true. . . . I'm just going to go back to work and do the best I can. . . . [T]he relationship was not improper. . . . [I]t is not an improper relationship and I know what the word means." When *Roll Call* pressed the issue, asking, "Was it in any way sexual?" Clinton retorted, "The relationship was not sexual. And I know what you mean, and the answer is no."[4]

The stakes were high. By Thursday, January 22, House Judiciary Committee Chairman Henry J. Hyde was already telling CNN that "impeachment might very well be an option."[5] Clinton's State of the Union address was less than a week away, and his repeated assertions that the relationship was "not improper" had led to unceasing speculation: according to the *Washington Post*, his "muted and seemingly opaque remarks" suggested that there might be "loopholes in the President's denials."[6] Under particular fire was Clinton's choice of wording in that initial statement to Jim Lehrer: "There is not a sexual relationship" seemed an evasion that did not deal with the past.

In an attempt to close these loopholes, Clinton held a press conference on January 26, the day before the State of the Union address. "I want you to listen to me," he said, in his second statement on the matter. "I'm going to say this again. I did not have sexual relations with that woman, Miss Lewinsky. I never told anybody to lie, not a single time—never. These allegations are false, and I need to go back to work for the American people."[7]

On March 5, the *Washington Post* carried a description of a Clinton statement the public had not yet seen—his deposition in the Paula Jones lawsuit, given to her lawyers on January 17, 1998, several days before his initial statement to Jim Lehrer. This deposition was private, and the *Post* neither quoted it directly nor explained how it had come into their hands. According to the March 5 story, in the deposition, "the President flatly denied ever having had sexual relations with Lewinsky. . . . For the purposes of the deposition, Jones's lawyers produced a written definition of sexual relations that encompassed acts such as fondling and oral sex but not kissing on the mouth—a definition that leaves little room to offer a revised explanation of his relationship with Lewinsky."[8] The story also pointed out that, despite Clinton's denials of having sex with Lewinsky, he "acknowledged for the first time in any known forum that he did have sexual relations with Gennifer Flowers, saying that it occurred just one time in 1977." Rumors about Clinton's affair with Flowers, a former employee of the state of Arkansas, had been circulating since 1992; Clinton had repeatedly denied that he had such a relationship with Flowers.

On March 13, the entire January 17 deposition was made public by Jones's lawyers, in response to a motion by Clinton's lawyers to have the Jones lawsuit dismissed.[9] Eighty-eight of the 215 pages were missing, as were the names of the women involved. In this statement, Clinton admitted to giving Lewinsky gifts, but denied any sexual involvement with her. Asked whether he and Lewinsky had ever been alone together in the Oval Office, he said, "I don't recall. . . . It's possible that she, in . . . while she was working there, brought something to me and that at that time she brought it to me, she was the only person there. That's possible."[10]

Clinton's deposition was criticized by content analysts for its evasive nature: Clinton "often lapsed into the present tense when answering critical questions," a habit they said was indicative of deception, and he constantly qualified his answers with "I think," "I believe," "it seemed," "not sure," and "my recollection is."[11]

Clinton's denials seemed to be catching up with him, and he retreated from responding directly to these new revelations. The day after the deposition was first leaked to the *Post*,

Clinton denounced its "illegal . . . publication. I have nothing else to say. I'm going to do my job. I'm going to follow
the law. That's what I wish everyone would do. Somebody in
this case ought to follow the law."[12] According to the *Washington Post*, Clinton announced at a May 1 press conference that
he was "absolutely prepared to leave Lewinsky questions
hanging for the rest of his presidency if that is what his lawyers advise."[13]

However, Clinton was not given the freedom to do this. He
was summoned by a grand jury to testify about his relationship
with Lewinsky. On August 17, he gave hours of testimony, all
of which were kept from the public.

Until this moment, Clinton's conduct had resembled the
self-defeating actions of Kennedy and Bakker. However, Clinton now chose a new strategy.

His first move was to go immediately to the public in a
display of willing openness. On the evening of August 17, he
broadcast a televised statement explaining his grand jury testimony. He had to confess that his previous denials of a sexual
relationship with Lewinsky were incorrect; a sexual relationship
had indeed existed. This posed two challenges: to get around
his unambiguous denials in press conferences (a public relations problem), and to explain how his deposition of January
17 and his grand jury testimony were consistent (a legal problem, since any contradiction would imply that he had perjured
himself).

"As you know," he said, in his broadcast of August 17, "in a
deposition in January, I was asked questions about my relationship with Monica Lewinsky. While my answers were legally accurate, I did not volunteer information. Indeed, I did have a
relationship with Miss Lewinsky that was not appropriate. In
fact, it was wrong. It constituted a critical lapse in judgment
and a personal failure on my part for which I am solely and
completely responsible. . . . I know that my public comments
and my silence about this matter gave a false impression. I misled people, including even my wife. I deeply regret that. . . .

Now, this matter is between me, the two people I love most—my wife and our daughter—and our God. I must put it right, and I am prepared to do whatever it takes to do so. Nothing is more important to me personally. But it is private, and I intend to reclaim my family life for my family. . . . It is time to stop the pursuit of personal destruction and the prying into private lives and get on with our national life."[14]

This initial stab at confession—Clinton's fourth statement on the matter, and the first to admit any kind of fault other than a bad memory—was widely viewed by the media as a failure. Clinton's choice of words, such as "misled" (a mild term for the absolute public denials which he now chose to ignore), "lapse in judgment" (a mistake, not a moral flaw), and "legally accurate" (rather than "factually untrue") seemed to be blame-dodging. In the *Washington Post*, one reporter blamed Clinton for "clinging to split hairs . . . the kind of dodge not permitted in true confession," while an editorial pointed out that reactions from Washington residents "made it clear they wanted nothing less than a full confession."[15]

Clinton then turned to give the public what it wanted. Ten days later, on August 28, he spoke to a primarily African-American audience at Union Chapel on Martha's Vineyard. The speech marked the thirty-fifth anniversary of the March on Washington, a civil rights landmark. Before addressing his sins, Clinton recalled watching the March on television in the summer of 1963: "I remember weeping uncontrollably during Martin Luther King's speech, and I remember thinking when it was over, my country would never be the same, and neither would I. There are people all across this country who made a more intense commitment to the idea of racial equality and justice that day than they had ever made before. And so, in very personal ways, all of us became better and bigger because of the work of those who brought that great day about."[16]

After identifying himself with King's work of racial reconciliation, Clinton went on to talk about America's need to relate peacefully to other countries, to resolve its own racial tensions, and to forgive its enemies. "All of you know," he told his audience, "I'm having to become quite an expert in this business of asking for forgiveness. It gets a little easier the more you do it. And if you have a family, an administration, a Congress and a whole country to ask you, you're going to get a lot of practice." This drew a huge ovation, and Clinton was applauded when he went on to say, "It is important that we are able to forgive those we believe have wronged us, even as we ask for forgiveness from people we have wronged. And I heard that first—first—in the civil rights movement." Although he did not directly talk about the Lewinsky affair, Clinton was widely seen as having apologized for it.

This was only the run-up to Clinton's most explicit confession, which took place on September 11 at the annual Washington prayer breakfast. Standing in the East Room of the White House, Clinton at last spoke the words, "I have sinned."

After welcoming the gathered ministers, he told them:

> I agree with those who have said that in my first statement after I testified I was not contrite enough. I don't think there is a fancy way to say that I have sinned. It is important to me that everybody who has been hurt know that the sorrow I feel is genuine: first and most important, my family; also my friends, my staff, my Cabinet, Monica Lewinsky and her family, and the American people. I have asked all for their forgiveness. But I believe that to be forgiven, more than sorrow is required—at least two more things. First, genuine repentance—a determination to change and to repair breaches of my own making. I have repented. Second, what my Bible calls a "broken spirit"; an understanding that I must have God's help to be the person that I want to be; a willingness to give the very forgiveness I seek; a renunciation of the pride and the anger which cloud judgment, lead people to excuse and compare and to blame and complain. . . . I will instruct my lawyers to mount a vigorous defense, using all available

appropriate arguments. But legal language must not obscure the fact that I have done wrong. . . . I will continue on the path of repentance, seeking pastoral support and that of other caring people so that they can hold me accountable for my own commitment.[17]

Clinton had now confessed three times—the last two times, successfully.

Clinton's path toward confession ran in the opposite direction to Swaggart's. Swaggart had succesfully confessed, and then refused to confess a second time; Clinton had denied, hesitated, and prevaricated before finally moving toward confession.

But Clinton, while avoiding a full admission of moral fault, played the other aspects of the public confession with enormous skill. Against all odds, his confessions managed to convince a significant segment of the American public that he was neither a predator nor an evildoer, and that he was fighting the good fight against evil. Most amazing, this white, male lawyer, this Rhodes Scholar, who held the highest elected office in the land, persuaded his followers that he was just like the country's poorest and most oppressed citizens.

• • •

In Bill Clinton's America, the intersection of Protestant practice, therapeutic technique, and talk-show ethos was complete. In order to survive, Clinton had to confess. He also had to marry this confession to the strategies used by scandal-survivors since Grover Cleveland—he had to put himself on the right side of a holy war, reject any implications that he was a sexual predator, and ally himself symbolically with the "common voter," particularly the victims and underdogs of society. Only in this way could he avoid the stigma of the predator.

Public confession was nothing new to Clinton. As a Southern Baptist, he had watched rituals of public repentance and confession all his life. In his autobiography, he tells of his childhood Sundays at the First Baptist Church of Hope, Arkansas and, a little later, at the Park Place Baptist Church; here he saw multiple altar calls, and, as a nine-year-old, he took part in the American Protestant ritual of public confession himself.

> In 1955 I had absorbed enough of my church's teachings to know that I was a sinner and wanted Jesus to save me. So I came down the aisle at the end of Sunday service, professed my faith in Christ, and asked to be baptized. The [Park Place minister] came to the house to talk to Mother and me. Baptists require an informed profession of faith for baptism; they want people to know what they are doing.[18]

Public confession in front of a large audience undoubtedly seemed quite natural to the Southern Baptist Clinton. He was, after all, part of that audience that saw thousands of sinners pour down to the front of the stadium to admit their wrong doings after a Billy Graham invitation:

> One of the Sunday-school teachers offered to take a few of the boys in our church to Little Rock to hear Billy Graham preach in his crusade in War Memorial Stadium. . . . Back then, Billy Graham was the living embodiment of Southern Baptist authority, the largest religious figure in the South, perhaps in the nation. I wanted to hear him preach. . . . Reverend Graham delivered a powerful message in his trademark twenty minutes. When he gave the invitation for people to come down onto the football field to become Christians or to rededicate their lives to Christ, hundreds . . . came down the stadium aisles. . . . For months after that I regularly sent part of my small allowance to support his ministry.[19]

However, Clinton's experience with public confession was convoluted. From his earliest days, his understanding of confession also involved the keeping of secrets. In his autobiography, he writes that the "secret I had in grade school and junior high was sending part of my allowance to Billy Graham. . . . I never told my parents or friends about that." Once, when he was getting ready to mail off his contribution to Graham, he took a long, circuitous route to the mailbox with the envelope in order to avoid being seen by his stepfather, who was working in the back yard.[20]

Furthermore, Clinton had viewed first-hand the results of a too-frank confession. Although he makes no mention of Carter's 1976 *Playboy* interview, Clinton describes his work as the Arkansas chair of the 1976 Carter presidential campaign:

> The fall campaign was a roller coaster. Carter came out of the convention in New York with a thirty-point lead over President Ford, but . . . President Ford made an impressive effort to catch up. . . . In the end, Carter defeated Ford by about 2 percent of the popular vote and by 297 electoral votes to 240.[21]

In the gap between the thirty-point and the two-percent lead lay the disastrous confession of the Southern Baptist Carter, an intersection of Baptist practice and political reality that Clinton was not likely to have missed.

From his earliest days, Clinton was imbued with the ideal of Protestant confession as both public and well-informed, involving full consent of both the will and the mind, and performed before a witnessing community that could testify to that full consent. Yet he was very much aware that an open confession such as Swaggart's was more likely to gain forgiveness from a religious congregation than from a national audience that (unlike Swaggart's followers) had no religious duty to forgive a sinner. As a Southern Baptist himself, Clinton came from a religious background where public admission of moral failing, along with public repentance, led inevitably to forgiveness. But as an occupant of the political realm, he had seen the disastrous effects that public confession could have on a candidacy.

Clinton may have realized that public confession was necessary for religious leaders accused of sexual sin, but his actions just after the scandal broke suggest that he had not yet realized its power in the secular political realm. He had immediately begun to place himself more and more explicitly within the religious community—inside the congregation of God's redeemed—those who were called to forgiveness. "Besieged by allegations about his personal life," the *Washington Post* had reported on January 26, "President Clinton yesterday left the White House for the first time in days to attend morning services . . . at Foundry United Methodist Church. . . . [He was] swept into a warm tide of smiles and hugs."[22] Once inside, Clinton "smiled and nodded his head" as the church choir "sang a song with the words, 'My God is a rock in a weary land, a shelter in the time of storm.'"[23] Clinton allied himself with Christianity not only visibly, but symbolically; in one of many gestures of identification with Christian voters, he had gathered advisors and aides together in the midst of the crisis to watch the movie *The Apostle*, a sympathetic portrayal of a Pentecostal evangelist, as a "morale-boosting session."[24]

When it became clear that details of the deposition were about to be leaked, Clinton went on television to address the American public directly. In his speech, he located himself within the Christian community as a sinner ("Now, this matter is between me, the two people I love most—my wife and our daughter—and our God. I must put it right, and I am prepared to do whatever it takes to do so. Nothing is more important to me personally"), but simultaneously located himself within the *secular* community as *legally blameless*. "I told the grand jury today and I say to you now," Clinton insisted, "that at no time did I ask anyone to lie, to hide or destroy evidence or to take any other unlawful action." On the following day, he snapped, in reference to the illegal leak, that he had nothing more to say: "I'm going to follow the law. . . . *Somebody* in this case ought to follow the law."

Clinton claimed that his response was shaped by a desire to preserve his privacy: "Even presidents have private lives," he remarked in his August 17 address. "It is time to stop the pursuit of personal destruction and the prying into private lives and get on with our national life." In fact, his response was more complex. He had a greater recognition of the need for confession of sin than Kennedy, who had refused to confess even a religious moral transgression. But he was attempting to separate a religiously-based standard of moral behavior (the damage done to his family life by his sexual immorality) from his secular political behavior, which he continued to insist was entirely ethical.

Some religious bodies were willing to accept this division. In late August, the National Council of Churches issued an official letter, "An Appeal for Healing," which pointed out the "common sinfulness" of all men, accepted Clinton's August apology, and suggested that Americans move on: "It is time once again to be led by our President," the letter said. "We need our country back."

But neoevangelicals rejected this strategy with scorn. The neoevangelical flagship magazine *Christianity Today* called the August 17 confession a "televised nonapology" in which the President "hid behind weasel words." "It was profoundly disturbing . . . [to hear] the President's attempt to excuse his stonewalling," the magazine editorialized. "What amazes us is that though Clinton comes from a conservative Christian background, he doesn't seem to understand the fundamentals of remorse and repentance."[25]

Clinton had indeed misunderstood something fundamental to American politicals. He had temporarily lost sight of the bond between "secular" political behavior and the goals of the new evangelical alliance.

Although neoevangelicals and their allies had continued to draw a clear battle line between the forces of God and the evil forces of Communism, humanism, and homosexuality, they had also shown an increasing willingness to welcome allies from outside the evangelical camp into their army—with the result that neoevangelicals were increasingly invested in seeing moral standards upheld within the "secular" political realm. In 1979, Jerry Falwell announced that the conservative voters in America made up a "moral majority," a name he adopted for his own Republican-loyal political organization. Falwell himself described the "moral majority" as

> religious conservatives who mobilized as a pro-life, pro-family, pro-Israel, and pro-strong national defense lobbying organization. . . . 80 million Americans committed to faith, family, and Judeo-Christian values.[26]

Notably, these members of the Moral Majority were *not evangelical believers*; rather, they were Americans who accepted "Judeo-Christian values," which could themselves be phrased as secular ethical goals.

Tim LaHaye, a founding member of the Moral Majority, wrote in his 1980 bestseller *The Battle for the Mind* that the "born-again adults" in America shared their moral standards with "pro-moral religious people from other churches," an estimated fifty million voters who "include Protestants who do not stress a born-again experience, Jews, Catholics, Mormons, and many other whose moral ideals are biblical." In addition, LaHaye claimed that another fifty million voters have no religious faith, but "were raised in a Christian consensus and possess a God-given, intuitive moral conscience." He called these voters "the nonchurch, promoral segment of society."[27]

The Moral Majority was designed to unite both converted and unconverted social conservatives in political activity that was not explicitly theological. Yet LaHaye's rhetoric makes very clear that the language of holy war was still central to this enterprise—even though it included those who were, conceivably, bound for hell.

> When I was assigned to a B-29 flight crew as a waist gunner, I didn't ask the other ten men whether they were Catholics, Jews, or Protestants. I merely wanted to know if they could fly the plane or shoot the 50-millimeter machine guns. Later I discovered that the other waist gunner was a Mormon, the turret gunner a Catholic, and the tail gunner a Southern Baptist. We could never have

worked together on a religious project (in fact, we could barely talk about theology without heating up), but on one fundamental we were in 100 percent agreement: We were all Americans interested in preserving our country's freedom.

Today the battle is not physical but essentially moral. Unless a sufficiency of pro-moral Americans acknowledge that and are willing to do battle on a basis of common moral conviction, I see no hope for freedom in the twenty-first century. If, however, pro-moral leaders of all religious persuasions are willing to stand together as fellow Americans concerned with preservation of the family and moral decency, we can still win this relentless battle for our minds and those of our children.[28]

This was a point of view that rapidly spread from neoevangelicalism into Pentecostalism; in 1981, Pentecostal televangelist Pat Robertson founded the "Freedom Council," an organization intended to teach conservative Protestants, Jews, and Catholics how to become political activists in alliance with their Pentecostal brethren.[29]

Esssentially, the Moral Majority, the Freedom Council, and other political action organizations that sprang from these roots were working to erase the very boundary that Bill Clinton was trying to draw—between private religious morality and behavior carried on within the secular political realm. In their rhetoric, morality was no longer religious. It was a shared ethical standard held by all decent people, be they secular, Catholic, Jewish. When this shared ethical standard was violated, confession was required.[30]

It was here that Clinton showed himself to be the most pragmatic of politicians. Rather than refusing to confess any more, as Swaggart had, he carried out the second act that Swaggart had refused to perform. Clinton invited over one hundred ministers to the September 11 prayer breakfast—ministers not only from the new evangelical alliance, but from all their allies in the culture wars. According to the *Washington Post*, the guest list included "leaders from most religions," including "Catholic, Christians, Jews, Muslims, [and] Hindus."[31]

In front of this ad hoc congregation, Clinton confessed his sins.

Although this confession was not made directly to the public, Clinton's decision to make it to a select group of ministers allowed it to filter through to a larger national audience, with examples of forgiveness already built in. The ministers who first heard the confession reacted to it with compassion, providing a model for the rest of the public. Minister Gordon MacDonald, addressing his Massachusetts congregation after returning from the prayer breakfast, demonstrates exactly how useful this strategy was to Clinton's cause:

> I was present at the breakfast when the President spoke. The experience will always remain as one of the most extraordinary experiences of my life. . . . I have chosen to believe that every word of the President's speech on Friday was out of a genuinely contrite heart. I have seen his private tears, heard his personal words of remorse. And I have chosen to embrace this man, as a sinner in need of mercy. I have received him as I would try to receive any of you, should you find yourself in similar circumstances.[32]

MacDonald and the other ministers at the breakfast not only placed Clinton's confession in a context of sincerity and biblical repentance, but identified Clinton as one Christian among many, a "sinner in need of mercy," just like "any of you," who might "find yourself in similar circumstances."

Clinton had chosen his ministers carefully. The *Post* pointed out that "most represent[ed] the more liberal traditions in their particular religion"; among the few neoevangelicals present were T. D. Jakes, black pastor of an enormous, Pentecostal-flavored nondenominational church in Dallas, and Gordon MacDonald, a neoevangelical minister who had himself confessed to adultery eleven years earlier, eventually regaining his pulpit after an extended period of "rehabilitation." Clinton then carefully wooed these Democratic-friendly neoevangelicals by using biblical phrases, the only vocabulary shared by a majority of those present. "I ask you to share my prayer that God will search me and know my heart," he told his listeners, quoting from Psalm 51, and went on to use familiar words from II Corinthians 2 ("Let me walk by faith and not sight") and Psalm 19 ("Let the words of my mouth . . . be pleasing"). At the same time he quoted from the Yom Kippur liturgy and from the Prayer of St. Francis ("I ask . . . to be an instrument of God's peace"), thus extending a rhetorical hand to Jews and Catholics as well.

That the confession was only the first half of his plan to disarm neoevangelical criticism became clear in the following days. On September 13, just two days after the breakfast, Gordon MacDonald told his Sunday morning congregation that the President had asked him and two other ministers to form an "accountability group that would deal with the spiritual realities of his life and help him walk his way through a personal restoration process."[33] On September 18, the *New York Times* reported that the other two ministers were Tony Campolo and J. Philip Wogaman.[34]

Although MacDonald and Campolo were theologically conservative neoevangelicals, neither was active in politically conservative, anti-Democrat organizations (in contrast to such vocal neoevangelical preachers as Jerry Falwell or James Dobson). MacDonald was the author of *Rebuilding Your Broken World*, a book written after his own confession of adultery and published by the very conservative neoevangelical publisher Thomas Nelson. Campolo, an independent Baptist, was also an academic: he taught sociology at a small college in Pennsylvania, and a few years earlier had publicly chastised Jerry Falwell for selling a video accusing Clinton of involvement in drug and murder conspiracies.[35] Wogaman was a Methodist minister and ethicist, and the pastor of the church the Clintons occasionally attended in Washington.

MacDonald's rhetoric drew Clinton into the neoevangelical circle. "Accountability groups" were common among neoevangelical men, and MacDonald's words to his congregation challenged them to accept this as proof of Clinton's desire for moral purity He told them that, at the Prayer Breakfast, he had seen the President

> re-enacting the biblical story of King David. . . . This public statement of repentance given on Friday was remarkable. . . . No one could have been present and retained a disbelieving, a cynical, a hardened attitude toward this man who opened his heart and acknowledged his realization of his sin. . . . Christ-following people have an obligation to treat seriously any attempt by a self-proclaimed sinner who asks for forgiveness.[36]

At the same time, Tony Campolo—a neoevangelical who voted Democrat and had earned himself the title of leader of the "Evangelical Left"—acted as reassurance to Democratic voters that it was possible to use neoevangelical rhetoric and still remain committed to liberal political ideals.

This effective strategy was soon eliciting complaints from those neoevangelicals who opposed Clinton on political grounds. At the Christian Coalition Convention in late September, delegates complained that American voters were not angry enough with Clinton. "Supposedly there are many Christians in this nation, God-fearing people," fumed a delegate from northern Virginia, "and yet Clinton can attend church and supposedly that makes him godly, even when every policy he's had has been ungodly."[37] Right-wing political luminaries Ralph Reed, Oliver North, and James Dobson all insisted that Clinton should forfeit the presidency for his behavior, and bemoaned the fact that the American people were "insufficiently outraged."

The ultimate success of Clinton's strategy is clear from the words of James Dobson, founder of the ultraconservative Focus on the Family: "What has alarmed me throughout this episode has been the willingness of my fellow citizens to rationalize the

President's behavior even as they suspected, and later knew, he was lying. I am left to conclude that our greatest problem is not in the Oval Office. It is with the people of this land."[38] Meanwhile, commentator Richard Schechner was writing, "The presidency . . . [has not] been indelibly stained and dishonored. The fundamentalist Christian talk-radio Right is not riding into power. Actually, I am happy with what's happened."[39] Clinton had beaten the new evangelical alliance at its own game. Through a carefully constructed confession and further rituals of repentance, he had acknowledged the existence of a "moral majority" and had answered its calls for repentance, placing himself on the right side of the holy war against evil—while still maintaining his independence from the political preferences of the most vocal segment of that "moral majority."

Clinton's confessions did more than place him on the side of good. They also worked, as good confessions must, to demonstrate that he was not a predator—something he seems to have kept in mind with every word he spoke.

Since the beginning of the scandal, a constant trickle of commentary pointed out that, by any measure, Clinton was guilty of sexual harassment. ("The President of the United States is a sexual predator," fumed Andrew Ferguson in *Time*, "the most powerful and famous man in the world. . . . [S]he is starstruck . . . and he takes her.")

Clinton did not actually portray himself as the sexual victim of an evil predator, but—as Grover Cleveland had done—he allowed others to do so on his behalf. Polls showed the majority of Americans did not entirely blame him for the affair,[40] in large part because media reports consistently portrayed Lewinsky as a predator in her own right. "Her former boss at the Pentagon calls her competent, reliable, and energetic," the *Washington Post* reported, right after the scandal broke. "But others there fault her for making sexually explicit jokes and time-wasting phone calls." She was a "rich kid" who attended Beverly Hills High School and an exclusive prep school, and who had already had at least one affair with a man "twice her age."[41] Less than ten days into the scandal, a teacher at her former high school announced to the press that he had had an affair with her, that she "talked obsessively about sex," and that she had "a pattern of twisting facts."[42] A "friend" insisted that Lewinsky had told him, months before going to work at the White House, "that she longed to have sex with the President on his Oval Office desk. . . . [A]cquaintances paint an image of a young woman . . . who read sexual meaning into the merest chance encounter."[43]

Meanwhile, Clinton himself never spoke disparagingly of Lewinsky, and his director of communications reportedly told the whole White House staff that she would "kill" anyone who tried to shift the focus onto Lewinsky's sexuality. This helped Clinton to avoid appearing to be a persecutor. In his only comments about Lewinsky, he managed to cast himself in the continuing role of victim: friends told reporters that the two had become close because they "shared stores about their turbulent family upbringings. . . . Lewinsky is the child of divorced parents, and Clinton grew up with an adoptive father who was an alcoholic and sometimes physically abusive."[44]

By February 1, a *Washington Post* poll found that 58 percent of respondents "had an unfavorable impression of Lewinsky, with only 7 percent saying that they "viewed her favorably"; the rest "were withholding judgment."[45] In the end, Lewinsky's persona as sexual predator made accusations of Clinton's harassment something the public was able to shrug off. "Maybe there is sexual harassment," a Florida voter told the *Washington Post*, "but it is negligible considering what [Clinton] has done for the country."[46]

Passively allowing others to picture him as a sexual victim, Clinton also actively portrayed himself as a legal victim. From the moment the scandal broke, Clinton insisted that the investigation of his affair with Lewinsky was an attempt by independent prosecutor Kenneth Starr to find some legal pretext for recommending impeachment—justified or not. This strategy—a politicized version of the holy-war strategy followed by Swaggart—allowed Clinton to survive the revelation that he had lied about the affair.

On September 21, Clinton's videotaped testimony before the grand jury—his sixth statement on the matter, and his third confession of fault—was released to the public. Transcripts of the most embarrassing bits, dealing with Clinton's exact sexual relationship with Lewinsky, appeared nationally in newspapers and on web sites; video clips of Clinton's evasions were broadcast on the newscasts and on talk shows for weeks afterward.

This grand jury testimony was obscure and confused when it came to his exact sexual relations, and ridiculously precise when it came to discussion of the earlier deposition. "Were you physically intimate with Monica Lewinsky?" asked one of the lawyers, to which Clinton answered that it would save "a lot of time" if he could "read a statement" that would "make it clear."

> When I was alone with Ms. Lewinsky on certain occasions in early 1996 and once in early 1997, I engaged in conduct that was wrong. These encounters did not consist of sexual intercourse. They did not constitute sexual relations as I understood that term to be defined at my January 17th, 1998 deposition. But they did involve inappropriate intimate contact. These inappropriate encounters ended, at my insistence, in early 1997. I also had occasional telephone conversations with Ms. Lewinsky that included inappropriate sexual banter. I regret that what began as a friendship came to include this conduct, and I take full responsibility for my actions. While I will provide the grand jury whatever other information I can, because of privacy considerations affecting my family, myself, and others, and in an effort to preserve the dignity of the office I hold, this is all I will say about the specifics of these particular matters. I will try to answer, to the best of my

ability, other questions including questions about my relationship with Ms. Lewinsky; questions about my understanding of the term "sexual relations," as I understood it
to be defined at my January 17th, 1998 deposition; and
questions concerning alleged subordination of perjury,
obstruction of justice, and intimidation of witnesses.[47]

The interrogating lawyer pointed out that "sexual relations"
had been defined, in the January 17 deposition, as "contact
with the genitalia, anus, groin, breast, inner thigh, or buttocks
of any person with an intent to arouse or gratify the sexual desire of any person," and wondered what kind of "intimate contact" could be considered "inappropriate" and yet not involve
any of these body parts. "I think it's clear," Clinton snapped. "I
do not believe it included conduct which falls within the definition I was given in the Jones deposition. . . . I thought the
definition included any activity by the person being deposed,
where the person was the actor and came in contact with those
parts of the body . . . and excluded any other activity. For example, kissing is not covered by that."

The many pages of the Starr Report, released at the same time
as Clinton's grand jury testimony, included Lewinsky's statements
that she had performed oral sex on the President (which would
not have been covered by Clinton's tortuous understanding of
the definition, since he, the "person being deposed," hadn't
touched Lewinsky in any of the areas mentioned), but also included statements making clear that a "sexual relation," as described by Jones's lawyers, *had* indeed existed. Clinton, pushed
to clarify, grew more incoherent ("I think what I thought there
was, since this was some sort of—as I remember they said in the
previous discussion—and I'm only remembering now, so if I
make a mistake you can correct me").

Finally, one of the lawyers present quoted an earlier statement by Clinton's attorney: "'There is no sex of any kind in
any manner, shape, or form, with President Clinton.' That
statement is made by your attorney in front of the judge. . . .

That statement is a completely false statement . . . an utterly false statement. Is that correct?"

"It depends," Clinton answered, "on what the meaning of the word 'is' is. . . . If 'is' means is and never has been . . . that is one thing. If it means that there is none, that was a completely true statement." (To this, the lawyer, apparently caught between incredulity and amusement, remarked, "Do you mean today that because you were not engaging in sexual activity with Ms. Lewinsky during the deposition that the statement. . . . might be literally true?")

This lawerly redefining of language succeeded in producing sympathy for Clinton's plight because Clinton was actively using his words to avoid being victimized by a vengeful legal system. In the version of events he was creating, Clinton was being oppressed by Starr's investigation, and was using his words carefully to avoid incriminating himself.

This was immediately understandable to every American watching him. The constitutional right against self-incrimination is central to the American sense of self-protection: "taking the Fifth" has become a slang phrase meaning "no comment." In American law, this right is connected to an ideal of valid confession as always voluntary. Kevin Crotty writes, "Voluntariness has been, in the words of one court, the 'ultimate test' for confessions, and 'the only clearly established test in Anglo-American courts for two hundred years.'"[48]

The Supreme Court's 1966 Miranda decision developed this further; in the Miranda case, a confession was ruled invalid, not because it was tortured or threatened out of a subject, but because a threat was implied by the presence of officers of the law. Such circumstances presented "an overwhelming impression of authority—one that is entitled not only to get an answer, but to use whatever means are necessary to obtain one."[49]

Clinton was not in police custody, nor was he helpless. He was, in fact, surrounded by teams of lawyers. But for months he had been objecting that the Starr investigation was pressuring him, looking for any excuse to file charges against him, and willing to do whatever was necessary to dig up enough legal dirt to discredit him. He had successfully portrayed himself as a man under attack. In these circumstances, he was able to arouse a certain public sympathy for his lies—in the same way a man might be excused for lying to the police out of fear that they might take advantage of him.

The kind of public confession that American television audiences had become familiar with was, after all, Augustinian confession—confession undertaken by the will, apart from the pressures of any external law system. This kind of confession is so widely valued because it demonstrates a certain idealized view of the human self: the self as freely deciding, free in will, and essentially independent from the surrounding legal system. Kevin Crotty concludes,

> The will constitutes an essential dimension of the person for contemporary Western societies. The will in some sense simply *is* the person, construed as an agent. Because of the will, our actions truly express who we are; they are a manifestation of our authentic self. [50]

Voluntary confession implies control over the self; it suggests that Augustine's evaluating self has asserted the upper hand.

Involuntary confession, on the other hand, strikes at the very heart of the individual self; if a man can be forced to confess against his will (the situation the Miranda decision addressed), the self itself has been eroded. Involuntary confession suggests that the autonomous self may actually be an illusion, that the self is far more dependent on the social pressures surrounding it than we like to think.

Clinton constantly excused the inaccuracy of his earlier statements by citing the need to resist pressures that might be forcing him toward coerced confession. Even the grand jury testimony—which might have been fatally damaging to Clinton's popularity, since it included him admitting that previous statements were untrue—showed Clinton desperately attempting to escape being forced into confession against his will.

Clinton then managed to place himself as the victim of a sexually rapacious woman, and also as the potential victim of legal pressures. Both of these implications were illusions (considering his age and experience as opposed to Lewinsky's, and also the team of lawyers he had on call). But perhaps the most extraordinary proof that Clinton had succeeded in identifying himself as a victim and underdog—extraordinary because he was a Rhodes Scholarship–winning white lawyer who occupied the highest American elected office–was the support of African-American voters.

This was not merely a matter of approval of his policies, although this played a part; just after the scandal was uncovered, 81 percent of black voters polled thought that the President was doing a good job. But 77 percent said that he shared America's moral values (twice as many as whites); after the release of the Starr Report, 63 percent of black voters polled *still* asserted that Clinton shared the "moral values of most Americans—while 22 percent of whites did."[51] Ishmael Reed wrote in the *Baltimore Sun* that Clinton had black style and a "black walk"; most famously, in the *New Yorker*, Toni Morrison called Clinton

> our first black President. Blacker than any actual black person who could ever be elected in our children's lifetime. After all, Clinton displays almost every trope of blackness: single-parent household, born poor, working-class, saxophone-playing, McDonald's-and-junk-food-loving boy from Arkansas.[52]

Morrison had her tongue in her cheek; Clinton's cultural affinity to black culture was as Southern as it was African-American. But her over-the-top rhetoric highlighted a peculiarity in Clinton's relationship to America. Despite the fact that he was the elected leader of the entire country, Clinton successfully positioned himself as attacked and opposed by mainstream American culture.

Clinton was a strong supporter of civil rights and, later, of affirmative action; this naturally ran him into a certain amount of political conflict. As the *Los Angeles Times* pointed out in 1998, "From the start of his political career in Arkansas, Clinton was hounded by superpatriotic, erstwhile, hard-line segregationists, notably the former state Supreme Court Justice Jim Johnson and his associates, whose hatred of Clinton's views on civil rights and the Vietnam War led them to charge him with all sorts of fantastic crimes, from drug smuggling to murder."[53] It was this sense of opposition, not just to far-right racists, but to mainstream American culture that impelled Chris Rock to come up with the original label "first black president," which Morrison borrowed, because said Rock, because everything he does is criticized. "He got his hair cut for $200 and people lost their minds," Rock said. "It's very simple. Black people are used to being persecuted. Hence, they relate to Clinton."[54]

In his August 28 speech at Martha's Vineyard, Clinton not only identified himself with Martin Luther King Jr., but also with Nelson Mandela, who taught him (he said) the importance of not hating one's enemies. Both men are black—and both are also victims of a dominant white culture. This, more than Clinton's ability to play the saxophone and "sing in black churches without a hymnal,"[55] was central to black support of Clinton during the scandal. The treatment of Clinton during the impeachment, a little later, was repeatedly referred to as "lynching,"[56] a term that certainly brings race, but also violence of a mob against a single person, into view.

Again and again, the language of Clinton supporters moved from specifically racial terms to more general terms of victimization. On September 15, 1998, Harvard sociologist Orlando Patterson objected in the *New York Times* that the focus on Clinton's sex life was an erosion of the right to privacy: "One reason African-Americans have so steadfastly stood by the President," he writes, ". . . is that their history has been one long violation of their privacy. . . . No one knows better than African-Americans just what freedom means." Four days later, the *Times* published a letter in response from Barbara Leah

Hartman, professor of English at Wellesley: "Orlando Patterson is right to identify as a fundamental privilege the right of privacy," she writes, and then points out that the intersection of news reporting and the Internet has made this privilege even harder to protect: "Mr. Clinton is the First Victim at the crossroad of our new technology and our belief in the right to privacy," she concludes.[57]

From the very beginning of the scandal back on January 21, 1998, Clinton kept repeating that although he was under attack by his political enemies, all he wanted was to "get back to work." To Jim Lehrer, he added, "What's important here is what happens to the American people. I mean, there are sacrifices to being president, and in some periods of history, the price is higher than others. I'm just doing the best I can for my country. . . . You know, I didn't come here for money or power or anything else. I came here to spend my time, to do my job, and go back to my life. That's all I want to do, and that's what I'm trying to do, for the best interests of America."[58]

By insisting that the unearthing of the Lewinsky scandal was an underhanded, unfair plot by his unprincipled political enemies to discredit him, Clinton was already positioning himself as a legally righteous man opposed by evil political forces. Neo-evangelical rhetoric had infiltrated the language of secular politics; now Clinton was secularizing the language of holy war for his own purposes. Six days later, Hillary Clinton insisted on the *Today* show that the allegations were the result of "a vast right-wing conspiracy." The public was soon picking up this language. "He has a lot of enemies that don't want him as president," a New York man told reporters.[59] A February 1 poll suggested that a "majority of Americans . . . agree that the president's political enemies are 'conspiring' to bring down his presidency."[60]

Clinton's insistence that he was being attacked allowed him to move the focus, as time went on, onto the effects of the rumors themselves rather than on the alleged wrongdoing. Like

McPherson had, he portrayed the scandal itself as a tool of the enemy. In his very first interview, he insisted that the rumors were distracting him from his real job. In effect, the scandal was hurting all of America. "I have got to get back to the work of the country," he told Jim Lehrer. ". . . I'll do my best to cooperate with this. . . . But meanwhile I've got to go on with the work of the country." In that one brief interview, Clinton repeated the phrase, "I've got to get back to work" ten times. In his August 17 statement to the public, he said, "It is time to stop the pursuit of personal destruction . . . and get on with our national life. Our country has been distracted by this matter for too long. . . . Now it is time—in fact, it is past time—to move on. We have important work to do." And even in his most explicit confession of wrongdoing, the September 11 Prayer Breakfast speech, Clinton said, "It is very important that our nation move forward . . . Unless we turn, we will be trapped forever in yesterday's ways."

Clinton, like McPherson, benefitted from this strategy. In the fall of 1998, the director of polling for CBS pointed out that, in her recent polls, Clinton was earning praise even from people who thought he was a liar because "he was remaining focused on his job despite the controversy."[61]

Despite the potentially predatory and self-serving nature of his offense, Clinton managed to reassure his constituency that he was "one of them," not an elite leader who would use the powers granted to him by the people to oppress them. His continual insistence that he needed to "go back to work for the American people" shifted his position from that of autocrat to servant; his protest that he (unlike his opponents) was "following the law" relieved the worst fears that he would abuse his power to circumvent justice.

And despite an absolute saturation of the media—almost 50 percent of the news stories aired on the major national networks between January 21 and April 20 of 1998 dealt with Clinton and some aspect of the Lewinsky scandal—Clinton's approval rates remained high.[62] A February 1 poll conducted by the *Washington Post* found that Clinton's "job approval rating and personal popularity have never been higher," and that public perception of his "honesty and integrity" stood at the exact same levels where they had been the preceding October.[63]

Many commentators suggested that this was because Americans were holding Clinton's personal morality apart from his performance as president; Kathleen Hall Jamieson voiced this widespread point of view in the *Washington Post,* just after the airing of a *60 Minutes* piece detailing Clinton's supposed sexual indiscretions.

> The explanation? . . . [T]he public is drawing a clear distinction between private and public character; between the personal and the presidential. . . . And it is possible that some have concluded that those who live in glass houses shouldn't throw stones, a notion borne out by the finding that half think that Clinton's moral standards are the same as that of the average married man.

Jamieson's analysis of Clinton's enduring popularity—that those who "live in glass houses" had decided "not to throw stones"—was accurate, but had nothing to do with a division between Clinton's private and public lives. Instead, this popularity stands as testimony to Clinton's success in convincing his followers that, despite his power and privilege, he had no desire to lord it over them. He lived, as they did, in the "glass house" of moral failure. His success in this was so extraordinary that he led his *opponents* into placing *themselves* as a moral elite, shifting the blame for Clinton's popularity onto "the American people."

Unlike Bakker, who had also changed his story again and again, Clinton used words successfully to portray himself as a victim, to position himself on the right side of a fight between good and evil, and to shift attention onto the effects of the rumors themselves and away from his alleged wrongdoing. Clinton's "great strength and weakness," opined the *New York Times*, "has been his powerful and often successful urge to be all things to all people."[64] In the end, Clinton's ability to change not only his words but even his story to fit the needs of his listeners kept him from being driven out of public life, as Swaggart and Bakker had been. He was able to project the image of an Augustinian public confession—one in which the evaluating self had gained control of the rebellious will by the grace of God—while at the same time engaging in exactly the sort of rhetoric that Augustine had rejected: rhetoric that allowed him to talk his way around a full and unstinting admission of wrongdoing.

Clinton showed enormous skill in continually adapting his words to a rapidly changing situation. As revelations occurred, Clinton consistently and successfully changed his story. The Prayer Breakfast confession (his most explicit) managed to shift the focus away from his actions with Lewinsky, and onto his August 17 confession; his true apology was for his lack of contrition, not for his sexual relationship with the White House intern. He was, in effect, constructing a new story on the fly: the story of a man brought low by pride and self-centeredness. This can be seen in the end of the Prayer Breakfast confession, when he explains what the children of America can learn from his difficulties: not that they should avoid having sex with the wrong person, but rather that they can "learn in a profound way that integrity is important and selfishness is wrong. . . . I want to embody those lessons for the children of this country."[65]

Even as he gave the impression of frankness, Clinton did not actually admit, at the prayer breakfast, to sex; he maintained the legal fiction of his innocence. His "I have sinned" statement was beautifully ambiguous: "I agree with those who have said that in my first statement after I testified I was not contrite enough. I don't think there is a fancy way to say that I have sinned." Parsed by a lawyer, the "I have sinned" would refer back to the lack of contrition, not to the relationship with Lewinsky. This apology, far more explicitly contrite than any before, apologized first and foremost, not for involvement with Lewinsky (which had still not been clarified by Clinton, who never used the words "adultery," or "affair," or, for that matter, "sexual relationship"), but for his own earlier confessional speech of August 17.[66]

Clinton's management of the scandal preserved his role in public life. The attempt to remove him from office failed. When it was over, the *Washington Post* reviewed the outcome:

> [B]y virtually every key measure, Clinton's job performance ratings are higher now than they were before the world heard the first reports of Clinton's relationship with former White House intern Monica S. Lewinsky. Today, his overall job approval rating stands at 68 percent, up 8 percentage points from a *Post* survey taken immediately before the scandal broke in mid-January 1998. Three in four currently approve of the way Clinton is handling the economy, up 11 percentage points from the January 1998 pre-scandal poll. Two in three say they like the way Clinton is managing foreign affairs, another double-digit increase from pre-scandal surveys.

Clinton's facility with words had allowed him to create an appearance of open confession that nevertheless stopped short of complete honesty. His Southern, neoevangelical Protestant upbringing taught him not only the importance of public confession, but also how to bring powerful rhetorical devices into play. In his confessions, he was able to align himself with the American underclass, reassuring his public that he was not claiming any essential superiority. As he did so, he placed himself on the side of good against evil.

Clinton's political success after Lewinsky was not solely the result of his confessions. But the confessions themselves show that Clinton had, in spades, the most important qualities any American politician could have: the flexibility to respond to the demands of the voters; the adaptability to be the leader they wanted (as opposed to the leader *he* wanted); the willingness to admit that ultimate power lay in *their* hands and not in his. Ultimately, Clinton's confessions and the rhetoric that surrounded them reassured the American people that his power over them was not oppressively strong. They could continue to support his presidency because—White House intern and perjury notwithstanding—he was not a predator who would overwhelm them against their will.

10

UNAWARE OF CHANGE

*The fundamental flaw was the assumption that a psychological
evaluation after treatment could be relied upon to reassign a priest.*

—CARDINAL LAW, 2002

THE OUTCRY FOR CLINTON'S ADMISSION of wrongdoing was
matched, four years later, by a call from the pews of the Catholic church: a demand that the Catholic hierarchy admit its own
sin in allowing known pedophiles to "minister" to children.

The first nationally-known scandal involving priest misconduct had actually erupted ten years earlier. On May 7, 1992,
the Boston station WBZ-TV Channel 4 broadcast a telephone
interview with former priest James Porter, in which Porter admitted to molesting somewhere between fifty and a hundred
children, both boys and girls, during his years as a parish priest
in Fall River, a Massachusetts city south of Boston.[1] The next
day, the *Boston Globe* also carried the story, reporting that nine
of the victims intended to sue the Catholic Church unless they
were compensated and Porter was brought to justice. The victims, according to the *Globe,* "said yesterday that the Fall River
diocese . . . knew that Porter had sexually molested several
children. . . . Yet, they said, church officials did not remove
Porter from the priesthood," instead transferring him to two
other parishes. "There's no question the Church covered it
up," one of the victims said.[2]

From this point on, the primary complaint made by the victims of abusive priests was not that the individual priests had
molested them, but that the Catholic Church had done nothing to protect them, to stop the abuse, or even to admit that
it was happening. James Porter had already confessed to his

involvement; now his victims were asking the Catholic Church to confess that it too had done wrong.

The type of confession needed was a full, evangelical-style admission of wrongdoing, along with a request for forgiveness. This was not a kind of confession that the American Catholic Church was accustomed to. Nor did the Church authorities see any need for a ceremonial laying down of power so that the laypeople of the affected parishes might pick it up and hand it back. The Church, after all, was neither a democracy nor a neoevangelical congregation. Power within the Catholic Church had never been located in the pews.

• • •

The tone for the Church's reaction was set at once: initial statements by Church spokespeople were defensive, insisting that Porter's actions in the 1960s could never have occurred in the 1990s. "Officials from the U.S. Catholic Conference say the Catholic Church takes the problem of sexual abuse much more seriously now than it did even five or ten years ago," the *Boston Globe* reported, and quoted a spokesperson as saying, "In past decades, child abuse may have been viewed as simply a moral failing for which one should be repentant rather than a psychological addiction for which treatment is mandatory. Today things are different. The mere hint of such a case is viewed by a bishop with alarm."[3]

On May 11, less than a week after the first story appeared, the *Globe* published its first editorial criticism of the Church: "Despite continuing disclosures about sexual misconduct by its priests," wrote reporter Alison Bass, ". . . the Catholic Church is not responding to the problem as aggressively or as uniformly as other religious denominations."[4] The story also pointed out that, in western Massachusetts alone, two other Roman Catholic priests had been arrested for sexual offenses in the previous year. In response, the Fall River diocese issued a one-paragraph statement admitting to no fault, taking no responsibility, but instead attacking the *Globe* for "the unfortunate manner in which allegations against a former priest have been made public. . . . Since this has become a legal matter, it is not appropriate to comment further."[5]

On May 14, Bernard Cardinal Law, ruling bishop of the Archdiocese of Boston (which includes Fall River) made his first public statement about the allegations. Like Kennedy's televised speech decades before, Law's remarks were explanatory, not confessionial.

His comments were made at the end of a speech on another subject, a homily celebrating twenty-five years of service by a group of ordained Catholic priests. "No one more than we join in the anguish of those most immediately affected by this betrayal," he told the priests, adding that the case was a "rare" one. The Church, he went on, already had in place "an effective policy . . . which attempts to respond to such cases in a holistic way, conscious as we are of the spiritual, moral, psychological, pastoral, and legal implications that are often present." The present celebration, he said, was "the best context in which to address the sad reality of those singular instances when the life of priestly service to which we have been called has been betrayed. We would be less than the community of faith and love which we are called to be, however, were we not to attempt to respond both to victim and betrayer in truth, in love and in reconciliation."[6]

On May 23, Law made a second statement on the matter, this time picking up on the Fall River statement and criticizing, not the Church or its priests, but the media coverage. "The papers like to focus on the faults of a few. . . . We deplore that," said Cardinal Law. "The good and dedicated people who serve the Church deserve better than what they have been getting day in and day out in the media. St. Paul spoke of the immeasurable power at work in those who believe. . . . We call down God's power on our business leaders, and political leaders and community leaders. By all means we call down God's power on the media, particularly the *Globe*."[7]

This was the same self-defeating strategy adopted by Jim Bakker—a strategy notably avoided by Jimmy Swaggart, who would refuse (until years later) to cast the media as an evil agent attempting to destroy him.[8] Criticism of the media practically guaranteed that reporters would intensify their attempts to dig out scandal. The *Boston Globe* continued to run critical stories; by July, the child-abuse story appeared in the *New York Times,* which by now was also scrutinizing the allegations that on July 26 James Porter had also molested children in New Mexico while "undergoing treatment for pedophilia at the Servants of the Paraclete center . . . and working weekends at Our Lady of Perpetual Help parish."[9]

On November 20, the *New York Times* reported that the semi-annual meeting of American Catholic bishops had "adopted a resolution pledging to re-examine and reinforce church policies designed to root out priests who sexually abuse minors . . . . It was the bishops' first collective statement on the problem." The resolution proposed five guidelines for handling future cases of abuse: the Church would respond promptly to allegations; if evidence confirmed the accusations, the offender would be suspended and undergo medical treatment; offenses would be reported to the civil authorities; the victims would receive emotional and spiritual support; and the public would receive "forthright" explanations, "within the limits of individuals' privacy."[10]

This was by no means a confession of wrongdoing; in fact, it asserted that Church policies were perfectly adequate to manage the problem. It was not a reformation, but a "re-examination and re-inforcement" of already-existing policies. But calls for reform were muted when, in December 1993, Porter was sentenced to an 18 to 20–year prison term. "Televisions across the country carried footage of him being locked away," writes reporter David France in his book on the scandal, ". . . And as swiftly as the subject of sex-abusing priests rose to the national stage, it sank off the front pages and evening news scrolls to become a problem of the past."[11]

For almost a decade, the issue subsided. But on Epiphany, January 6, 2002, the *Globe* unveiled the new scandal.

The headline of the first *Boston Globe* story was "Church allowed abuse by priest for years." The accusers had shifted their focus: the wrongdoing that demanded confession was no longer simply that of one priest, the defrocked John J. Geoghan, but that of the Catholic Church hierarchy, which had known of the abuse for years and had done nothing to stop it.

The *Globe* story went on to reveal that, in 2001, Cardinal Law had admitted in a legal deposition giving former priest John J. Geoghan a job working with youth groups in 1984. He had taken this step in full knowledge that Geoghan had already been repeatedly accused of child abuse.

Geoghan's behavior had continued into his new assignment. In 1989, he had been admitted to institutional treatment for "sexually abusive priests," but had then been returned to his same parish, where he continued to abuse children. The *Globe* story next moved directly to the question that would remain central to the scandal: "Why did it take a succession of three cardinals and many bishops thirty-four years to place children out of Geoghan's reach?"[12]

The *Globe* pointed out that other Church officials had warned Law that Geoghan was dangerous. Five other bishops—Thomas Daily, Robert Banks, William Murphy, John McCormack, and Alfred Hughes—were also identified as having kept Geoghan's actions secret. But blame soon became centered on the person of Bernard Law, who would come to represent the entire Catholic hierarchy in the eyes of many American Catholics. The sins of which Law was accused were the transgressions of the American Catholic Church as a whole: concealing wrongdoing, ignoring the safety of the children in its parishes, and disregarding the pathological nature of pedophilia. "The transcripts [of depositions in Geoghan's trial] reflect a consistent institutional failure by the archdiocese to deal decisively with the problem presented by Geoghan," wrote Stephen Kurkjian in the *Boston Globe*, three weeks later. "In their depositions, the priests indicate that there was little effort by the archdiocese or . . . Cardinal Bernard F. Law, to determine how extensive [Geoghan's] abuses might have been or whether the problem was pervasive among other priests."[13]

The coverage widened immediately from the *Boston Globe* to newspapers and television news programs across the country. But in contrast to his actions in 1992, Cardinal Law did not delay a full apology. Going directly to the press, he held an hour-long press conference on January 9. "I wish to address the issue of sexual abuse of minors by clergy," he began. "At the outset, I apologize once again to all those who have been sexually abused as minors by priests."[14]

Like his 1992 speech, Law's 2001 "apology" was an explanation that sought to show he had committed no grave sin. By exposing children to sexual abuse, he had breached an *important* (not trivial) law. But he had done so without full mental knowledge of the sin's gravity, and his will had certainly not given full consent. "However much I regret having assigned him," he told the press, "it is important to recall that John Geoghan was never assigned by me to a parish without psychiatric or medical assessments indicating that such assignments were appropriate." Moral blame, such as it was, belonged to the medical and scientific authorities he had consulted—not to him.

Law made no mention of the letters received throughout the 1980s from other clergy, advising him against returning Geoghan to parish work. He added, "Before God, however, it was not then, nor is it my intent now, to protect a priest accused of misconduct." Then Law came to the center of his apology: "With all my heart, I wish to apologize once again for the harm done to the victims of sexual abuse by priests. I do so in my own name, but also in the name of my brother priests. These days are particularly painful for the victims of John Geoghan. My apology to them and their families, and particularly to those who were abused in assignments which I made, comes from a grieving heart. I am indeed profoundly sorry."

Law's statement was characterized by the *Boston Globe* as "an extraordinary public expression of remorse."[15] However, outside the Boston area the reception was more skeptical. The skepticism grew louder when Law, despite his pledge to bring a new openness and a "zero tolerance policy of abuse" to the Boston archdiocese, refused to allow police and prosecutors access to Church records on clergy behavior. "[F]or all of his apologies and claims of having a 'grieving heart,'" commentator Derrick Jackson wrote in the *Globe*, "Law said nothing about past incidents that the church knows about. . . . Law said there will be no mandated reporting of the past. . . . [But] it was the archdiocese's abuse of "confidentiality" that landed them in the Geoghan mess. . . . Geoghan moved without question to one parish because the archdiocese, in its 'confidentiality,' did not tell that parish about Geoghan's past. That kind of 'confidentiality' has got to go, along with Law."[16]

Law was responding to the scandal within a purely Catholic framework. He had *not* confessed the actual wrongdoing of which he was accused, the transgression of keeping Geoghan's sins private. Within his own schema for understanding moral transgressions, he had committed no "sin" that required confession. Furthermore, he was determined to uphold the privacy of secrets revealed by clergy within the confessional. Increasingly, these two traditional Catholic positions came to be seen as inadequate not only by non Catholics, but by the Catholic public beyond Boston.

Law held another press conference on January 24, to insist that he had no intention of resigning. Once again he talked of new policies that the diocese was implementing, including the establishment of "an interdisciplinary center for the prevention of sexual abuse of children."[17] Once again, he apologized for the past while pointing out that he was acting according to Church policies: "I have acknowledged that, in retrospect, I know that I made mistakes in the assignment of priests. I have said that I have come to see that our policy was flawed. . . . I wish I could undo what I now see to have been mistakes. However, that is not a possibility. What is possible is to apologize again to victims and their families and also to learn from those mistakes as we plan for the future." He then announced that he had decided to make the reporting of allegations of abuse retroactive: his office would release the records of those complaints.

On January 30, Church lawyers delivered an inventory of the allegations brought against Boston-area priests over the last forty years to local law enforcement offices. The list of allegations was incomplete and included no names of victims, and Law insisted that "no priests accused of sexual abuse were currently in the church's employ."[18] At the end of the month, Law also published an open letter to the members of the Archdiocese of Boston, and read the letter during Sunday Mass at Boston's Cathedral of the Holy Cross. Yet again, the same justifications were repeated as part of his apology: Law had made a mistake, but committed no sin. "[T]he Archdiocese of Boston has failed to protect one of our most precious gifts, our children," he said, expanding the blame to the entire Catholic community. "As Archbishop, it was and is my responsibility to ensure that our parishes be safe havens for our children. . . . In retrospect, I acknowledge that, albeit unintentionally, I have failed in that responsibility. The judgments which I made, while made in good faith, were tragically wrong."[19]

Most of the rest of the letter was dedicated to an outline of Law's proposed reforms. When he returned, at the letter's end, to the current scandal, he used the passive voice—which allowed him to avoid assigning fault: "Trust in the Church has been shattered. . . .[A]ll of the faithful have suffered. Faith has been shaken and relationships of affection and trust between the faithful and clergy have been frayed." He then described his own part in the scandal, again in words that shifted blame— this time from himself personally, to the Church as a whole: "My acknowledgment, in retrospect, that the response of the Archdiocese and me personally to the grave evil of the sexual abuse of children by priests was flawed and inadequate," Law wrote, "has contributed to this profoundly difficult moment in the life of this Archdiocese."

By early February, calls for Law's resignation had grown louder, and anger over the scandal had focused itself even more intensely on his behavior. A poll taken in the first week of February by a local research firm showed that 48 percent of Boston-area Catholics wanted Law to resign, while 38 percent thought he should stay. The poll, according to the *Boston Globe*, also showed that "local Catholics are making a clear distinction between their beliefs and practices as Catholics, which remain strong, and their assessment of Law's conduct, which is extraordinarily weak. They appear largely to have personalized their anger, criticizing the cardinal but saying that being upset with him has not affected their broader feelings about the church."[20]

Law's three apologies had not averted blame. Over the next few months, he refrained from expanding on his earlier statements. "I wonder if the hierarchy knows how gravely the Roman Catholic Church, especially the American church, has been wounded," marvelled *Time* magazine reporter Lance Morrow in March. "There's massive internal bleeding, a hemorrhage of credibility—yet, in the face of all that, a squirming official attitude mixing anguish and evasion. At least Jimmy Swaggart had the good grace to bawl on television and beat his breast and otherwise oblige the audience with the theatrics of repentance."[21]

Law did none of these things. The previous year, he had insisted in a communication to other Catholic priests that he had made no "effort" to "shift a problem from one place to the next."[22] He stood by this assertion. After February he refused to take further questions from the media, and in his occasional remarks to Catholic gatherings, he repeated the language of his three early apologies: His failure had been a "flaw" and a "mistake in judgment" that nevertheless had been in compliance with "inadequate" Church policies then in place.

As multiple cases of abuse, most notably involving serial molesters Joseph Birmingham and Paul Shanley, hit the headlines one after another, Law appointed an articulate and telegenic aide to be his public face. When he was embarassed by the release of Church documents showing Shanley had been retained in active ministry even though Law had acknowledged Shanley's record as an abuser, Law met with bishops to discuss the possibility of his resignation. But on April 12 he delivered a two-page statement to Boston priests, informing them that he intended to stay on. Photocopies of the letter soon reached the press, and were published by the *Boston Globe* on April 13. In this fourth letter, Law did not apologize again, but his confession of "mistakes" took on a new dimension: "The case of Father Paul Shanley is particularly troubling for us," he wrote. "For me personally, it has brought home with painful clarity how inadequate our record-keeping has been. A continual institutional memory concerning allegations and cases of abuse of children was lacking. Trying to learn from the handling of this and other cases, I am committed to ensure that our records are kept in a way that those who deal with clergy personnel in the future will have the benefit of a full, accurate, and easily accessible institutional memory."[23]

The shift of blame for Shanley's abuse onto clerical error struck most Catholics as a retreat even from Law's earlier, inadequate confessions. "This is like a criminal telling me, 'Listen, I am the best person to prevent break-ins because I've done them in the past,'" one of Birmingham's victims told the *Globe*.[24]

Law made one more public apology before his resignation. On Pentecost 2002 he sent an open letter to the priests of the Boston Archdiocese and asked that it be read from every pulpit. This letter was even less frank than his previous explanations. Backpedalling from any personal responsibility, Law apologized for decisions made by some seemingly obscure agency: "I am profoundly sorry that the inadequacy of past policies and flaws in past decisions have contributed to this situation," he wrote. "I wish I could undo the hurt and harm."[25]

This Pentecost letter contained the most blatant blame-shifting yet—attempting even to implicate Law's predecessor. To the Catholics of Boston, Law insisted:

[T]he case of Father Paul Shanley has been particularly disturbing. . . . When I arrived in Boston in 1984, I assumed that priests in place had been appropriately appointed. It did not enter into my mind to second-guess my predecessors. . . . I was not aware until these recent months of the allegations against [Paul Shanley] from as early as 1966. . . . It is only possible to act based on what is known. . . . Mistakes have . . . been made when facts which should have been before me were not. I often have made decisions based on the best information available to me at the time, only to find that new details later became available which some may argue I should have had previously. Obviously, I wish that I had been aware of all pertinent facts before making any past decisions.

This statement was a rebuttal of allegations made by Shanley's victims, who had produced Church documents acknowledging official awareness of Shanley's history of sexual abuse.

Law continued to refuse direct contact with the media. In June of 2002, the *Boston Globe* reported that Law had apologized to American bishops in Dallas at the United States Conference of Catholic Bishops, but the session was closed to the public and detailed reports of his words were not published. *Globe* reporters were barred from the Conference entirely, as punishment for an earlier editorial decision to publish a copy of the draft policy on sexual abuse before it had been formally announced by Church authorities.[26]

Law did not address the issue again until October, when he met with victims of Joseph Birmingham in another private session; reporters were again barred from the meeting, but one *Globe* writer managed to get in. She did not make a transcript of Law's words, and the *Globe* story, published the next day, offered only indirect testimony. "This is the first time I ever heard him say publicly he was at fault, and ask forgiveness," one of the attendees was quoted as saying.[27]

Four days later, Law began his sermon at Mass at the Cathedral of the Holy Cross with a confession and apology—the first in six months. This statement, which was broadcast on BCTV (the official network channel of the Archdiocese of Boston)[28] included some of the same passive language used in Law's earlier apologies ("Our relationships have been damaged. Trust has been broken").[29] However, Law seemed to be inching toward a fuller admission of blame—while still insisting that his intentions had been good.

> Once again I want to acknowledge publicly my responsibility for decisions which I now see were clearly wrong. While I would hope that it would be understood that I never intended to place a priest in a position where I felt he would be a risk to children, the fact of the matter remains that I did assign priests who had committed sexual abuse. Our policy does not allow this now, and I am convinced that this is the only correct policy. Yet in the past, however well intentioned, I made assignments which I now recognize were wrong. With all my heart I apologize for this, once again. . . . I would also ask forgiveness. I address myself to all the faithful. Particularly do I ask forgiveness of those who have been abused, and of their parents and other family members. I acknowledge my own responsibility for decisions which led to intense suffering. While that suffering was never intended, it could have been avoided had I acted differently. I see this now with a clarity that has been heightened through the experience of these past 10 months. I ask forgiveness in my name and in the name of those who served before me. . . . The forgiving love of God gives me the courage to beg forgiveness of those who have suffered because of what I did.

Had this been the first of Law's apologies, it might have been received differently. But it was his sixth public apology; against the backdrop of the previous five, it rang false.

Any public inclination to accept Law's confession as genuine was squelched on December 4, when the *Globe* published findings that other "rogue priests," including one who had beaten his housekeeper and another with a cocaine addiction, had been treated with "gentleness and sensitivity" by Law, who had "quietly" transferred them elsewhere. The *Globe* quoted from a number of "sympathetic, reassuring notes" sent by Law to priests accused of violence and sexual abuse; one of these notes, sent to a priest who had admitted abuse and was facing defrocking, indicated that Law might restore the priest's ministry because of "the wisdom which emerges from difficult experience."[30]

Law made no public apology this time. Instead he flew to Rome to meet with Vatican officials. On December 13, 2002, he resigned from Archbishop of Boston and then left Rome for "an unknown destination."

• • •

Bernard Law's multiple apologies for his part in the 2002 scandal took place in an American Catholic Church that had been in upheaval for a quarter century. In the years following Vatican II, the Church hierachy still continued to maintain the Church's institutional resistance to changes advocated by many American Catholics: these included not only acceptance of artificial birth control, but also of "political activity by clergy, the ordination of women, a married clergy, and the marriage annulment procedures recently utilized in the United States."[31] In these years, voices both within and without the American Catholic Church complained that the Vatican's continuing top-down control of Catholic practice was not reflective of the actual Catholic community in the United States. Priest Andrew Greeley, one of the most vocal of the critics, described a kind of American Catholicism that he called "communal Catholicism" and defined as "informal networks of Catholics going their own way and worshipping together without reference to assigned parishes or other authority structures."[32] This was a more democratic Catholicism: a self-constituted, Americanized Catholic community with greater and greater lay participation, and a less rigid and hierarchical authority structure. Jaroslav Pelikan called this the "Protestantization of Catholicism"; it was a shift not only in practice, but also in theology, as individuals claimed the privilege of following personal conscience and praying directly to God.[33]

In fact, within American Catholicism, appearances were battling with reality. The existence of "communal Catholics" and the post-Vatican II increase in lay participation gave the impression of a more democratic authority structure, with the Catholic leadership responsible to Catholic worshippers in the manner of elected officials (or Protestant ministers) who were obliged to satisfy their constituencies. By its very existence, Vatican II had demonstrated that the Church's members and priests had the right to criticize it. In the words of Ruth A. Wallace, the "changes initiated by Vatican II de-reified Catholic church norms, for these changes revealed that they were the product of human decisions, rather than immutable and God-given."[34]

In the American Catholic church, the "empowerment" of lay Catholics after Vatican II was reflected in a number of changes: the growing use of a vernacular Mass, a shift in the priest's orientation (so that now he *faced* his congregation); an increased involvement of the laity in singing, responding, and otherwise taking part in the services of Catholic churches. The Vatican Council had underlined that the Church's task in worship was a team effort: "the *joint* worship of priest and people."[35] Between 1966 and the late 1970s, lay people and priests also met together for prayer and discussion of church practices, in a series of "living room dialogues.[36] This gave laypeople an ongoing model for making their own decisions about what was and was not moral.

But studies of the Catholic church such as Jean-Guy Vaillancourt's *Papal Power* and Peter Nichols's *The Pope's Divisions* concluded that, despite the American Church's adoption of some democratic forms and the "*apparent* collegiality and participative format of the post–Vatican II congresses," the "traditional Church bureaucrats" were "still in charge"[37] of both doctrine and practice—even in areas in which the majority of American Catholics disagreed with Church strictures. The church's approach to the issue of artificial birth control was the most obvious site of this clash, and reveals the ongoing tension between lay conscience and Church authority.

In 1962 John XXIII had appointed a papal commission to re-examine the Church's stance on artificial birth control. The commission, which continued its task into the papacy of Paul VI, reported in 1966 that the majority of its members, including nineteen theologians, believed that the Church should rethink its teaching: although marriage should still be "oriented towards the procreation and education of children," artificial birth control was not intrinsically evil and should be permitted under certain conditions. Furthermore, married couples should be properly educated in church doctrine and then allowed "to make their own judgment about what is best in their particular situation." Four of the nineteen theologians dissented.[38]

In 1968, Paul VI issued the papal bull *Humanae Vitae*, which (against all expectation) disregarded this majority opinion and forbade Catholics to use artificial family-planning methods. "Could it not be admitted," the encyclical begins, "that procreative finality applies to the totality of married life rather than to each single act?" The conclusion was that it *could not*, and that artificial contraception *was* intrinsically immoral. Priests were specifically reminded that they were "bound to . . . obey the magisterium of the Church" on this mattter, and were not permitted to dissent.[39]

Priests and laypeople in the United States at once protested. Eighty-seven prominent Catholic theologians signed a statement criticizing the Pope's decision. In the District of Columbia alone, forty priests were suspended for protesting *Humanae Vitae*.[40] Paul VI's declaration was not merely about the intrinsic moral nature of birth control; it also rejected the commission's recommendation that Catholic couples be allowed to come to their own decision about what was moral. In fact, *Humanae Vitae* specifically denied that the layperson had any right to make such a decision: "[Has] the time . . . come when the transmission of life should be regulated by their intelligence and will?" the encyclical asked, and answered with an unambiguous *no*: "[Catholic couples] are not free to act . . . as if it were wholly up to them to decide what is the right course to follow."

At the same time that American Catholics were struggling with a top-down enforcement of regulations that stood in tension with the convictions of many, the practice of confession saw a revival. However, it was in many ways more therapeutic than ever before.

In 2001, the year before Law's struggles with public confession, Father Francis Randolph published a confessional guide for the new decade, titled *Pardon and Peace* (just like Wilson's earlier volume). In it, he described confession as having three parts: repentance ("regret for the stupid mistakes we made before"), penance ("a resolution that we will take steps to ensure they do not happen again"), and the acceptance of grace ("the positive acceptance of the love of God"). Together, these three make up an adequate confession. Randolph argued that confession moves the sinner progressively closer and closer to salvation—just as sessions with a therapist move a patient close and closer to mental health. "[N]early all our confessions," writes Randolph, "are a continuation of a smooth progress toward the love of God and neighbor, rather than a series of radically new beginnings."[41]

However, the traditional emphasis on secrecy remained. Confession is "a private affair between you, the priest, and God. Everyone now has the right to choose his own confessor," Randolph writes, and adds that many parishioners may feel more comfortable going to another parish where their confessions will be completely anonymous. He then repeats the injunction to privacy. "In no way is it intended that people should confess their sins publicly," he writes. ". . . We admit publicly that we are sinners, we admit that we have failed to live up to our expectations, but we certainly do not go into details!"[42]

There is one exception to this: "When whatever we have done is public knowledge . . . it can be necessary to make a public apology." In fact, this is not really an exception. The apology may be public, but the admission of fault and the open confession of sin remain private. Law's public statements reflected this division. In offering apologies, he offered no real confession; the apology was public, the confession (if any) remained private.

Randolph also offers an insight into the difference between grave and trivial sin, which he distinguishes as "formal" and "material" sin. "A material sin is any action, word, or thought that in itself causes unhappiness, whether we are aware of it or not," he writes. "A formal sin is committed when we are aware of it and intend it." He then gave an example which eerily prefigures Law's own defense, a year later: Slave-holders were committing material sin because slavery "was normal in their society, and it never occurred to them that there could be anything wrong with it."[43] The following year, Law would tell his listeners:

> Given the horrible details that have been reported concerning it, the case of Father Paul Shanley has been particularly disturbing. I, too, am profoundly disturbed by these details, and wish to share some facts concerning this case. When I arrived in Boston in 1984, I assumed that priests in place had been appropriately appointed. It did not enter into my mind to second-guess my predecessors, and it simply was not in the culture of the day to function otherwise.[44]

Law's apologies were all made for material sins: "In retrospect, I acknowledge that, albeit unintentionally I have failed in that responsibility," he told Boston Catholics in 2002. "The judgments which I made, while made in good faith, were tragically wrong."[45] This, while an admission, was not truly a confession; Randolph points out that it is not even necessary to confess material sins.

Like Kennedy, Law did not appear to think that a public confession of sin was needed—despite the public demand for just such a speech. Like Kennedy, Law seemed to have in mind the difference between material and formal sin, and if he confessed to the latter, it was in private.

This tension between an appropriate Catholic response and an appropriate *public* response was visible in another area of Law's confessions as well. While he continued to insist that the Church was taking the advice of doctors and psychologists in dealing with abusive priests, apparently he had been responding to the confessions of abuse by priests themselves in a theological, not psychological, fashion.

Law's apologies again and again acknowledged the importance of psychiatric diagnosis and treatment for priests accused of abuse. "John Geoghan was never assigned by me to a parish without psychiatric or medical assessments indicating that such assignments were appropriate.," he insisted, in his first public explanation.[46] His April 12, 2002, letter took his endorsement of psychiatric treatment even further:

> There was a time many years ago when instances of sexual abuse of children were viewed almost exclusively as moral failures. A spiritual and ascetical remedy, therefore, was deemed sufficient. . . . In more recent years, which would certainly include my tenure as Archbishop, there has been a general recognition that such cases reflect a psychological and emotional pathology. It has been this recognition which has inspired our reliance on medical professionals. . . . The medical profession itself has evolved in the understandings and treatment of this pathology, or perhaps, more accurately, "pathologies,"

and we are able gratefully to benefit from that increased knowledge.[47]

But in fact Law's tenure as Archbishop included a number of instances in which priests were given spiritual counseling and then sent back to work. This was not necessarily a wrong decision from a theological point of view: the sinners had confessed their sins and been forgiven, which wiped the slate clean. From a psychological (and pastoral) point of view, though, the treatment of child abuse as a sin *exclusively,* rather than as a symptom of a psychiatric condition, was completely inadequate. Sin could be absolved, and its memory wiped away. A psychological condition that required a *cure* was a different matter.

James Porter, the priest accused in 1992, had been undergoing treatment at a "church counselling center," which the plaintiff's lawyer—speaking from the point of view of law, rather than of psychology—rejected as inadequate. "Pedophilia is not a curable condition," he said, and the lawsuit filed by Porter's victims claimed that "the Catholic hierarchy knew of accusations that Mr. Porter molested children but 'systematically and clandestinely' transferred him from parish to parish without reporting any misdeeds to police or to parishioners."[48]

Certainly in the 1960s, when James Porter was being transferred from place to place, his compulsion was treated more as "a moral failing" than as "a psychological addiction," as the U.S. Catholic Conference put it.[49] He was sent to a counseling center, but it was a Church center that focussed on spiritual rather than psychological treatment.

Church officials other than Law insisted that this could never happen in the present day. "[T]reatment is mandatory," said the spokesman for the U.S. Catholic Conference. "Today things are different. The mere hint of such a case is viewed by a bishop with alarm."[50] In other words, the Church was promising the public that, in these cases, it would rely on psychiatric advice *rather than* offering a purely theological response. Yet at least once, in his January 24 press conference, Law *blamed* psychology for the scandal; after saying that he had made "mis-takes in the assignment of priests," he added, "The fundamen-tal flaw was the assumption that a psychological evaluation after treatment could be relied upon to reassign a priest."

Law's reaction to the 1992 scandal had already shown him as unwilling to admit blame, either on his own behalf or on behalf of the Church. The 2002 scandal revealed that he still had no concept of the value of an open and willing confession as a means of appeasing followers who feared that they were being taken advantage of.

This popular demand for confession ran counter to Catho-lic practice—but more than that, it ran counter to the Catholic Church hierarchy's view of itself. It was a democratic demand, ordering the Church to render itself accountable. The media and the American public wanted a confession; the victims and their families wanted not just a confession, but also an assur-ance that the church would no longer continue to operate as it had. They demanded that the church alter itself, in response to the needs of its members.

Law's response was to protect both his own authority and the Church's power. His reversion to theologically based decision-making (forgiveness and restoration) in the cases of the abusive priests reveals a system uneasily balanced between accepting secular standards and holding to its own separate methods of governance. Acceptance of the validity of psychiatric diagnoses had been a kind of accommodation, since it allowed decisions to be made on the basis of something other than traditional authority.[51] To publicly reject the erring priests would have demonstrated that the Church was accepting psychiatry's final diagnosis—that pedophilia could never be "cured," but only "managed." To retain such priests in service was to demonstrate faith in the ultimate redemptive power of confession, penance, and reconciliation.

The secrecy that surrounded this decision shows a Church deeply worried about its ability to keep power. To admit publicly that a non-Catholic field of study might dictate Church practice would have removed authority from its residence in the Catholic hierarchy; ultimately, this would have exposed the Church to more challenges from lay people, already agitating for more say in Church affairs.

In fact, the strategy apparently followed by the Massachusetts hierachy—moving priest from parish to parish—could only be carried out by a strongly top-down organization which has the power to do as it pleases without interference from the masses of people lower down in the system. When the 1992 allegations surfaced, attorney Jeffrey Anderson pointed out that "Protestant denominations, while not perfectly forthcoming, haven't dealt with [sexual abuse by clergy] in that fashion, in part because they didn't have the same power as a Catholic bishop does."[52] Law continued to insist that he had acted according to the policy of the Church; and while he saw this as an adequate defense, lay Catholics saw it as an intolerable assertion of autocratic moral authority, in complete disregard of lay demands for accountability. In appealing to Church polity, Law—himself *not* a predator—was placing himself (as had Carter) in apparent sympathy with sexual predators. He was giving priority to the rehabilitation of priests, rather than to the protection of helpless children.

The tension between laity and hierarchy underlies much of the conversation about the 2002 revelations. After Law's second press conference, commentator Brian McGrory complained in the *Boston Globe*,

Catholic doctrine says we need to forgive Geoghan, which is fine, especially after he's hauled off to jail. But Law? It's now stunningly clear that his allegiance wasn't to his flock, but to himself and the hierarchy. He was afraid of controversy and publicity, and that fear drove him to reassign Geoghan rather than defrock him. These weren't mistakes, or bad decisions, or flawed policies, as Law calls them. No, they represent a fundamental disregard for the people—the rank and file parishioners—who put their trust in the Catholic Church and sought its help.[53]

And after Law's open letter was read in the Cathedral of the Holy Cross, another *Globe* editorial remarked, "Law will no doubt try to ride out the tide of people turning against him. He never paid much attention to the people in the first place."[54]

Public outrage over Law's concealments were mingled with calls for the Church to change its positions on clerical marriage, the ordination of women, and other longstanding positions enforced from the top down. Boston College theologians suggested that the Church revisit its positions on sexuality. Massachusetts Women-Church, an organization supporting women's ordination, put out an open letter of its own, declaring, "When Catholic women are ordained to the diaconate and the priesthood—and they will be—travesties such as these will never be hidden."[55] Lance Morrow of *Time* magazine concluded: "The church ought to have learned, after all these years, not to push Catholics toward the place where, in their disillusioned hearts, they will . . . listen for the unmediated voice of God and decide that the church, with too many squalors and secrets, is untrustworthy and perhaps an irrelevance."[56]

In early March, nearly three thousand lay Catholic leaders met with Cardinal Law and demanded reform. Parish council member Patricia Casey told the *Globe*, "In a strange way, this whole situation has really empowered Catholic people and priests at the parish level. I think we've kind of crossed a line, and I don't think we're going to go back." Religious education teacher Bonnie Ciambotti Newton said, "We need to change the whole power structure of the church. We need more women. The power, and the male dominance, and the secrecy are how this whole thing started."[57]

Law seemed unaware of the laity's need for participation in Church life and in Church decisions. In his Pentecost letter, he wrote, "We are the Church. That 'We' must never be understood in an exclusive sense, however. It is not just 'We the Laity,' or 'We the Hierarchy,' or 'We the Clergy,' or 'We the Religious,' or 'We the Prophetic Voice.' It is all of us together." But at the height of the scandal, Law told Boston parish priests that family members should no longer deliver eulogies at funerals, and that only liturgical music could be used: the focus in a funeral should be the glory of God, not the life of the deceased.[58]

Even had he made a full confession in the Protestant style, this insistence on lay submission would have undermined Law's attempts to stay in power. Law seemed *unable* to take any position other than that of unquestioned leader. Yet he was offering his apologies to an American Catholic population that had, to some degree, become "Protestantized"—particularly in its view of the relationship between laity and clergy.

Protestant congregations not only were allowed a voice in their own governance, but were able to hold their ministers accountable to certain standards of behavior. Public confession of wrongdoing by a Protestant minister allowed a congregation to decide whether or not the minister's authority—ultimately derived from the consent of the congregation—should continue to hold good. A similar dynamic exists between the electorate and political leaders, who also receive their authority from their constituencies. In both cases, the performance of confession recognizes the existence of a complex power relationship: the leader has authority over the group, but only because the group is willing to grant that authority. As Archbishop, Bernard Law did not serve at the pleasure of Boston's Catholics, but Boston's Catholics reacted to his wrongdoing as though he *did*: they reacted in the same way Swaggart's congregation and Clinton's constituency reacted to the missteps of *their* leaders.

In addition, Boston's Catholics were demanding for themselves a Protestant-type role not only in church governance, but also in the admission and evaluation of sin. Like Protestant congregations, they wanted to be asked for forgiveness. In Law's framework, there could be no role for the Catholics of

Boston, no need for them to respond to his confession—and so no need for him to confess.

In the end, Law offered his non-confessions to an American Catholic population that had gradually accepted other models— a psychological approach to pathological sin, a tendency to expect open public confession of sins as the norm, and the conviction that ordained leaders should be answerable to the congregation. His apologies were consonant with Catholic practice, but failed to satisfy America's "Protestantized" Catholics.

• • •

Clinton's successful management of his own scandal was made possible by his willingness to respond to the demands of his public. He asked them for forgiveness, in an act of humility that demonstrated that he understood his subordinate relationship to them: he had no authority that had not been given to him by the people of the United States. Not only did he confess and give the voters the role they demanded in forgiving him, but he managed to do so in the most effective manner possible: he allied himself symbolically with the interests of the powerless, and he placed himself on the right side of a struggle between good and evil.

But Law, insisting on his privacy, appeared to be an autocratic shepherd who refused to acknowledge his essential *sameness* with his flock. He positioned himself as divinely ordained to dictate law to his sheep; he refused to give them the chance to forgive; he symbolically allied himself with the interests of the powerful; and he placed himself on the side of sexual predators and evildoers.

Ultimately, Law's assertion of his authority led directly his resignation.

CONCLUSION

PREDICTIONS

I am a deceiver and a liar.
—TED HAGGARD

*This was a very serious sin in my past for which I am,
of course, completely responsible.*
—SEN. DAVID VITTER (R-LA.)

*He reiterates unequivocally that he has never had sexual
contact with a minor.*
—DAVID ROTH, ATTORNEY FOR MARK FOLEY

IN THE FALL OF 2006, minister Ted Haggard—president of the
National Association of Evangelicals, pastor of one of the largest neoevangelical churches in America, and outspoken opponent of gay rights—was outed by the male prostitute who had
allegedly provided him with both sex and crystal meth.

Within a week of the accusation, Haggard stepped down from
his pulpit and grovelled. His written confession, read out to his
congregation on the Sunday morning after his resignation,
showed an almost complete mastery of the confessional ritual.
He confessed his wrongdoing without excuse, but in a way that
identified him with his congregation; he offered reassurances that
he had no intention of using his power for personal gain; he situ-
ated himself firmly on the side of good in the American holy war.

It was an almost picture-perfect confession.

Ted Haggard's Letter to New Life Church

The following letter from Ted Haggard, former senior pastor of New
Life Church, was read to the congregation this morning at the 9 a.m.

and 11 a.m. services. [*The Swaggart strategy: Haggard gave the letter to an-other church official to read, showing that he had the support of other Chris-tians, and thus beginning the effort to keep himself on the right side of the American holy war.*]

November 05, 2006

To my New Life Church family:

I am so sorry. I am sorry for the disappointment, the betrayal, and the hurt. I am sorry for the horrible example I have set for you.

I have an overwhelming, all-consuming sadness in my heart for the pain that you and I and my family have experienced over the past few days. I am so sorry for the circumstances that have caused shame and embarrassment to all of you. [*Not yet confession, but notice the repetition of "sorry," reminiscent of Swag-gart's "I have sinned."*]

I asked that this note be read to you this morning so I could clarify my heart's condition to you. The last four days have been so difficult for me, my family and all of you, and I have further confused the situation with some of the things I've said during interviews with reporters who would catch me coming or going from my home. But I alone am responsible for the confusion caused by my inconsistent statements. The fact is, I am guilty of sexual immorality, and I take responsibility for the entire problem. [*Open confession, yet without details which would tend to make the listeners recoil.*]

I am a deceiver and a liar. There is a part of my life that is so repulsive and dark that I've been warring against it all of my adult life. [*More confession, this time using Augustinian terms to firmly entrench himself on the righteous side of the holy war against evil: in his essence, he wars against evil, while the sin was committed by a part of him.*]

For extended periods of time, I would enjoy victory and re-joice in freedom. Then, from time to time, the dirt that I thought was gone would resurface, and I would find myself thinking thoughts and experiencing desires that were contrary to everything I believe and teach.

Through the years, I've sought assistance in a variety of ways, with none of them proving to be effective in me. Then, because of pride, I began deceiving those I love the most because I didn't want to hurt or disappoint them. [*Translation: I am not a predator. I was hurting myself, but no one else.*]

The public person I was wasn't a lie; it was just incomplete. [*A reinforcing of Augustinian terms used earlier.*] When I stopped communicating about my problems, the darkness increased and finally dominated me. As a result, I did things that were contrary to everything I believe.

The accusations that have been leveled against me are not all true, but enough of them are true that I have been appropriately and lovingly removed from ministry. Our church's overseers have required me to submit to the oversight of Dr. James Dobson, Pastor Jack Hayford, and Pastor Tommy Barnett. Those men will perform a thorough analysis of my mental, spiritual, emotional, and physical life. They will guide me through a program with the goal of healing and restoration for my life, my marriage, and my family. [*A Clinton-style accountability group, which demonstrates that these three neoevangelical superstars are ready to accept and forgive.*]

I created this entire situation. The things that I did opened the door for additional allegations. But I am responsible; I alone need to be disciplined and corrected. An example must be set.

It is important that you know how much I love and appreciate my wife, Gayle. What I did should never reflect in a negative way on her relationship with me. She has been and continues to be incredible. The problem is not with her, my children or any of you. It was created 100 percent by me. [*No blame shifting here.*]

I have been permanently removed from the office of Senior Pastor of New Life Church. [*Reassures the congregation that he will not grasp power or use his personal charisma to make an inappropriate*

return to leadership.] Until a new senior pastor is chosen, our Associate Senior Pastor Ross Parsley will assume all of the the responsibilities of the office. On the day he accepted this new
role, he and his wife, Aimee, had a new baby boy. A new life in
the midst of this circumstance—I consider the confluence of
events to be prophetic. Please commit to join with Pastor Ross
and the others in church leadership to make their service to
you easy and without burden. They are fine leaders. You are
blessed.

I appreciate your loving and forgiving nature, and I humbly
ask you to do a few things.

1. Please stay faithful to God through service and giving.
2. Please forgive me. I am so embarrassed and ashamed. I
   caused this and I have no excuse. I am a sinner. I have
   fallen. I desperately need to be forgiven and healed.
   [*An appeal to them to fulfill the traditional role of the Protestant congregation, joining together in support; the appeal is
   continued in the next paragraph.*]
3. Please forgive my accuser. He is revealing the deception and sensuality that was in my life. Those sins, and
   others, need to be dealt with harshly. So, forgive him
   and, actually, thank God for him. I am trusting that his
   action will make me, my wife and family, and ultimately
   all of you, stronger. He didn't violate you; I did.
4. Please stay faithful to each other. Perform your functions well. Encourage each other and rejoice in God's
   faithfulness. Our church body is a beautiful body, and
   like every family, our strength is tested and proven in
   the midst of adversity. Because of the negative publicity I've created with my foolishness, we can now demonstrate to the world how our sick and wounded can
   be healed, and how even disappointed and betrayed
   church bodies can prosper and rejoice.

Gayle and I need to be gone for a while. We will never return to a leadership role at New Life Church. [*Repetition of the*

promise that he will not exploit his pastoral power for gain.] In our hearts, we will always be members of this body. We love you as our family. I know this situation will put you to the test. I'm sorry I've created the test, but please rise to this challenge and demonstate the incredible grace that is available to all of us.

Ted Haggard

AS HE MADE A FULL AND OPEN CONFESSION of his moral fault, asking the congregation to join in forgiving him, portraying himself as a warrior for righteousness (despite his failings), and assuring the members of his church that he would not take advantage of their loyalty, Haggard avoided making direct mention of his homosexual acts, which neoevangelicals might have particular difficulty in squaring with his insistence that he still stood on the side of the righteous. He also avoided confessing to anything that might get him into *legal* trouble. As *Christianity Today* reported, Haggard, "admitted that allegations against him are true," but "not all true. . . . Haggard did not specify [which] allegations he denies, and did not mention drug use in his letter."[1]

At once his colleagues fell into line with his insistence that he was a righteous warrior who had been temporarily overcome by evil forces, and whose restoration could play an important part in the spiritual renewal of America. His assistant pastor immediately told reporters, "God is not angry at Ted. He loves him. He's wrapping His arms around him," while another church official insisted, "God chose to reveal Pastor Ted's sin. . . . Now we can be mad at God. We can say that's not fair. The timing is terrible. Or we can say, Blessed be the name of the Lord. . . . God is a holy God and He chose this incredibly important timing for this sin to be revealed, and I actually think it's a good thing. I believe America needs a shaking, spiritually."[2] Even Haggard's sin had become part of the holy war for America's soul, with the potential to bring revival.

The aftershocks of Haggard's fall suggest two things.

In the first place, the positive response to Haggard's reasonably prompt and well-designed confession confirms what my examination of the previous century has revealed: the public confession has evolved into an essential ritual for any leader caught in sexual sin. An additional detail, buried in a *New York Times* story of November 19, 2006, provides yet more corroboration: According to reporter Laurie Goodstein, the board members who voted to accept Haggard's resignation were initially divided over the proper course of action. Haggard had "promptly" confessed his sin to them; they had the option of dismissing him as New Life's pastor, or retaining him while forcing him to take a leave of absence so that he could "repent, receive spiritual counseling and return to ministry." But on the second day of their deliberations, they saw a news report from the previous evening. After confessing to them, Ted Haggard had stopped to speak to reporters and had denied both the immorality and the drug use. "The overseers said they watched Mr. Haggard, affable as ever, smile grimly into the television camera and lie," Goodstein wrote. "'We saw the other side of Ted that Friday morning,' said the Rev. Michael Ware, one of the overseers. 'It helped us to know whether this would be a discipline or a dismissal.' The Rev. Mark Coward, another overseer, agreed. 'It was a defining moment.'"[3] Haggard's confession itself was powerful enough to retain his ministry; it was his failure to confess shortly afterward that sealed his fate. Jimmy Swaggart would have recognized the pattern.

Second, Haggard's actions since his fall suggest that consistent holy-war language, following a confession, might well serve to return a fallen leader to power. Less than three months afterward, Haggard told the New Life leadership that three weeks of counseling had rendered him "completely heterosexual." In an email, he wrote that the three weeks had seemed like "three years' worth of analysis and treatment. . . . I have spent so much time in repentance, brokenness, hurt and sorrow."[4] The mention of three years is significant because, months earlier, one of the ministers appointed to help in Haggard's spiritual counseling had

told the *New York Times* that "it could take at least three years before a fallen minister was 'restored' to 'spiritual, emotional, and
physical health.'"[5]

It is also significant because the number three represents resurrection to new life, by analogy to the resurrection of Christ
after three days. Haggard's announcement implied that supernatural power had been at work in him in an unusual and significant way ("Jesus is starting to put me back together," he
wrote). The decision to repudiate completely all homosexual
urges was the strongest possible way for Haggard to place himself back at the frontlines of the culture wars. As Jim Bakker
had discovered two decades earlier, neoevangelicals tend to
view homosexuality as a partner to secular humanism, the two
posing a joint threat to Christian America. "Humanists demand
complete rights for those who choose the homosexual life-style,"
Tim LaHaye warned, in *Battle for the Mind*. "If they succeed . . .
in forcing the pro-moral majority to accept homosexuality as
normal behavior, contrary to biblical teaching . . . and over 300
years of American history, they will go on to . . . legalizing pros-
titution, drugs, gambling, and who knows what else?"[6] By announcing his cure, Haggard was aligning himself with his fellow
believers once more.

That this announcement was a holy-war strategy is clear from
the reactions; Haggard's New Life board agreed that he was
now "completely heterosexual," while celebrity psychiatrist Jack
Drescher insisted from the other side of the frontlines that any
"cure" for homosexuality was a complete illusion. "There's not
a debate in the profession on this issue," Drescher snapped.
"This is like creationism. You create the impression to the public as if there was a debate in the profession, which there is
not."[7] Meanwhile, another of the ministers taking part in Haggard's spiritual restoration told *People* Magazine that he firmly
believed that Haggard would return to the pulpit–although
probably not the pulpit at New Life itself.[8]

As of this writing, Haggard has made no attempt to return to
the ministry. Yet this study suggests that if Haggard can manage

to refrain from excusing himself or prematurely seizing his job back without support of his colleagues, he may well return to public life through the power of public confession.

...

Clinton's virtuoso performance aside, it has taken a little longer for politicians to recognize the need for public confession. Since that September 11 Prayer Breakfast, no other politicians has so successfully made use of the ritual of public confession, or so skillfully combined the language of confession with the rhetoric of holy war and the goals of secular political gain.

But it is instructive to glance at two political scandals that unfolded within a year of Haggard's implosion. On September 29, 2006, Representative Mark Foley resigned after it became clear that he had spent years harassing underage Congressional pages, sending them sexually explicit emails, and asking for photographs. Unlike Haggard, Foley did everything wrong. His initial public statement read, in full:

> Today I have delivered a letter to the Speaker of the House informing him of my decision to resign from the U.S. House of Representatives, effective today. I thank the people of Florida's 16th Congressional District for giving me the opportunity to serve them for the last twelve years; it has been an honor. I am deeply sorry and I apologize for letting down my family and the people of Florida I have had the privilege to represent.[9]

The statement contained no confession; it made no mention of the pages, who were the victims of his attentions; in fact, it showed no awareness of the predatory nature of Foley's misdeeds.

Rather than following Clinton's example and making amends with increasing frankness, Foley then retreated further. He asked his attorney, David Roth, to read his next statement; unlike the ministers who had read Ted Haggard's statement to the New Life congregation, the lawyer could not help to place Foley on the side of righteousness. The new statement from Foley began, "Mark explicitly reaffirms his acceptance of responsibility and remorse"—a meaningless remark, given that Foley had not yet expressed responsibility for any wrongdoing—and one that was negated by the next sentence: "He reiterates unequivocally that he has never had sexual contact with a minor."

Roth continued, "Mark has asked that you be told that between the ages of 13 and 15 he was molested by a clergyman."[10] He concluded by announcing that Foley was not merely a victim of child abuse, but also an addict: Foley had just entered a mental health facility for treatment. Roth added that Foley "acknowledged that he is an alcoholic."[11]

The Catholic Church (having learned their lesson after Cardinal Law's catastrophic performances) immediately announced it had suspended, pending investigation, the retired priest whom Foley accused. But Foley's attempt to align himself with victims was negated by his complete refusal to admit to any sexual misbehavior. Foley's Florida constituency, and voters nationwide, accused him of blameshifting and dishonesty; even his friends told the *Washington Post* that they did not believe Foley was an alcoholic. As of this moment, Foley's career lies in complete ruin.

On July 9th of 2007, Senator David Vitter of Louisiana answered accusations that he had used the services of a District of Columbia madam and her prostitutes with a confession. Only a few hours after the accusation was first made (by *Hustler* magazine), Vitter issued a statement to the Associated Press that read, "This was a very serious sin in my past for which I am, of course, completely responsible. Several years ago, I asked for and received forgiveness from God and my wife in confession and marriage counseling. Out of respect for my family, I will keep my discussion of the matter there—with God and with them. But I certainly offer my deep and sincere apologies to all I have disappointed and let down in any way."[12]

Vitter's statement openly confessed his wrongdoing, calling it sin and taking responsibility. Vitter wasted no time in evasion; in fact, he confessed so quickly that the attorney for the "D.C. Madam" said, "I'm stunned that someone would be apologizing for this already." Unlike Foley, whose only reference to religion was to accuse an anonymous clergyman of molestation, Vitter put himself on the side of the good: he had received forgiveness from God (and from his wife).

Vitter also benefited from the nature of the attack: although the offense had been sexual, Vitter appeared as a victim rather than a predator. His connection with the D.C. Madam was made public only because Larry Flynt, publisher of *Hustler*, had offered a $1 million reward to anyone who could prove they had had a sexual relationship with a member of Congress. After Vitter's confession *Hustler* confirmed that the story had been "the result of a multi-pronged investigation launched and run by Larry Flynt."[13] With Flynt and *Hustler* as his opponents, Vitter undoubtedly found it much simpler to align himself with God.

Vitter's confession was followed by stories pointing out that he hadn't actually run afoul of the law ("Legal trouble unlikely for Vitter," announced the *New Orleans Times-Picayune* on July 12), and reported that he was on his way back to a normal schedule. "Sen. Vitter Quietly Returns to Work" the *Washington Post* proclaimed on July 17, noting that Vitter "briefly spoke" to a private luncheon for senators at the Capitol and "received a round of applause audible outside the room." "I look foward today to being back at work," Vitter said, in an echo of Clinton's words, "really focused on a lot of important issues for the people of Louisiana." Two days later, a reporter for Gannett News Service wrote that Vitter's colleagues appeared ready to forgive and forget: "'I'm a great believer in redemption,' said U. S. Sen. Orrin Hatch."[14] A mere week after Vitter's confession, the affair was already fading from public view.

Open confession of sin is not an automatic get-out-of-jail-free card; because Foley's offense was the worst kind of predatory sexual behavior—directed against children—it is likely that no confession could have saved his career. But although confession of sin cannot rescue every politician and preacher, it seems clear that erring leaders can no longer survive *without* confessing.

Evangelical forms of public confession have saturated American public life. Protestant ministers are under obligation to satisfy their followers that they are not a set-apart priesthood, but ordinary sinners saved by grace. The Catholic Church in America is under increasing pressure to yield to the demands of the laypeople in the pews; Catholic leaders who treat confession as only a Church affair risk appearing insensitive and arrogant. Scandal-marked politicians cannot preserve a dignified silence; they must prove, through humble confession, that they are willing to acknowledge the power of the voters at whose pleasure they serve.

American democracy is not essentially evangelical, but American evangelicalism is essentially democratic, so that its rituals translate seamlessly into rituals of American public life. Now, at the beginning of the twenty-first century, huge numbers of Americans who would never identify themselves with Protestantism, let alone its evangelical forms, have unconsciously accepted not only the form of the confession, but the religious language of holy war that accompanies it.

APPENDIXES

The Texts of the Confessions

APPENDIX A

EDWARD KENNEDY'S CONFESSION

Broadcast from the home of Joseph P. Kennedy. Transcript carried in the *New York Times*, July 26, 1969, p. 10, under the headline "Kennedy's Television Statement to the People of Massachusetts."

July 25, 1969

My fellow citizens:

I have requested this opportunity to talk to the people of Massachusetts about the tragedy which happened last Friday evening. This morning I entered a plea of guilty to the charge of leaving the scene of an accident. Prior to my appearance in court it would have been improper for me to comment on these matters; but tonight I am free to tell you what happened and to say what it means to me.

On the weekend of July 18, I was on Martha's Vineyard Island participating with my nephew, Joe Kennedy—as for thirty years my family has participated—in the annual Edgartown Sailing Regatta. Only reasons of health prevented my wife from accompanying me.

On Chappaquiddick Island, off Martha's Vineyard, I attended on Friday evening, July 18, a cook-out I had encouraged and helped sponsor for a devoted group of Kennedy campaign secretaries. When I left the party around 11:15 p.m., I was accompanied by one of these girls, Miss Mary Jo Kopechne. Mary Jo was one of the most devoted members of the staff of Senator Robert Kennedy. She worked for him for four years and was broken up over his death. For this reason, and because she was such a gentle, kind and idealistic person, all of us tried to help her feel that she still had a home with the Kennedy family.

There is no truth, no truth whatever, to the widely circulated suspicions of immoral conduct that have been leveled at my behavior and hers regarding that evening. There has never been a private relationship between us of any kind. I know of nothing in Mary Jo's conduct on that or any other occasion—the same is true of the other girls at that party—that would lend any substance to such ugly speculation about their character.

Nor was I driving under the influence of liquor.

Little over one mile away, the car that I was driving on an unlit road went off a narrow bridge which had no guard rails and was built on a left angle to the road.

The car overturned in a deep pond and immediately filled with water. I remember thinking, as the cold water rushed in around my head, that I was for certain drowning. Then water entered my lungs and I actually felt the sensation of drowning, but somehow I struggled to the surface alive.

I made immediate and repeated efforts to save Mary Jo by diving into the strong and murky current but succeeded only in increasing my state of utter exhaustion and alarm. My conduct and conversations during the next several hours, to the extent that I can remember them, make no sense to me at all.

Although my doctors informed me that I suffered a cerebral concussion as well as shock, I do not seek to escape responsibility for my actions by placing the blame either on the physical, emotional trauma brought on by the accident or on anyone else. I regard as indefensible the fact that I did not report the accident to the police immediately.

Instead of looking directly for a telephone after lying exhausted in the grass for an undetermined time, I walked back to the cottage where the party was being held and requested the help of two friends, my cousin, Joseph Gargan, and Phil Markham, and directed them to return immediately to the scene with me—this was some time after midnight—in order to undertake a new effort to dive down and locate Miss Kopechne. Their strenuous efforts, undertaken at some risks to their own lives, also proved futile.

All kinds of scrambled thoughts—all of them confused, some of them irrational, many of them which I cannot recall and some of which I would not have seriously entertained under normal circumstances—went through my mind during this period. They were reflected in the various inexplicably inconsistent and inconclusive things I said and did, including such questions as whether the girl might still be alive somewhere out of that immediate area, whether some awful curse did actually hang over all the Kennedys, whether there was some justifiable reason for me to doubt what had happened and to delay my report, whether somehow the awful weight of this incredible incident might in some way pass from my shoulders. I was overcome, I'm frank to say, by a jumble of emotions, grief, fear, doubt, exhaustion, panic, confusion and shock.

Instructing Gargan and Markham not to alarm Mary Jo's friends that night, I had them take me to the ferry crossing. The ferry having shut down for the night, I suddenly jumped into the water and impulsively swam across, nearly drowning once again in the effort, and returned to my hotel about 2 a.m. and collapsed in my room.

I remember going out at one point and saying something to the room clerk.

In the morning, with my mind somewhat more lucid, I made an effort to call a family legal adviser, Burke Marshall, from a public telephone on the Chappaquiddick side of the ferry and belatedly reported the accident to the Martha's Vineyard police.

Today, as I mentioned, I felt morally obligated to plead guilty to the charge of leaving the scene of an accident. No words on my part can possibly express the terrible pain and suffering I feel over this tragic incident. This last week has been an agonizing one for me and the members of my family and the grief we feel over the loss of a wonderful friend will remain with us the rest of our lives.

These events, the publicity, innuendo and whispers which have surrounded them and my admission of guilt this morning—raises the question in my mind of whether my standing among

the people of my state has been so impaired that I should resign my seat in the United States Senate. If at any time the citizens of Massachusetts should lack confidence in their Senator's
character or his ability, with or without justification, he could
not in my opinion adequately perform his duty and should
not continue in office.

The people of this state, the state which sent John Quincy
Adams and Daniel Webster and Charles Summer and Henry
Cabot Lodge and John Kennedy to the United States Senate,
are entitled to representation in that body by men who inspire
their utmost confidence. For this reason, I would understand
full well why some might think it right for me to resign. For
me this will be a difficult decision to make.

It has been seven years since my first election to the Senate.
You and I share many memories—some of them have been glo-
rious, some have been very sad. The opportunity to work with
you and serve Massachusetts has made my life worthwhile.

And so I ask you tonight, people of Massachusetts, to think
this through with me. In facing this decision, I seek your advice and opinion. In making it, I seek your prayers, for this is a
decision that I will have finally to make on my own.

It has been written, a man does what he must in spite of personal consequences, in spite of obstacles and dangers and pressures, and that is the basis of all human morality. Whatever
may be the sacrifices he faces, if he follows his conscience—the
loss of his friends, his fortune, his contentment, even the esteem of his fellow man—each man must decide for himself the
course he will follow. The stories of the past courage cannot
supply courage itself. For this, each man must look into his
own soul.

I pray that I can have the courage to make the right decision. Whatever is decided and whatever the future holds for
me, I hope that I shall have, be able to put this most recent
tragedy behind me and make some further contribution to
our state and mankind, whether it be in public or private life.

Thank you and goodnight.

APPENDIX B

JIMMY CARTER'S CONFESSION OF
"LUST IN MY HEART"

"*Playboy* Interview: Jimmy Carter," by Robert Scheer, in *Playboy*, November 1976

PLAYBOY: Do you feel you've reassured people with this interview, people who are uneasy about your religious beliefs, who wonder if you're going to make a rigid, unbending President?
CARTER: I don't know if you've been to Sunday school here yet; some of the press has attended. I teach there about every three or four weeks. It's getting to be a real problem because we don't have room to put everybody now when I teach. I don't know if we're going to have to issue passes or what. It almost destroys the worship aspect of it. But we had a good class last Sunday. It's a good way to learn what I believe and what the Baptists believe.

One thing the Baptists believe in is complete autonomy. I don't accept any domination of my life by the Baptist Church, none. Every Baptist church is individual and autonomous. We don't accept domination of our church from the Southern Baptist Convention. The reason the Baptist Church was formed in this country was because of our belief in absolute and total separation of church and state. These basic tenets make us almost unique. We don't believe in any hierarchy in church. We don't have bishops. Any officers chosen by the church are defined as servants, not bosses. They're supposed to do the dirty work, make sure the church is clean and painted and that sort of thing. So it's a very good, democratic structure.

When my sons were small, we went to church and they went, too. But when they got old enough to make their own decisions, they decided when to go and they varied in their devoutness. Amy really looks forward to going to church, because she gets to see all her cousins at Sunday school. I never knew anything except going to church. My wife and I were born and raised in innocent times. The normal thing to do was to go to church.

What Christ taught about most was pride, that one person should never think he was better than anybody else. One of the most vivid stories Christ told in one of his parables was about two people who went into a church. One was an official of the church, a Pharisee, and he said, "Love, I thank you that I'm not like all those other people. I keep all your commandments; I give a tenth of everything I own. I'm here to give thanks for making me more acceptable in your sight." The other guy was despised by the nation, and he went in, prostrated himself on the floor and said, "Lord, have mercy on me, a sinner. I'm not worthy to lift my eyes to heaven." Christ asked the disciples which of the two had justified his life. The answer was obviously the one who was humble.

The thing that's drummed into us all the time is not to be proud, not to be better than anyone else, not to look down on people, but to make ourselves acceptable in God's eyes through our own actions and recognize the simple truth that we're saved by grace. It's just a free gift through faith in Christ. This gives us a mechanism by which we can relate permanently to God. I'm not speaking for other people, but it gives me a sense of peace and equanimity and assurance.

I try not to commit a deliberate sin. I recognize that I'm going to do it anyhow, because I'm human and I'm tempted. And Christ set some almost impossible standards for us. Christ said, "I tell you that anyone who looks on a woman with lust has in his heart already committed adultery."

I've looked on a lot of women with lust. I've committed adultery in my heart many times. This is something that God recognizes I will do—and I have done it—and God forgives me for it. But that doesn't mean that I condemn someone who not only looks on a woman with lust, but who leaves his wife and shacks up with somebody out of wedlock.

Christ says, don't consider yourself better than someone else because one guy screws a whole bunch of women while the other guy is loyal to his wife. The guy who's loyal to his wife ought not to be condescending or proud because of the relative degree of sinfulness. One thing that Paul Tillich said was that religion is a search for the truth about man's existence and his relationship with God and his fellow man; and that once you stop searching and think you've got it made—at that point you lose your religion. Constant reassessment, searching in one's heart—it gives me a feeling of confidence.

I don't inject these beliefs in my answers to your secular questions; but I don't think I would *ever* take on the same frame of mind that Nixon or Johnson did—lying, cheating and distorting the truth. Not taking into consideration my hope for my strength of character, I think that my religious beliefs alone would prevent that from happening to me. I have that confidence. I hope it's justified.

APPENDIX C

JIM BAKKER'S ORIGINAL CONFESSION

The Charlotte Observer, March 20, 1987

Memo: The following correction was published on March 21, 1987: In reporting that the Rev. Richard Dortch succeeds Jim Bakker as PTL president and talk show host, Friday's *Observer* erroneously attributed the information to Dortch. Lawyer Norman Roy Grutman said it.

JIM BAKKER RESIGNS FROM PTL

CHARLES E. SHEPARD, Staff Writer; Staff writer Liz Chandler contributed to this article.

PTL President Jim Bakker, who built a fledgling Christian TV show in Charlotte into one of the nation's most popular TV ministries, resigned Thursday from PTL "for the good of my family, the church and all of our related ministries."

Bakker, 47, his voice trembling by the end of a telephone statement to *The Observer,* said fellow TV evangelist Jerry Falwell of Lynchburg, Virginia would replace him as chairman of PTL's board.

Falwell immediately announced a new board of directors and PTL Executive Director Richard Dortch told employees at the Heritage USA headquarters south of Charlotte that he will succeed Bakker as president. He also said he will host PTL's weekday talk show, now called the "Jim and Tammy Show" after Bakker and his wife.

In the statement, Bakker said that seven years ago he was "wickedly manipulated by treacherous former friends" who "conspired to betray me into a sexual encounter." He did not identify those people.

Then Bakker said he "succumbed to blackmail to protect and spare the ministry and my family.

"Unfortunately, money was paid in order to avoid further suffering or hurt to anyone to appease these persons who were determined to destroy this ministry.

"I now, in hindsight, realize payment should have been resisted and we ought to have exposed the blackmailers to the penalties of the law."

Bakker made the comments as *The Observer* was investigating allegations that a New York woman and her representatives received $115,000 in 1985 after she told PTL she had sexual relations with Bakker in a Florida hotel room.

Bakker also said he was resigning from his Pentecostal denomination, the Assemblies of God.

"I am not able to muster the resources needed to combat a new wave of attack that I have learned is about to be launched against us by *The Charlotte Observer*, which has attacked us incessantly for the past 12 years," he said. Rich Oppel, editor of *The Observer*, responded in a statement:

"We were investigating allegations about PTL's Jim Bakker at the time of his resignation. . . . No article would have been published unless we were convinced of the accuracy and fairness of the information, which did involve allegations of a sexual encounter and subsequent payments.

"Mr. Bakker often has questioned our motives in pursuing coverage of PTL's activities. The accuracy of our coverage has never been successfully challenged.

"We have covered PTL closely for more than 10 years because it is a major institution in our community. It has many employees, substantial real estate holdings, and an image that is projected nationally and raises millions of dollars from public broadcasts."

A lawyer representing PTL, Norman Roy Grutman of New York, refused Thursday to answer whether PTL, Bakker personally or some other source supplied the money Bakker said was paid.

Grutman said payment was made under a pledge of secrecy and PTL would not violate that.

The Observer first sought comment from Bakker and other PTL officials Feb. 24. Dortch canceled an interview, declined to answer questions submitted in advance and issued a three-paragraph statement:

"We refuse to become bitter and respond to rumors, conjecture and false accusations," Dortch's statement said then. "We place ourselves and our ministry in the hands of those who have spiritual rule over us and submit to their disposition of any matters brought before them concerning us."

On March 13, however, lawyer Grutman agreed to make Bakker and Dortch available for an interview.

The interview began with Bakker's statement Thursday at 2:30 p.m.

PTL employees gasped and cried when told of Bakker's resignation two hours later, during a closed staff meeting in the church at Heritage USA.

Falwell also spoke by phone to the employees, who numbered about 400.

The developments open a new chapter for PTL, which reported $129 million in revenues in 1986, employs about 2,000 people and owns the 2,300-acre Heritage USA retreat between Charlotte and Fort Mill, SC. PTL reported 6 million visitors last year.

Bakker, a Michigan-born preacher, moved to Charlotte in early 1974 and soon became the top figure at fledgling PTL.

He became PTL's senior pastor, preaching before overflow crowds Sunday mornings.

He used his personality and gift for TV to raise hundreds of millions of dollars from viewers. The weekday broadcast once known as the "PTL Club," for Praise The Lord or People That Love, was renamed after Bakker and his wife.

He was Heritage USA's master planner, conceiving two 500-room hotels, a water amusement park, homes for single mothers and street people and other buildings. There are plans for developments worth hundreds of millions of dollars more.

In other developments Thursday:

- PTL and Dortch also are leaving the Springfield, MO–based Assemblies of God, lawyer Grutman said. Dortch will serve on the new PTL board.

  Denomination officials told *The Observer* in the past week that they had begun formally investigating allegations against PTL, including the charge of sexual misconduct by Bakker. The investigation will continue, despite the resignations, church officials said Thursday.

- Bakker disclosed that "my and Tammy's physical and emotional resources have been so overwhelmed that we are presently under full-time therapy at a treatment center in California.

  "Tammy Faye and I and our ministries have been subjected to constant harassment and pressures by various groups and forces whose objective has been to undermine and to destroy us. I cannot deny that the personal toll that these pressures have exerted on me and my wife and family have been more than we can bear," he said.

  On March 6, in a videotape shown to PTL viewers, Bakker and his wife of 26 years disclosed that Tammy Bakker was being treated for drug dependency.

  Since mid-January the Bakkers have been in the Palm Springs, CA, area where they own a home. PTL viewers had been told in recent broadcasts that Bakker would be returning from California.

- The entire board of directors at PTL, which Bakker had chaired, resigned. At least two of eight members of the board had resigned in recent weeks.

  One of those, the Rev. Charles Cookman of Dunn, is the NC district superintendent for the Assemblies of God. In that role, he is responsible for the investigation of Bakker and PTL.

Cookman, a longtime personal friend and colleague of Dortch's, confirmed Monday he had resigned from PTL. He did so, he said, to avid a conflict of interest, not because he had reached any conclusion on the allegations' merits.

When an Assemblies of God minister is found guilty of a moral indiscretion, church procedure says, the minister will, at minimum, be suspended for two years. For at least some of that time, ministers are barred from preaching if they want to return to the ministry in the denomination, church officials say. In more extreme cases, the minister is dismissed from the denomination.

* Falwell, speaking from Virginia on the same telephone hookup with Bakker and *The Observer*, said he agreed to take the PTL post, in part because he feared "a backwash that would hurt every gospel ministry in America, if not the world."

Falwell, who will continue his ministry in Virginia, pledged the new PTL leadership will have an open-door stance toward the news media.

PTL officials have for years regarded many reporters with suspicion, accusing *The Observer* and its parent corporation, Knight Ridder Inc., of a conspiracy to destroy PTL and Bakker.

Thursday's events have their roots on a sunny, breezy Saturday afternoon in Clearwater Beach, Florida six years ago.

Bakker, then 40, was in Florida December 6, 1980, to appear on a broadcast for a nearby Christian TV station.

At the time, his marriage was troubled—a fact Bakker touched on Thursday. Among those accompanying Bakker in Florida was Oklahoma City evangelist, John Wesley Fletcher, then a friend of Bakker's and a regular guest on PTL broadcasts.

Also at Bakker's hotel in Clearwater Beach was a 21-year-old church secretary from New York named Jessica Hahn. Fletcher had arranged for her to fly to Florida to meet Bakker and see the broadcast, according to Fletcher and Hahn.

She said she was emotionally troubled by the encounter, which she said she did not expect, and by gossip that she said had followed.

In his statement Thursday, Bakker said:

"I sorrowfully acknowledge that seven years ago in an isolated incident, I was wickedly manipulated by treacherous former friends and then colleagues who victimized me with the aid of a female confederate.

"They conspired to betray me into a sexual encounter at a time of great stress in my marital life. Vulnerable as I was at the time, I was set up as part of a scheme to co-opt me and obtain some advantage for themselves over me in connection with their hope for position in the ministry."

Hahn said Thursday, "There was no blackmail, no extortion. Jim Bakker is obviously trying to protect himself. . . . I know what the truth is and I don't want Jim Bakker to leave PTL."

Fletcher could not be reached Thursday. In a February 24 interview, Fletcher told *The Observer* that Bakker was depressed by his marital troubles.

"Anything I did for Jim, I did, honest to God, because I thought I was helping him. I believed it," Fletcher said.

Fletcher, crying during portions of the interview, said he regrets his actions.

"My vocabulary fails me, the word 'sorry' is so inadequate. But if no one forgives me down here, if no one on earth forgives me, I know that I found forgiveness in God's hands," Fletcher said.

Fletcher was dismissed from the Assemblies of God in October 1981 for what he describes as a drinking problem. He has not reappeared on PTL programs.

In a 1984 interview, Hahn said she had complained to PTL and met twice with Dortch in New York. In the second meeting in November 1984, she said, she signed a document recanting her allegations.

She later said she felt pressured to sign.

In late 1984 or early 1985, Hahn met with Paul Roper, an Anaheim, California, businessman. Roper's activities have included managing a 10,000-member Anaheim church and running a Seattle savings and loan. He is one of more than 20 people who have been sued by a federal agency in connection with the thrift's failure.

Roper once announced a campaign to investigate TV evangelists. Roper also knew the New York woman's pastor and had spoken at her church.

By early February 1985, Roper had sent PTL officials the draft of a lawsuit detailing the woman's allegations and seeking millions of dollars in damages from PTL, Bakker and others.

He did so, he said in an interview, because he was unable to get PTL officials to return his telephone calls.

"All I did was threaten to place it (the complaint) in the hands of an attorney for whatever action that attorney might take," Roper said.

Bakker did not mention a draft lawsuit in his statement Thursday.

But he said, "I categorically deny that I've ever sexually assaulted or harassed anyone. . . . Anyone who knows Jim Bakker knows that I never physically assaulted anyone in my life."

Oppel, *The Observer* editor, said the newspaper's investigation didn't involve allegations of sexual assault or harassment.

At least twice in February 1985, Roper met with Dortch or Los Angeles lawyer, Howard Weitzman, and his partner, Scott Furstman. Roper said he presented the woman's allegations and suggested compensation, including a trust fund, if her story was true. Also discussed was a provision that the woman forfeit the money if she sued or otherwise made her charges public.

On February 27, 1985, a check for $115,000 drawn on the "Howard L. Weitzman clients trust account" was given to Roper on the woman's behalf, Roper confirmed on March 11.

APPENDIX D

JIMMY SWAGGART'S SERMON
OF CONFESSION

Reverend Jimmy Swaggart: Apology Sermon, February 21, 1988, Family Worship Center, Baton Rouge, Louisiana

Everything that I will attempt to say to you this morning will be from my heart. I will not speak from a prepared script. Knowing the consequences of what I will say and that much of it will be taken around the world, as it should be, I am positive that all that I want to say I will not be able to articulate as I would desire; but I would pray that you will somehow feel the anguish, the pain, and the love of my heart. I have always—every single time that I have stood before a congregation and a television camera—I have met and faced the issues head-on. I have never sidestepped or skirted unpleasantries. I have tried to be like a man and to preach this gospel exactly as I have seen it, without fear or reservation or compromise. I can do no less this morning.

I do not plan in any way to whitewash my sin. I do not call it a mistake, a mendacity; I call it sin. I would much rather, if possible—and in my estimation it would not be possible—to make it worse than less than it actually is. I have no one but myself to blame. I do not lay the fault or the blame of the charge at anyone else's feet. For no one is to blame but Jimmy Swaggart. I take the responsibility. I take the blame. I take the fault.

Many times I have addressed the media in a very stern manner, and I have chastised them for what I thought and believed was error in their reporting or their investigation even. This time I do not. I commend them. I feel that the media, both in print and by television, radio, have been fair and objective and even compassionate. Ted Koppel on *Nightline*, I feel, did everything within his power, in going the second, third, fourth, fifth, tenth mile to make doubly certain that what he reported was at least as fair and as honest as he, the spokesman for this world-famed news program, could make it. And I thank him for his objectivity, his kindness, and his fairness.

And I also want to express appreciation to the entire media everywhere, but especially here in Baton Rouge—channels 9, 2, and 33, the newspapers, the radio stations. They've been hard, but they have been fair. They have been objective and at time, I believe, they have even been compassionate—even my old nemesis, John Camp, that we have disagreed with very strongly. And I love you, John. And in spite of our differences, I think you are one of the finest investigative reporters in the world—and I mean that.

I want to address myself as best as I know how to those that I have wronged, that I have sinned against. First of all, my wife, Frances—God never gave a man a better helpmate and companion to stand beside him. And as far as this gospel has been taken through the airwaves to the great cities of the world and covered this globe, it would never have been done were it not for her strength, her courage, her consecration to her Redeemer, the Lord Jesus Christ. I have sinned against you. And I beg your forgiveness.

God said to David 3,000 years ago, you have done this thing in secret, but I will do what I do openly before all of Israel. My sin was done in secret, and God has said to me, "I will do what I do before the whole world." Blessed be the name of the Lord.

God could never give a man, a father, a minister of the Gospel, a finer son than he has given me and his mother—Donnie and my beautiful and lovely daughter-in-law, Debbie. Donnie has stood with me. I have relied upon him. And in these trying days, his mother and myself, we do not know what we would have done without his strength, his courage, and his utter devotion to the Lord Jesus Christ. Donnie and Debbie, I have sinned against you and I beg you to forgive me.

To the Assemblies of God, which helped bring the Gospel to my little beleaguered town when my family was lost without Jesus—this movement and fellowship that . . . has been more instrumental in taking this gospel through the . . . night of darkness to the far-flung hundreds of millions than maybe in the effort in annals of human history. Its leadership has been compassionate and kind and considerate and long-suffering toward me with, without exception, but never for one moment condoning sin, both on the national level and this esteemed district level. But to its thousands and thousands of pastors that are godly, that uphold the standard of righteousness, its evangelists that are heralds and criers of redemption, its missionaries on the front lines . . . holding back the path of hell—I have sinned against you and I have brought disgrace and humiliation and embarrassment upon you. I beg your forgiveness.

This church [Family Worship Center], this ministry, this Bible college [Jimmy Swaggart Bible College], these professors, this choir, these musicians, these singers that have stood with me on a thousand crusade platforms around the world, that have labored unstintedly [*sic*] and tirelessly to lift up that great name of Jesus Christ, to tell the weary that He is rest, and the sin-cursed that He, Jesus, is victory, my associates—and no evangelist ever had a greater group of men and women, given by the hand of God—have stood with me unstintedly [*sic*], unflaggingly. I have sinned against you. I have brought shame and embarrassment to you. I beg your forgiveness.

To my fellow television ministers and evangelists, you that are already bearing an almost unbearable load, to continue to say and tell the great story of Jesus' love, I have made your load heavier and I have hurt you. Please forgive me for sinning against you.

And to the hundreds of millions that I have stood before in over a hundred countries of the world, and I've looked into the cameras and so many of you with a heart of loneliness, needing help, have reached out to the minister of the gospel as a beacon of light. You that are nameless—most I will never be able to see except by faith. I have sinned against you. I beg you to forgive me.

And most of all, to my Lord and my Savior, my Redeemer, the One whom I have served and I love and I worship. I bow at His feet, who has saved me and washed me and cleansed me. I have sinned against You, my Lord. And I would ask that Your precious blood would wash and cleanse every stain, until it is in the seas of God's forgetfulness, never to be remembered against me anymore.

I say unto you that watch me today, through His mercy, His grace and His love, the sin of which I speak is not a present sin; it is a past sin. I know that so many would ask why, why? I have asked myself that 10,000 times through 10,000 tears. Maybe Jimmy Swaggart has tried to live his entire life as though he were not human. And I have thought that with the Lord, knowing He is omnipotent and omniscient, that there was nothing I could not do—and I emphasize with His help and guidance. And I think this is the reason (in my limited knowledge) that I did not find the victory I sought because I did not seek the help of my brothers and my sisters in the Lord. I have had to come to the realization that this Gospel is flawless, even though it is ministered at times by flawed men. If I had sought the help of those that loved me, with their added strength, I look back now and know that factory would have been mine. They have given me strength along with the compassion of our Savior in these last few days that I have needed for a long, long time.

Many ask, as I close, this: will the ministry continue? Yes, the ministry will continue. Under the guidance, leadership, and directives (as best we know how and can) of the Louisiana District of the Assemblies of God, we will continue to take this Gospel of Jesus Christ all over the world. I step out of this pulpit at the moment for an indeterminate period of time and we will leave that in the hands of the Lord.

The Bible College of these young men and young ladies whom I have tried to set a standard for and have miserably failed, its most esteemed president, Ray Tresk—I, too, beg you, the future pastors, evangelists and missionaries, to forgive me. But this Bible College will continue.

I close this today with the words of another man that lived 3,000 years ago—and I started to say who committed sin that was worse than mine, but I take that back. And if the Holy Spirit will allow me to borrow His words, I will review that which is as real now as when it was penned in Jerusalem:

Have mercy upon me, O God. According to thy lovingkindness; according unto the multitude of thy tender mercies, blot out my transgressions. Wash me thoroughly from mine iniquity, and cleanse me from my sin. For I acknowledge my transgressions; and my sin is ever before me. Against thee, thee only, have I sinned and done this evil in thy sight, that thou mightest be justified when thou speakest, and be clear when thou judgest. Behold, I was shapen in iniquity; and in sin did my mother conceive me. Behold, thou desireth truth in the inward parts; and in the hidden parts thou shalt make me to know wisdom. Purge me with hyssop, and I shall be clean; wash me, and I shall be whiter than snow. Make me to hear joy and gladness; that the bones which thou hast broken may rejoice. Hide thy face from my sins, and blot out all mine iniquities. Create in me a clean heart, O God; and renew a right spirit within me. Cast me not away from thy presence; and take not thy holy spirit from me. Restore unto me the joy of thy salvation; and uphold me with thy free spirit. Then will I teach transgressors thy ways; and sinners shall be converted unto thee. Deliver me from bloodguiltiness, O God, thou God of my salvation: and my tongue shall sing aloud of thy righteousness. O Lord, open thou my lips; and my mouth shall shew forth thy praise. For thou desireth not sacrifice; else would I give it; thou delightest not in a broken spirit; a broken and a contrite heart, O God, thou wilt not despise. Do good in thy good pleasure unto Zion; build thou the walls of Jerusalem. Then shalt thou be pleased with the sacrifices of righteousness, with burnt offering and with the whole burnt offering; then shall they offer bullocks upon thine altar. [Psalm 51]

Thank you. Thank you and God bless you.

APPENDIX E

PRESIDENT CLINTON'S STATEMENTS
AND CONFESSIONS

STATEMENT ONE, Jim Lehrer, *Newshour*, January 21, 1998

LEHRER: The news of this day is that Kenneth Starr, independent counsel, is investigating allegations that you suborned perjury by encouraging a 24-year-old woman, former White House intern, to lie under oath in a civil deposition about her having had an affair with you. Mr. President, is that true?

CLINTON: That is not true. That is not true. I did not ask anyone to tell anything other than the truth. There is no improper relationship. And I intend to cooperate with this inquiry, but this is not true.

LEHRER: No improper relationship. Define what you mean by that.

CLINTON: Well, I think you know what it means. It means that there is not a sexual relationship, an improper sexual relationship, or any other kind of improper relationship.

LEHRER: You had no sexual relationship with this young woman?

CLINTON: There is not a sexual relationship. That is accurate. We are doing our best to cooperate here, but we don't know much yet. And that's all I can say now. What I'm trying to do is to contain my natural impulses and get back to work. I think it's important that we cooperate. I will cooperate. But I want to focus on the work at hand.

LEHRER: Just for the record, to make sure I understand what your answer means, so there's no ambiguity about it. . . .

CLINTON: There is no . . .

LEHRER: All right. You had no conversations with this young woman, Monica Lewinsky, about her testimony or possible testimony before in giving a deposition . . .

CLINTON: I did not urge—I did not urge anyone to say anything that was untrue. I did not urge anyone to say anything that was untrue. That's my statement to you.

LEHRER: Did you talk to her?

CLINTON: And on that . . .

LEHRER: Excuse me. I'm sorry.

CLINTON: And beyond that, I think it's very important that we let the investigation take its course. But I want you to know that that is my clear position. I didn't ask anyone to go in there and say something that's not true.

LEHRER: What about your having had—another one of the allegations is that you may have asked, or the allegation that's being investigated is that you asked your friend Vernon Jordan. . . .

CLINTON: To do that.

LEHRER: . . . to do that.

CLINTON: I absolutely did not do that. I can tell you I did not do that. I did not do that. He is in no ways involved in trying to get anybody to say anything that's not true at my request. I didn't do that. Now, I don't know what else to tell you. I don't even know—all I know what is what I have read here. But I'm going to cooperate. I didn't ask anybody not to tell the truth. There is no improper relationship. The allegations I have read are not true. I do not know what the basis of them is other than just what you know. We'll just have to wait and see. And I will be vigorous about it, but I have got to get back to the work of the country. I was up past midnight with Prime Minister Netanyahu last night. I've got Mr. Arafat coming in. We've got action all over the world and a State of the Union to do. I'll do my best to cooperate with this, just as I have through every other issue that's come up over the last several years. But I have got to get back to work.

LEHRER: Would you acknowledge, though, Mr. President, this is very serious business, this charge against you that's been made?

CLINTON: And I will cooperate in the inquiry of it.

LEHRER: What's going on? What—what—if it's not true, that means somebody made this up. Is that—is that—is that . . .

CLINTON: Look. You know as much about this as I do right now. We'll just have to look into it and cooperate, and we'll see. But meanwhile, I've got to go on with the work of the country. I got hired to help the rest of the American people.

LEHRER: But on a more personal level, Mr. President, you're beginning—you're a week from your State of the Union address, and here . . . you're under investigation for a very, very serious crime and—allegation of a serious crime. I mean, what does that do to your ability to do all of these things that we've been talking about, whether it's the Middle East or whether it's child-care reform or what?

CLINTON: Well, I've got to do my best. You know, I'd be—I'd be less than candid if I said it was, you know, just hunky dory. You know, these—but I've been living with this sort of thing for a long time. And my experience has been, unfortunately, sometimes, you know, when one charge dies, another one just lifts up to take its place. But I can tell you, whatever I feel about it, I owe it to the American people to put it in a little box and keep working for them. This job is not like other jobs, in that sense. You can't—it's not—you don't get to take a vacation from your obligations to the whole country. You just have to, you know, remember why you ran, understand what's happening and why, and, you know, go back and hit it tomorrow. That's all you can do.

LEHRER: But going back to what we said at the beginning when we were talking about it, isn't this one different than all the others? This one isn't about a land deal in Arkansas, or it's not even about sex; it's about other things, about a serious matter. Do you—I mean . . .

CLINTON: Well, but all the others, a lot of them were about serious matters. They just faded away.

LEHRER: I'm not suggesting that they weren't serious. But I mean . . .

CLINTON: I don't mean—I just—all I can tell you is, I'll do my best to help them get to the bottom of it. I did not ask anybody to lie under oath. I did not do that. That's the allegation. I didn't do it. And we'll just get to the bottom it, we'll go on. And meanwhile, I've got to keep working at this. I can't just—you know, ignore the fact that every day that passes is one more day that I don't have to do what I came here to do. And I think the results that America has enjoyed indicates it's a pretty good argument for doing what I came here to do.

LEHRER: That whatever the personal things may be, the polls show that the people approve of your job as president, even though they may not have that high regard—that high regard of you as a person.

CLINTON: Well, hardly anyone has ever been subject to the level of attack I have. You know, it made a lot of people mad when I got elected president. And the better the country does, it seems like the madder some of them get. But that's—you know, that's not important. What's important here is what happens to the American people. I mean, there are sacrifices to being president, and in some periods of history, the price is higher than others. I'm just doing the best I can for my country.

LEHRER: We're sitting here in the Roosevelt Room in the White House. It's 4:15 Eastern Time. All of the cable news organizations have been full of this story all day. The newspapers are probably going to be full of it tomorrow. And the news may—this story is going to be there and be there and be there. The Paula Jones trial coming up in May. And you're going to be. . . .

CLINTON: I'm looking forward to that.

LEHRER: Why?

CLINTON: Because I believe that the evidence will show what I have been saying; that I did not do what I was accused of doing. It's very difficult. You know, one of the things that people learn is you can charge people with all kinds of things; it's almost impossible to prove your innocence. That's almost impossible to do. I think I'll be able to do that. We're working hard at it.

LEHRER: What about the additional element here? You're the president of the United States. Certainly you've got personal things that you want to prove or disprove, et cetera. But when does it—just the process, become demeaning to the presidency? I mean, somebody said—in fact, just said it on our program, that this trial in May will be tabloid nirvana and . . .

CLINTON: Well, I tried to spare the country that. That's the only reason that we asked the Supreme Court to affirm that absent some terrible emergency, the president shouldn't be subject to suits so that he wouldn't become a political target. They made a different decision. And they made a decision that this was good for the country. And so I'm taking it and dealing with it the best I can.

LEHRER: And the new thing? They're going to be—you know, pour it on, nothing's going to change?

CLINTON: I have got to go to work every day. You know, whatever people say about me, whatever happens to me, I can't say that people didn't tell me they were going to go after me because they thought I represented a new direction in American politics and they thought we could make things better. And I can't say that they haven't been as good as their word every day, you know. Just a whole bunch of them are trying to make sure that I get done. But I just have to keep working at it. You know, I didn't come here for money or power or anything else. I came here to spend my time, to do my job, and go back to my life. That's all I want to do, and that's what I'm trying to do, for the best interests of America. And so far the results have been good, and I just hope the people keep that in mind

STATEMENT TWO, Deposition of January 17, 1988, released to the public March 13, 1998, portions having to do with President Clinton's relationship with Monica Lewinsky

Q: Now, do you know a woman named Monica Lewinsky?
A: I do.

Q: How do you know her?

A: She worked in the White House for a while, first as an intern, and then in–as the–in the legislative affairs office.

Q: She began—excuse me.

A: So that's how I know her.

Q: Excuse me for interrupting you, sir. Did she begin to work as an intern in the White House in the summer of 1995?

A: I don't know when she started working at the White House.

Q: Do you recall when you met her for the first time?

A: It would be sometime, I'd think, in later 1995.

Q: She began to work in the White House office of legislative affairs around December of 1995, correct?

A: I have no idea.

Q: Do you know how she obtained that job?

A: No.

Q: Is it true that when she worked at the White House she met with you several times?

A: I don't know about several times. There was a period when the, when the Republican Congress shut the government down that the whole White House was being run by interns, and she was assigned to work back in the chief of staff's office, and we were all working there, and so I saw her on two or three occasions then, and then when she worked at the White House, I think there was one or two other times when she brought some documents to me.

Q: Well, you also saw her at a number of social functions at the White House, didn't you?

A: Could you be specific? I'm not sure. I mean when we had, when we had like big staff things for, if I had a, like in the summertime, if I had a birthday party and the whole White House staff came, then she must have been there. If we had a Christmas party and the whole White House staff was invited, she must have been there. I don't remember any specific social occasions at the White House, but people who work there when they're invited to these things normally come. It's a—they work long hours, it's hard work, and it's one of the nice things about being able to work there, so I assume she was there, but I don't have any specific recollection of any social events.

Q: Mr. President, before the break, we were talking about Monica Lewinsky. At any time were you and Monica Lewinsky alone together in the Oval Office?

A: I don't recall, but as I said, when she worked at the legislative affairs office, they always had somebody there on the weekends. I typically worked some on the weekends. Sometimes they'd bring me things on the weekends. She—it seems to me she brought things to me once or twice on the weekends. In that case, whatever time she would be in there, drop it off, exchange a few words and go, she was there. I don't have any specific recollections of what the issues were, what was going on, but when the Congress is there, we're working all the time, and typically I would do some work on one of the days of the weekends in the afternoon.

Q: So I understand, your testimony is that it was possible, then, that you were alone with her, but you have no specific recollection of that ever happening?

A: Yes, that's correct. It's possible that she, in, while she was working there, brought something to me and that at the time she brought it to me, she was the only person there. That's possible.

Q: Did it ever happen that you and she went down the hallway from the Oval Office to the private kitchen?

A: Well, let me try to describe the facts first, because you keep talking about this private kitchen. The private kitchen is staffed by two naval aides. They have total, unrestricted access to my dining room, to that hallway, to coming into the Oval Office.

The people who are in the outer office of the Oval Office can also enter at any time.

I was, after I went through a presidential campaign in which the far right tried to convince the American people I had committed murder, run drugs, slept in my mother's bed with four prostitutes, and done numerous other things, I had a high level of paranoia.

There are no curtains on the Oval Office, there are no curtains on my private office, there are no curtains or blinds that can close the windows in my private dining room. The naval aides come and go at will. There is a peephole on the office that George Stephanopoulos first and then Rahm Emanuel occupied that looks back down that corridor. I have done everything I could to avoid the kind of questions you are asking me here today, so to talk about this kitchen as if it is a private kitchen, it's a little cubbyhole, and these guys keep the door open. They come and go at will. Now that's the factual background here.

Now, to go back to your question, my recollection is that, that at some point during the government shutdown, when Ms. Lewinsky was still an intern but was working the chief staff's office because all the employees had to go home, that she was back there with a pizza that she brought to me and to others. I do not believe she was there alone, however. I don't think she was. And my recollection is that on a couple of occasions after that she was there but my secretary Betty Currie was there with her. She and Betty are friends. That's my, that's my recollection. And I have no other recollection of that.

MR. FISHER: While I appreciate all of that information, for the record I'm going to object. It's nonresponsive as to the entire answer up to the point where the deponent said, "Now back to your question."

Q: At any time were you and Monica Lewinsky alone in the hallway between the Oval Office and this kitchen area?

A: I don't believe so, unless we were walking back to the back dining room with the pizzas. I just, I don't remember. I don't believe we were alone in the hallway, no.

Q: Are there doors at both ends of the hallway?

A: They are, and they're always open.

Q: At any time have you and Monica Lewinsky ever been alone together in any room in the White House?

A: I think I testified to that earlier. I think that there is a, it is—I have no specific recollection, but it seems to me that she was on duty on a couple of occasions working for the legislative affairs office and brought me some things to sign, something on the weekend. That's—I have a general memory of that.

Q: Have you ever met with Monica Lewinsky in the White House between the hours of midnight and six a.m.?

A: I certainly don't think so.

Q: Have you ever met. . . .

A: Now, let me just say, when she was working there, during, there may have been a time when we were all—we were up working late. There are lots of, on any given night, when the Congress is in session, there are always several people around until late in the night, but I don't have any memory of that. I just can't say that there could have been a time when that occurred, I just j—but I don't remember it.

Q: . . . . [H]ave you ever given any gifts to Monica Lewinsky?

A: I don't recall. Do you know what they were?

Q: A hat pin?

A: I don't, I don't remember. But I certainly, I could have.

Q: A book about Walt Whitman?

A: I give—let me just say, I give people a lot of gifts, and when people are around I give a lot of things I have at the White House away, so I could have given her a gift, but I don't remember a specific gift.

Q: Do you remember giving her a gold brooch?

A: No.

Q: Do you remember giving her an item that had been purchased from The Black Dog store at Martha's Vineyard?

A: I do remember that, because when I went on vacation, Betty said that, asked me if I was going to bring some stuff back from The Black Dog, and she said Monica loved, liked that stuff and would like to have a piece of it, and I did a lot of Christmas shopping from The Black Dog, and I bought a lot of things for a lot of people, and I gave Betty a couple of the pieces, and she gave I think something to Monica and something to some of the other girls who worked in the office. I remember that because Betty mentioned it to me.

Q: What in particular was given to Monica?

A: I don't remember. I got a whole bag full of things that I bought at The Black Dog. I went there, they gave me some things, and I went and purchased a lot at their store, and when I came back I gave a, a big block of it to Betty, and I don't know what she did with it all or who got what.

Q: But while you were in the store you did pick out something for Monica, correct?

A: While I was in the store—first of all, The Black Dog sent me a selection of things. Then I went to the store and I bought some other things, t-shirts, sweatshirts, shirts. Then when I got back to home, I took out a thing or two that I wanted to keep, and I took out a thing or two I wanted to give to some other people, and I gave the rest of it to Betty and she distributed it. That's what I remember doing.

Q: Has Monica Lewinsky ever given you any gifts?

A: Once or twice. I think she's given me a book or two.

Q: Did she give you a silver cigar box?

A: No.

Q: Did she give you a tie?

A: Yes, she had given me a tie before. I believe that's right. Now, as I said, let me remind you, normally, when I get these ties, I get ties, you know, together, and they're given to me later, but I believe that she has given me a tie.

Q: Did you have an extramarital sexual affair with Monica Lewinsky?

A: No.

Q: If she told someone that she had a sexual affair with you beginning in November of 1995, would that be a lie?

A: It's certainly not the truth. It would not be the truth.

Q: I think I used the term "sexual affair." And so the record is completely clear, have you ever had sexual relations with Monica Lewinsky, as that term is defined in Deposition Exhibit 1, as modified by the Court.

MR. BENNETT: I object because I don't know that he can remember.

JUDGE WRIGHT: Well, it's real short. He can—I will permit the question and you may show the witness definition number one. [*See explanatory note, below.*]

A: I have never had sexual relations with Monica Lewinsky. I've never had an affair with her.

[*Explanatory note*] "Definition of Sexual Relations" to the court: For the purposes of this deposition, a person engages in "sexual relations" when the person knowingly engages in or causes—

1. contact with the genitalia, anus, groin, breast, inner thigh, or buttocks of any person with an intent to arouse or gratify the sexual desire of any person;
2. contact between any part of the person's body or an object and the genitals or anus of another person; or
3. contact between the genitals or anus of the person and any part of another person's body. "Contact" means intentional touching, either directly or through clothing.

STATEMENT THREE, President Clinton's statement of August 17, 1998, provided by the Federal Document Clearing House

Good evening. This afternoon in this room, from this chair, I testified before the Office of Independent Counsel and the grand jury.

I answered their questions truthfully, including questions about my private life, questions no American citizen would ever want to answer.

Still, I must take complete responsibility for all my actions, both public and private. And that is why I am speaking to you tonight.

As you know, in a deposition in January, I was asked questions about my relationship with Monica Lewinsky. While my answers were legally accurate, I did not volunteer information.

Indeed, I did have a relationship with Miss Lewinsky that was not appropriate. In fact, it was wrong. It constituted a critical lapse in judgment and a personal failure on my part for which I am solely and completely responsible.

But I told the grand jury today and I say to you now that at no time did I ask anyone to lie, to hide or destroy evidence or to take any other unlawful action.

I know that my public comments and my silence about this matter gave a false impression. I misled people, including even my wife. I deeply regret that.

I can only tell you I was motivated by many factors. First, by a desire to protect myself from the embarrassment of my own conduct. I was also very concerned about protecting my family. The fact that these questions were being asked in a politically inspired lawsuit, which has since been dismissed, was a consideration, too.

In addition, I had real and serious concerns about an independent counsel investigation that began with private business dealings 20 years ago, dealing, I might add, about which an independent federal agency found no evidence of any wrongdoing by me or my wife over two years ago.

The independent counsel investigation moved on to my staff and friends, then into my private life. And now the investigation itself is under investigation.

This has gone on too long, cost too much and hurt too many innocent people.

Now, this matter is between me, the two people I love most— my wife and our daughter—and our God. I must put it right, and I am prepared to do whatever it takes to do so. Nothing is more important to me personally. But it is private, and I intend to reclaim my family life for my family. It's nobody's business but ours. Even presidents have private lives.

It is time to stop the pursuit of personal destruction and the prying into private lives and get on with our national life.

Our country has been distracted by this matter for too long, and I take my responsibility for my part in all of this. That is all I can do. Now it is time—in fact, it is past time—to move on.

We have important work to do—real opportunities to seize, real problems to solve, real security matters to face.

And so tonight, I ask you to turn away from the spectacle of the past seven months, to repair the fabric of our national discourse, and to return our attention to all the challenges and all the promise of the next American century.

Thank you for watching. And good night.

STATEMENT FOUR, Grand Jury Testimony of President Clinton, August 17, 1998, released to the public September 21, 1998, questions and answers dealing with the President's earlier statements about his relationship with Monica Lewinsky

Q: Mr. President, were you physically intimate with Monica Lewinsky?

A: Mr. Bittman, I think maybe I can save the–you and the grand jurors a lot of time if I read a statement, which I think will make it clear what the nature of my relationship with Ma. Lewinsky was and how it related to the testimony I gave, what I was trying to do in that testimony. And I think it will perhaps make it possible for you to ask even more relevant questions from your point of view. And, with your permission, I'd like to read that statement.

Q: Absolutely. Please, Mr. President.

A: When I was alone with Ms. Lewinsky on certain occasions in early 1996 and once in early 1997, I engaged in conduct that was wrong. These encounters did not consist of sexual intercourse. They did not constitute sexual relations as I understood that term to be defined at my January 17th, 1998, deposition. But they did involve inappropriate intimate contact.

These inappropriate encounters ended, at my insistence, in early 1997. I also had occasional telephone conversations with Ms. Lewinsky that included inappropriate sexual banter.

I regret that what began as a friendship came to include this conduct, and I take full responsibility for my actions.

While I will provide the grand jury whatever other information I can, because of privacy considerations affecting my family, myself, and others, and in an effort to preserve the dignity of the office I hold, this is all I will say about the specifics of these particular matters.

I will try to answer, to the best of my ability, other questions including questions about my relationship with Ms. Lewinsky; questions about my understanding of the term "sexual relations", as I understood it to be defined at my January 17th, 1998 deposition; and questions concerning alleged subornation of perjury, obstruction of justice, and intimidation of witnesses.

That, Mr. Bittman, is my statement.

Q: Thank you, Mr. President. And, with that, we would like to take a break.

Q: Was this contact with Ms. Lewinsky, Mr. President, did it involve any sexual contact in any way, shape, or form?

A: Mr. Bittman, I said in this statement I would like to stay to the terms of the statement. I think it's clear what inappropriately intimate is. I have said what it did not include. I—it did not include sexual intercourse, and I do not believe it included conduct which falls within the definition I was given in the Jones deposition. [*See explanatory note, above.*] And I would like to stay with that characterization. . . .

Q: It was at page 19, Mr. President, beginning at line 21, and I'll read it in full. This is from the Jones attorney. "Would you please take whatever time you need to read this definition, because when I use the term 'sexual relation,' this is what I mean today."

A: Alright. Yes, that starts on 19. But let me say that there is a—just for the record, my recollection was accurate. There is a long discussion here between the attorney and the Judge. It goes on until page 23. And in the end the Judge says, "I'm talking only about part one in the definition," and "Do you understand that"? And I answer, "I do." The Judge says part one, and then the lawyer for Ms. Jones says he's only talking about part one and asked me if I understand it. And I say, I do, and that was my understanding. I might also note that when I was given this and began to ask questions about it, I actually circled number one. This is my circle here. I remember doing that so I could focus only on those two lines, which is what I did.

Q: Did you understand the words in the first portion of the exhibit, Mr. President, that is, "For the purposes of this deposition, a person engages in 'sexual relations' when the person knowingly engages in or causes"? Did you understand, do you understand the words there in that phrase?

A: Yes. My—I can tell you what my understanding of the definition is, if you want me to . . .

Q: Sure.

A: . . . do it. My understanding of this definition is it covers contact by the person being deposed with the enumerated areas, if the contact is done with an intent to arouse or gratify. That's my understanding of the definition.

Q: What did you believe the definition to include and exclude? What kinds of activities?

A: I thought the definition included any activity by the person being deposed, where the person was the actor and came in contact with those parts of the bodies with the purpose or intent or gratification, and excluded any other activity. For example, kissing is not covered by that, I don't think.

Q: Did you understand the definition to be limited to sexual activity?

A: Yes, I understood the definition to be limited to, to physical contact with those areas of the bodies with the specific intent to arouse or gratify. That's what I understood it to be.

Q: What specific acts did the definition include, as you understood the definition on January 17, 1998?

A: Any contact with the areas there mentioned, sir. If you contacted, if you contacted those parts of the body with an intent to arouse or gratify, that is covered.

Q: What did you understand . . .

A: The person being deposed. If the person being deposed contacted those parts of another person's body with an intent to arouse or gratify, that was covered.

Q: What did you understand the word "causes," in the first phrase? That is, "For the purposes of this deposition, a person engaged in 'sexual relations' when the person knowingly" causes contact?

A: I don't know what that means. It doesn't make any sense to me in this context, because—I think what I thought there was, since this was some sort of—as I remember, they said in the previous discussion—and I'm only remembering now, so if I make a mistake you can correct me. As I remember from the previous discussion, this was some kind of definition that had something to do with sexual harassment. So, that implies it's forcing to me, and I—and there was never any issue of forcing in the case involving, well, any of these questions they were asking me. They made it clear in this discussion I just reviewed that what they were referring to was intentional sexual conduct, not some sort of forcible abusive behavior. So, I basically—I don't think I paid any attention to it because it appeared to me that that was something that had no reference to the facts that they admitted they were asking me about.

Q: So, if I can be clear, Mr. President, was it your understanding back in January that the definition, now marked as Grand Jury Exhibit 2, only included consensual sexual activity?

A: No. My understanding—let me go back and say it. My understanding—I'll tell you what it did include. My understanding was, what I was giving to you, was that what was covered in those first two lines was any direct contact by the person being deposed with those parts of another person's body, if the contact was done with an intent to arouse or gratify. That's what

I believed it meant. That's what I believed it meant then reading it. That's what I believe it means today.

Q: I'm just trying to understand, Mr. President. You indicated that you put the definition in the context of a sexual harassment case.

A: No, no. I think it was not in the context of sexual harassment. I just reread those four pages, which obviously the grand jury doesn't have. But there was some reference to the fact that this definition apparently bore some, had some connection to some definition in another context, and that this was being used not in that context, not necessarily in the context of sexual harassment.

So, I would think that this "causes" would be, would mean to force someone to do something. That's what I read it [*sic*]. That's the only point I'm trying to make. Therefore, I did not believe that anyone had suggested that I had forced anyone to do anything, and that—and I did not do that. And so that could not have had any bearing on any questions related to Ms. Lewinsky.

Q: I suppose, since you have now read portions of the transcript again, that you were reminded that you did not ask for any clarification of the terms. Is that correct? Of the definition?

A: No, sir. I thought it was a rather—when I read it, I thought it was a rather strange definition. But it was the one the Judge decided on and I was bound by it. So, I took it.

Q: So, your definition of sexual relationship is intercourse only, is that correct?

A: No, not necessarily intercourse only. But it would include intercourse. I believe, I believe that the common understanding of the term, if you say two people are having a sexual relationship, most people believe that includes intercourse. So, if that's what Ms. Lewinsky thought, then this is a truthful affidavit. I don't know what was in her mind. But if that's what she thought, the affidavit is true.

Q: What else would sexual relationship include besides intercourse?

A: Well, that—I think—let me answer what I said before. I think most people when they use that term include sexual relationships and whatever other sexual contact is involved in a particular relationship. But they think it includes intercourse as well. And I would have thought so. Before I got into this case and heard all I've heard, and seen all I've seen, I would have thought that that's what nearly everybody thought it meant.

Q: Well, I ask, Mr. President, because your attorney, using the very document, Grand Jury Exhibit 4, WJC-4, represented to Judge Wright that his understanding of the meaning of that affidavit, which you've indicated you thought Ms. Lewinsky thought was, she was referring just to intercourse, he says to Judge Wright that it meant absolutely no sex of any kind in any manner, shape or form.

A: Well, let me say this. I didn't have any discussion obviously at this moment with Mr. Bennett. I'm not even sure I paid much attention to what he was saying. I was thinking, I was ready to get on with my testimony here and they were having these constant discussions all through the deposition. But that statement in the present tense, at least, is not inaccurate, if that's what Mr. Bennett meant. That is, at the time that he said that, and for some time before, that would be a completely accurate statement.

Now, I don't believe that he was I don't know what he meant. You'd have to talk to him, because I just wasn't involved in this, and I didn't pay much attention to what was being said. I was just waiting for them to get back to me. So, I can't comment on, or be held responsible for, whatever he said about that, I don't think.

Q: Well, if you—do you agree with me that if he mislead Judge Wright in some way that you would have corrected the record and said, excuse me, Mr. Bennett, I think the Judge is getting a misimpression by what you're saying?

A: Mr. Bennett was representing me. I wasn't representing him. And I wasn't even paying much attention to this conversation, which is why, when you started asking me about this, I asked to see the deposition, I was focusing on my answers to the questions. And I've told you what I believe about this deposition, which I believe to be true. And it's obvious, and I think by your questions you have betrayed that the Jones lawyers' strategy in this case had nothing to do with uncovering or proving sexual harassment.

By the time this discovery started, they knew they had a bad case on the law and they knew what our evidence was. They knew they had a lousy case on the facts. And so their strategy, since they were being funded by my political opponents, was to have this dragnet of discovery. They wanted to cover everybody. And they convinced the Judge, because she gave them strict orders not to leak, that they should be treated like other plaintiffs in other civil cases, and how could they ever know whether there had been any sexual harassment, unless they first knew whether there had been any sex.

And so, with that broad mandate limited by time and employment in the federal or state government, they proceeded to cross the country and try to turn up whatever they could; not because they thought it would help their case. By the time they did this discovery, they knew what this deal was in their case, and they knew what was going to happen. And Judge Wright subsequently threw it out. What they . . .

Q: With all respect, Mister . . .

A: Now, let me finish, Mr. Bennett [*sic*]. I mean, you brought this up. Excuse me, Mr. Bittman. What they wanted to do, and what they did do, and what they had done by the time I showed up here, was to find any negative information they could on me, whether it was true or not; get it in a deposition; and then leak it, even though it was illegal to do so. It happened repeatedly. The judge gave them orders.

One of the reasons she was sitting in that deposition was because she was trying to make sure that it didn't get out of hand. But that was their strategy, and they did a good job of it, and they got away with it. I've been subject to quite a lot of illegal leaking, and they had a very determined deliberate strategy, because their real goal was to hurt me. When they knew they couldn't win the lawsuit, they thought, well, maybe we can pummel him. Maybe they thought I'd settle. Maybe they just thought they would get some political advantage out of it. But that's what was going on here.

Now, I'm trying to be honest with you, and it hurts me. And I'm trying to tell you the truth about what happened between Ms. Lewinsky and me. But that does not change the fact that the real reason they were zeroing in on anybody was to try to get any person in there, no matter how uninvolved with Paula Jones, no matter how uninvolved with sexual harassment, so they could hurt me politically. That's what was going on. Because by then, by this time, this thing had been going on a long time. They knew what our evidence was. They knew what the law was in the circuit in which we were bringing this case. And so they just thought they would take a wrecking ball to me and see if they could do some damage.

[BY MR. WISENBERG] Q: Mr. President, I want to, before I go into a new subject area, briefly go over something you were talking about with Mr. Bittman. The statement of your attorney, Mr. Bennett, at the Paula Jones deposition, "Counsel is fully aware"—it's page 54, line 5—"Counsel is fully aware that Ms. Lewinsky has filed, has an affidavit which they are in possession of saying that there is absolutely no sex of any kind in any manner, shape or form, with President Clinton." That statement is made by your attorney in front of Judge Webber, , correct?

A: That's correct.

Q: That statement is a completely false statement. Whether or not Mr. Bennett knew of your relationship with Ms. Lewinsky, the statement that there was "no sex of any kind in any manner, shape or form, with President Clinton," was an utterly false statement. Is that correct?

A: It depends on what the meaning of the word "is" is. If the— if he—if "is" means is and never has been that is not—that is one thing. If it means there is none, that was a completely true statement. But, as I have testified, and I'd like to testify again, this is—it is somewhat unusual for a client to be asked about his lawyer's statements, instead of the other way around. I was not paying a great deal of attention to this exchange. I was focusing on my own testimony. And if you go back and look at the sequence of this, you will see that the Jones lawyers decided that this was going to be the Lewinsky deposition, not the Jones deposition. And, given the facts of their case, I can understand why they made that decision. But that is not how I prepared for it. That is not how I was thinking about it. And I am not sure, Mr. Wisenberg, as I sit here today, that I sat there and followed all these interchanges between the lawyers. I'm quite sure that I didn't follow all the interchanges between the lawyers all that carefully. And I don't really believe, therefore, that I can say Mr. Bennett's testimony or statement is testimony and is imputable to me. I didn't—I don't know that I was even paying that much attention to it.

Q: You are the President of the United States and your attorney tells a United States District Court Judge that there is no sex of any kind, in any way, shape or form, whatsoever. And you feel no obligation to do anything about that at that deposition, Mr. President?

PRESIDENT CLINTON: I don't . . .

[MR. KENDALL] Q: I'm going to object to any questions about communications with private counsel.

[MR. WISENBERG] Q: Well, the witness has already testified, I think, that Mr. Bennett didn't know about the inappropriate relationship with Ms. Lewinsky. I guess . . .

A: Well, you'll have to ask him that, you know. He was not a sworn witness and I was not paying that close attention to what he was saying, I've told you that repeatedly. I was—I don't—I never even focused on that until I read it in this transcript in preparation for this testimony. When I was in there, I didn't think about my lawyers. I was, frankly, thinking about myself and my testimony and trying to answer the questions.

Q: I just want to make sure I understand, Mr. President. Do you mean today that because you were not engaging in sexual activity with Ms. Lewinsky during the deposition that the statement of Mr. Bennett might be literally true?

A: No, sir. I mean that at the time of the deposition, it had been—that was well beyond any point of improper contact between me and Ms. Lewinsky. So that anyone generally speaking in the present tense, saying there is not an improper relationship, would be telling the truth if that person said there was not, in the present tense; the present tense encompassing many months. That's what I meant by that.

Not that I was—I wasn't trying to give you a cute answer, that I was obviously not involved in anything improper during a deposition. I was trying to tell you that generally speaking in the present tense, if someone said that, that would be true. But I don't know what Mr. Bennett had in his mind. I don't know. I didn't pay any attention to this colloquy that went on. I was waiting for my instructions as a witness to go forward. I was worried about my own testimony.

STATEMENT FIVE, President Clinton, Prayer Breakfast Speech, Friday, September 11, 1998, transcript provided by the Associated Press

Thank you very much, ladies and gentlemen. Welcome to the White House and to this day to which Hillary and the vice president and I look forward so much every year.

This is always an important day for our country, for the reasons that the vice president said. It is an unusual and, I think, unusually important day today. I may not be quite as easy with my words today as I have been in years past, and I was up rather late last night thinking about and praying about what I ought to say today. And rather unusual for me, I actually tried to write it down. So if you will forgive me, I will do my best to say what it is I want to say to you–and I may have to take my glasses out to read my own writing.

First, I want to say to all of you that, as you might imagine, I have been on quite a journey these last few weeks to get to the end of this, to the rock bottom truth of where I am and where we all are. I agree with those who have said that in my first statement after I testified I was not contrite enough. I don't think there is a fancy way to say that I have sinned.

It is important to me that everybody who has been hurt know that the sorrow I feel is genuine: first and most important, my family; also my friends, my staff, my Cabinet, Monica Lewinsky and her family, and the American people. I have asked all for their forgiveness.

But I believe that to be forgiven, more than sorrow is required—at least two more things. First, genuine repentance—a determination to change and to repair breaches of my own making. I have repented. Second, what my Bible calls a "broken spirit"; an understanding that I must have God's help to be the person that I want to be; a willingness to give the very forgiveness I seek; a renunciation of the pride and the anger which cloud judgment, lead people to excuse and compare and to blame and complain.

Now, what does all this mean for me and for us? First, I will instruct my lawyers to mount a vigorous defense, using all available appropriate arguments. But legal language must not obscure the fact that I have done wrong. Second, I will continue on the path of repentance, seeking pastoral support and that of other caring people so that they can hold me accountable for my own commitment.

Third, I will intensify my efforts to lead our country and the world toward peace and freedom, prosperity and harmony, in the hope that with a broken spirit and a still strong heart I can be used for greater good, for we have many blessings and many challenges and so much work to do.

In this, I ask for your prayers and for your help in healing our nation. And though I cannot move beyond or forget this—indeed, I must always keep it as a caution light in my life—it is very important that our nation move forward.

I am very grateful for the many, many people—clergy and ordinary citizens alike—who have written me with wise counsel. I am profoundly grateful for the support of so many Americans who somehow through it all seem to still know that I care about them a great deal, that I care about their problems and their dreams. I am grateful for those who have stood by me and who say that in this case and many others, the bounds of privacy have been excessively and unwisely invaded. That may be. Nevertheless, in this case, it may be a blessing, because I still sinned. And if my repentance is genuine and sustained, and if I can maintain both a broken spirit and a strong heart, then good can come of this for our country as well as for me and my family.

The children of this country can learn in a profound way that integrity is important and selfishness is wrong, but God can change us and make us strong at the broken places. I want to embody those lessons for the children of this country—for that little boy in Florida who came up to me and said that he wanted to grow up and be President and to be just like me. I want the parents of all the children in America to be able to say that to their children.

A couple of days ago when I was in Florida a Jewish friend of mine gave me this liturgy book called *Gates of Repentance*. And there was this incredible passage from the Yom Kippur liturgy. I would like to read it to you:

> Now is the time for turning. The leaves are beginning to turn from green to red to orange. The birds are beginning to turn and are heading once more toward the south. The animals are beginning to turn to storing their food for the winter. For leaves, birds and animals, turning comes instinctively. But for us, turning does not come so easily. It takes an act of will for us to make a turn. It means breaking old habits. It means admitting that we have been

wrong, and this is never easy. It means losing face. It means starting all over again. And this is always painful. It means saying I am sorry. It means recognizing that we have the ability to change. These things are terribly hard to do. But unless we turn, we will be trapped forever in yesterday's ways. Lord, help us to turn, from callousness to sensitivity, from hostility to love, from pettiness to purpose, from envy to contentment, from carelessness to discipline, from fear to faith. Turn us around, O Lord, and bring us back toward you. Revive our lives as at the beginning, and turn us toward each other, Lord, for in isolation there is no life.

I thank my friend for that. I thank you for being here. I ask you to share my prayer that God will search me and know my heart, try me and know my anxious thoughts, see if there is any hurtfulness in me, and lead me toward the life everlasting. I ask that God give me a clean heart, let me walk by faith and not sight.

I ask once again to be able to love my neighbor—all my neighbors—as my self, to be an instrument of God's peace; to let the words of my mouth and the meditations of my heart and, in the end, the work of my hands, be pleasing. This is what I wanted to say to you today.

Thank you. God bless you.

APPENDIX F

BERNARD LAW'S APOLOGIES

**STATEMENT ONE, Cardinal Bernard Law,
Press Conference, January 9, 2002**

I wish to address the issue of sexual abuse of minors by clergy. At the outset, I apologize once again to all those who have been sexually abused as minors by priests. Today that apology is made in a special way with heartfelt sorrow to those abused by John Geoghan.

There is no way for me to describe adequately the evil of such acts. All sexual abuse is morally abhorrent. Sexual abuse of minors is particularly abhorrent. Such abuse by clergy adds to the heinous nature of the act. It affects a victim's relationship to the Church. A child's ability to trust is shattered by such abuse, and self-esteem is damaged.

Today the issue of sexual abuse is a matter of open and public discussion. While this is often painful, it has allowed us to address the issue more directly. Only in this way can all of us be more alert to its dangers, protect potential victims, respond more effectively with those responsible for such abuse.

Here in this archdiocese, I promulgated a policy to deal with sexual abuse of minors by clergy. This went into effect on January 15, 1993. All priest personnel records were reviewed in light of this policy. In those instances in which a charge of abuse had not been processed earlier with the rigor of our present policy, the case was reopened, and the policy followed.

I am aided in such cases by a priest-delegate and by an interdisciplinary review board that examines each case and makes a recommendation to me. This review board includes the mother of a victim, another parent, a clinical social worker, a clinical psychologist, a psychotherapist, a retired justice of the Supreme Judicial Court, a priest, a civil attorney and, usually, a canon lawyer.

While the response of the Church understandably focuses on the removal of the threat of future acts of abuse, it is also concerned with providing psychological and spiritual counsel to victims as well as assistance to parishes coping with such incidents. Victims who come forward are offered confidential psychological counseling and spiritual support. It is my desire that the Church be present in whatever way possible to all those who have suffered such abuse.

While our policy has been effective, we continue to refine our procedures. Since our knowledge and experience in dealing with such cases have evolved both within the Church and society as a whole, I want to be certain that our policy is as effective as it might be. In August, I directed that our policy be reviewed. In September, a panel of persons with special expertise began the review process. Except for one priest, this panel consists of lay men and women. The work of this group has nearly been completed. I anticipate that the revised policy will be promulgated and made available within the next three to four weeks.

I wish we had had such a policy 50 years ago, or when I first came here as archbishop. Cases were handled then in a manner that would not be acceptable according to our present policy. I know of nothing that has caused me greater pain than the recognition of that fact.

I am announcing today a new archdiocesan policy that will mandate all clergy, employees, and volunteers to report any allegations of abuse against a minor, following the procedures set forth in the statutes of the Commonwealth of Massachusetts. In particular, this mandated reporting would include any knowledge of abuse learned by a priest outside of the sacrament of penance or through spiritual counseling. In addition, a number of archdiocesan agencies are in the process of developing and implementing a comprehensive child protection program, Keeping Children Safe. These additions to our present policy will underscore our archdiocesan commitment to a zero tolerance policy of abuse of minors by clergy.

The many acts that have been alleged against John Geoghan constitute a heart-rending pattern. These acts have been reported in some detail in recent media stories. The horror of these acts speaks for itself.

However much I regret having assigned him, it is important to recall that John Geoghan was never assigned by me to a parish without psychiatric or medical assessments indicating that such assignments were appropriate. It is also important to state that it was I who removed him from parish ministry, that I then placed him on retirement, and that I finally asked the Holy See to dismiss him from the priesthood without possibility of appeal, even though he had not requested laicization. This extraordinary act of the Holy See went beyond the usual procedures for the laicization of priests.

That some should criticize my earlier decisions I can easily understand. Before God, however, it was not then, nor is it my intent now, to protect a priest accused of misconduct against minors at the expense of those whom he is ordained to serve.

Judgments were made regarding the assignment of John Geoghan which, in retrospect, were tragically incorrect. These judgments were, however, made in good faith and in reliance upon psychiatric assessments and medical opinions that such assignments were safe and reasonable.

With all my heart, I wish to apologize once again for the harm done to the victims of sexual abuse by priests. I do so in my own name, but also in the name of my brother priests. These days are particularly painful for the victims of John Geoghan. My apology to them and their families, and particularly to those who were abused in assignments which I made, comes from a grieving heart. I am indeed profoundly sorry.

The trust that was broken in the lives of those suffering the effects of abuse is a trust which was built upon the selfless lives of thousands of priests who have served faithfully and well in this archdiocese throughout its history. One of the sad consequences of these instances of abuse, a consequence which pales in comparison to the harm done to these most innocent of victims, is that they have placed under a cloud of suspicion the faithful priests who serve the mission of the Church with integrity.

I can only hope that victims and their families can take some heart from the fact that not only the Church but society as a whole are responding more effectively to this overwhelming tragedy.

For the Archdiocese of Boston, I pledge a policy of zero tolerance for such behavior. Any priest known to have sexually abused a minor simply will not function as a priest in any way in this archdiocese.

Please pray for all those who have been victimized as minors by clergy, as well as for their families. Pray that those responsible may come to conversion of heart and self-awareness. Pray for the hundreds of faithful priests of this archdiocese who bear with me the burden of a few.

Before God, we are trying to do the best we can. In your kindness, pray also for me.

STATEMENT TWO, Cardinal Bernard Law, Press Conference, January 24, 2002

As you know, we've just concluded the third assembly of priests in this archdiocese . . . And I would say that the consensus was that it could not have come at a more providential time. It was very, very good for us to be together. It was a positive time. We dealt realistically with the sad events of the past, which bring you together here today. We assessed the present, and we agreed in moving forward confidently to the future. . . .

Let me just make a series of points that, from my perspective, help position us moving forward.

I have acknowledged that, in retrospect, I know that I made mistakes in the assignment of priests.

I have said that I have come to see that our policy was flawed. The fundamental flaw was the assumption that a psychological evaluation after treatment could be relied upon to reassign a priest.

I have come to recognize that it is simply not appropriate to assign a priest guilty of such an act to a parish or to any other assignment. Our revised policy reflects this conviction, as I have indicated before and repeat again: There is no priest known to us to have been guilty of the sexual abuse of a minor holding any position in this archdiocese.

I wish I could undo what I now see to have been mistakes. However, that is not a possibility. What is possible is to apologize again to victims and their families and also to learn from those mistakes as we plan for the future. And our policy moving forward seeks to do that, and it is that policy which I was able to outline to the priests yesterday, and it is that policy which I outline to you in some more detail now.

I have made the decision that the archdiocese will report retroactively on priest offenders. Obviously we want to do this in a way that respects the confidentiality of the victims.

Dr. Michael Collins, who is the president and CEO of Caritas Christi, is representing me in convening a group of distinguished physicians and educators whom I have asked to assist in developing a strategy for the protection of all children from sexual abuse. I will ask this group to consider four basic . . . questions:

First, the feasibility of establishing an interdisciplinary center for the prevention of sexual abuse of children.

Secondly, I will ask this group to put forth the goals for such a center.

Thirdly, the objectives for reaching those goals.

And then, fourthly, I will ask this group of distinguished physicians and educators to suggest the names of those most qualified who can move this project forward.

There are several things that I would also ask this group to do, if not this group itself then the group of people who they will suggest, as, if you will, a blue [ribbon] panel national group of experts. And I would ask them, first of all, to critique our present policy. We think it's a good policy, but we want it critiqued nonetheless.

Secondly, to help us in enhancing our outreach to victims and to families.

Thirdly, to assist us in enhancing our outreach to parishes and schools most affected.

And then, fourthly, to help us enhance our spiritual care of all of those affected.

This is a tall order and what I'm sharing with you now is the beginning of a process, the beginning of a journey. . . .

I indicated yesterday to the priests that the solution to this problem, as I see it, does not include my resignation as archbishop. The relationship of the bishop to his diocese is signified by the ring he wears, and you don't walk away when the problem is difficult. That's when you need to be together.

STATEMENT THREE, Text of Bernard Cardinal Law's open letter, Cardinal's residence, 2101 Commonwealth Avenue, Brighton, Massachusetts, January 26, 2002

Dearly Beloved in Christ,

I write to you on what has become a major issue of public attention: the manner in which the Archdiocese and I in particular, have handled allegations of sexual abuse of children by priests.

In the terrible instances of sexual abuse, the Archdiocese of Boston has failed to protect one of our most precious gifts, our children. As Archbishop, it was and is my responsibility to ensure that our parishes be safe havens for our children, places where they can experience all that the Church is called to be.

In retrospect, I acknowledge that, albeit unintentionally, I have failed in that responsibility. The judgments which I made, while made in good faith, were tragically wrong. Because of this, some have called for my resignation. I do not believe that submitting my resignation to the Holy Father is the answer to the terrible scourge of sexual abuse of children by priests. I intend to implement a comprehensive and aggressive child protection program in order to better uncover and prevent the sexual abuse of children. This program will focus on our children. In going forward and responding to this horrible reality, the number one priority of the Archdiocese and me personally will be to ensure the safety of our children and to make every conceivable effort to see that no more of our young people become the victims of such abuse. I am committed to do all in my power to implement a policy of zero tolerance for the sexual abuse of children by priests or any agent of the Archdiocese.

Some of these tragedies occurred on my watch, and I cannot and will not avoid my responsibility to ensure the prevention of such tragedies in the future. As was announced on Thursday, the deans of the Medical Schools at Boston University, Harvard, Tufts, and the University of Massachusetts, as well as the dean of the Boston College School of Social Work have agreed to work with me. Together we will plan our program (and) identify experts in a broad range of disciplines who are nationally recognized in dealing with the issue of the sexual abuse of children, and who are willing to serve as members of a blue ribbon committee. I will ask the members to review and critique the manner in which the Archdiocese, on all levels, deals with the problem of sexual abuse of children. I will ask them to conduct their study as quickly and as effectively as possible and then to make recommendations for a comprehensive and aggressive child protection program to uncover and prevent any further abuse of children.

It is my firm expectation that the sexual abuse prevention program to be developed will contain written policies and procedures which will address, among other things, the following:

REPORTING SEXUAL ABUSE: All priests, deacons, as well as all Archdiocesan employees and volunteers, shall be obligated to report to me all complaints of sexual abuse of children (learned in any forum other than in the Sacrament of Penance), including allegations against any priest, former priest, or priest who is no longer in active service, and I, in turn, shall forward those reports to appropriate public authorities. Moreover, the names of any priest perpetrators of such abuse which are in the records of the Archdiocese and which have never been turned over to public authorities will immediately be conveyed to such authorities.

DETECTION AND DETERRENCE OF SEXUAL ABUSE: With the help of experts, I will review the present program of mandatory screening of applicants to the seminary with a view to improving that process. All Archdiocesan personnel, including priests, deacons, religious, seminarians, and lay staff will receive appropriate training about sexual abuse, including early detection of conduct characteristic of both victims and perpetrators of such abuse.

EDUCATION REGARDING SEXUAL ABUSE: The Archdiocese will create and implement an educational program for parishes regarding sexual abuse and offer resources for victims of sexual abuse by priests or any agents of the Archdiocese. I have asked the Director of our Catholic Schools Office, Sister Kathleen Carr, CSJ, to gather educational experts of diverse backgrounds who will develop a curriculum which will be a practical and effective resource for students, parents, teachers, and staff in our parochial schools and religious education programs.

CONTINUING PASTORAL CARE FOR VICTIMS AND THEIR FAMILIES: The victims of sexual abuse, and their families, are the ones who have been most directly and severely affected. The Archdiocese and I personally want and need to offer our apology, consolation, and support. I will make myself available to meet privately with those victims and their families who desire to do so. Dr. Joseph Doolin, Secretary for Social Services, will assist me in gathering experts to suggest ways to enhance our provision of psychiatric counseling and psychotherapy to all victims and their families, as well as ways to offer enhanced counseling outreach to parishes and schools directly impacted, and to all those who may have been affected. The Archdiocesan Office of Spiritual Development will assist me in providing an appropriate program of spiritual counseling for victims and their families.

THE LEGAL PROCESS FOR VICTIMS OF SEXUAL ABUSE: The Archdiocese will strive to eliminate the need for victims of sexual abuse to endure protracted and painful litigation. We are committed to resolving cases expeditiously, fairly, and equitably. At the same time, I can assure you that no monies from parish collections, the Cardinal's Appeal, the Promise for Tomorrow Capital Campaign, or any other donated funds, unless specifically designated for this purpose, have been or will be used to resolve such cases.

The terrible tragedy of sexual abuse of children by priests has caused deep pain and profound suffering. Most traumatically and severely impacted have been the victims and their families. The failure of the Archdiocese to protect one of God's greatest gifts to us, our children, has been devastating. Trust in the Church has been shattered in many cases. With God's help we must strive to restore that trust.

In a profound manner, although it pales in comparison to what has been endured by victims and their families, all of the faithful have suffered. Faith has been shaken and relationships of affection and trust between the faithful and clergy have been frayed in some cases. Considerable effort must and will be expended to repair the breakdown in trust and confidence which the faithful properly expect to have in the Church and her ministers.

Considerable damage has also been done to the hundreds of priests of this Archdiocese who, on a daily basis, offer humble, generous, faithful, and loving service to their people. These good and holy priests have been deeply wounded by the reprehensible actions of some of their number who sexually abused children, as well as by an Archdiocesan response to such tragic incidents which, in retrospect, was flawed and deficient. The relationship between a bishop and his diocese, in our case between me and this Archdiocese, is a sacred and serious one. It seeks to reflect the relationship between Christ and the Church in much the same way as the Sacrament of Matrimony does. The Bishop's ring, like the wedding ring, symbolizes the commitment and love of the bishop to the faithful of his diocese.

My acknowledgment, in retrospect, that the response of the Archdiocese and me personally to the grave evil of the sexual abuse of children by priests was flawed and inadequate has contributed to this profoundly difficult moment in the life of this Archdiocese, and has affected the relationship between us.

With humble sorrow and hopeful faith, I turn to our loving God and to you, the faithful of this Archdiocese, and seek your forgiveness and support. With all my heart, with every fiber of my being, I pledge to you that I am committed to protect our children and restore the relationship of trust on which the faith life of this Archdiocese is founded. I humbly beg your prayers and support as together, with God's help, we try to work through this difficult and challenging situation.

I wish to underscore, once again, my commitment to do all in my power to implement and ensure a policy of zero tolerance for the sexual abuse of children by priests or any agents of the Archdiocese.

May our resolve help to console and reassure victims and their families, and may God's blessing be with them. May God grant His peace to all of us who struggle with this issue. May God bless our efforts as we move forward.

Devotedly yours in Christ,

Bernard Cardinal Law
Archbishop of Boston

STATEMENT FOUR, Bernard Cardinal Law, open letter to priests of the Boston Archdiocese, April 12, 2002

My dear brother priests,

The expression of support and the assurance of prayer which have come from so many of you in recent weeks have been, for me, a source of strength and consolation. Please know of my esteem for you and my deep appreciation for your faithful priestly ministry in a most challenging time for us all, and my constant prayers for you and those whom you serve. If ever there were a time when the unity in ministry which is ours through ordination should be evident, it is now. I cherish that communion as a great grace.

The case of Father Paul Shanley is particularly troubling for us. For me personally, it has brought home with painful clarity how inadequate our record keeping has been. A continual institutional memory concerning allegations and cases of abuse of children was lacking. Trying to learn from the handling of this and other cases, I am committed to ensure that our records are kept in a way that those who deal with clergy personnel in the future will have the benefit of a full, accurate, and easily accessible institutional memory.

Like many of you, I have had the moving and painful experience of meetings with those who have been abused as children as well as with their parents, spouses, and other family members. The unbelievable horror of these accounts can only dimly reflect the awful and often on-going pain of the reality. Each of these encounters makes me more determined than ever to do all in my power to ensure, as far as is humanly possible, that no child is ever abused again by a priest in this Archdiocese. Obviously, the best of policies cannot provide an infallible assurance. We can, however, learn from our experience, the experience of others, and from our mistakes in formulating the best of policies.

Looking back, I see that we were too focused on the individual components of each case, when we should have been more focused on the protection of children. This would have changed our emphasis on secrecy as a part of legal settlements. While this focus was inspired by a desire to protect the privacy of the victim, to avoid scandal to the faithful, and to preserve the reputation of the priest, we now realize both within the Church and in society at large that secrecy often inhibits healing and places others at risk.

There was a time many years ago when instances of sexual abuse of children were viewed almost exclusively as moral failures. A spiritual and ascetical remedy, therefore, was deemed sufficient. While the moral aspect of such cases is always present, these cases cannot be reduced only to a moral component.

In more recent years, which would certainly include my tenure as Archbishop, there has been a general recognition that such cases reflect a psychological and emotional pathology. It has been this recognition which has inspired our reliance on medical professionals. I remember so clearly the insistence made by my seminary professors that our seminary education did not constitute us as psychologists, and we were warned not to assume a competence we did not possess. The medical profession itself has evolved in the understandings and treatment of this pathology, or perhaps, more accurately, "pathologies," and we are able gratefully to benefit from that increased knowledge.

There is a third dimension to these cases and it is their criminal nature. In an effort to give a pastoral response, we have not taken into sufficient account the criminality involved in abuse. In a desire to encourage victims who might not desire to enter a criminal process to come forward to us, we did not communicate cases to public authorities. While our reason for not doing so seemed reasonable, I am convinced it was not adequate. Public authorities have the obligation not only to prosecute, but also to defend the public from harm. It is for these reasons that we have pledged to report all allegations going forward, and have provided the names of all priests against whom a credible allegation had been made, going back 53 years.

We have now, I believe, in proper balance the three dimensions: the moral, the pathological and the criminal.

There is much more all of us need to learn about this pathology so that we can protect children. I am pledged to do all in my power to provide the most effective educational materials for all in the Church: clergy, pastoral staffs, teachers, children, parents and the faithful in general.

As long as I am your Archbishop, I am determined to provide the strongest leadership possible in this area. I know that there are many who believe my resignation is part of the solution. It distresses me greatly to have become a lightning rod of division when mine should be a ministry of unity. My desire is to serve this Archdiocese and the whole Church with every fiber of my being. This I will continue to do as long as God gives me the opportunity.

I depend more than ever on your prayers and support in these days so trying to us all.

With warm personal regards, and asking God to bless you and those whom you serve, I am

Sincerely yours in Christ,

Bernard Cardinal Law
Archbishop of Boston

STATEMENT FIVE, Bernard Cardinal Law, open letter to the Archdiocese of Boston, Pentecost, May 19, 2002

Dearly Beloved in Christ,

Today is Pentecost. With all my heart I pray that the Church in Boston might be given new life by a fresh outpouring of the

Spirit's gifts. I would first like to thank you for maintaining your faith despite what you are seeing and reading about the current situation facing the Catholic Church. Difficult times come for each of us in different ways, and we need to draw on our faith in prayer in order to face these difficulties.

All of us are burdened by the seemingly never ending repercussions of the sexual abuse of children by clergy. The scandalous and painful details which have emerged sear our hearts. The harm done to victims and their families is overwhelming. Bewilderment has given rise to anger and distrust. In the process, my credibility has been publicly questioned and I have become for some an object of contempt. I understand how this is so, and I am profoundly sorry that the inadequacy of past policies and flaws in past decisions have contributed to this situation. I wish I could undo the hurt and harm.

As a result of civil suits in process and the various depositions being taken, many documents are currently in the public domain. It often appears that these cases are being tried in the press during this discovery period rather than being more appropriately tried later in court. Because only selected passages of many documents have been made public, I would like to give again an account of my stewardship in handling these cases.

Since becoming Archbishop in March of 1984, I have viewed such acts as the result of a psychological pathology. In dealing with such cases, my colleagues and I have been aided by the insights and recommendations of those with a medical competence which we did not have. Furthermore, since 1993 every case has also been examined by a review board consisting mainly of lay persons with a variety of backgrounds that would ensure that theirs be an informed counsel as to how to deal with the particular case before them.

In 1993, as you know, an Archdiocesan written policy for dealing with such cases was formulated on the basis of our past experience, our review of other diocesan policies, and on consultation. After this policy was promulgated, I directed that all past cases of allegations against priests be reviewed in accord with the new policy.

The 1993 policy did not mandate reporting to public authorities because it was felt that doing so would inhibit some victims from coming forward. It was our judgment at the time that such reporting was more appropriately the victim's choice. As you know, our current policy is that any allegation is immediately reported to the proper public authority. Furthermore, we have brought forward the names of all living priests known to us against whom credible allegations of sexual abuse of minors have been made.

Another major change in policy which I introduced at the beginning of this year is that no priest against whom a credible allegation has been made may hold any Church assignment whatsoever. That policy has been implemented, and I recommended a similar policy during the Cardinal's meeting in Rome last month.

Given the horrible details that have been reported concerning it, the case of Father Paul Shanley has been particularly disturbing. I, too, am profoundly disturbed by these details, and wish to share some facts concerning this case. When I arrived in Boston in 1984, I assumed that priests in place had been appropriately appointed. It did not enter into my mind to second-guess my predecessors, and it simply was not in the culture of the day to function otherwise. Despite the quantity of documents released and statements on the part of some indicating they believe otherwise, before God I assure you that my first knowledge of an allegation of sexual abuse against this priest was in 1993. It was immediately acted upon, and the authorization for him to serve as a priest in California was rescinded. I was not aware until these recent months of the allegations against him from as early as 1966.

In 1990, when Fr. Shanley left Boston, it was at his request that he was given a sick leave. It had nothing to do with an issue of sexual abuse. The attestation that he was a priest in good standing at the time was in accord with the facts as I knew them then. In addition, it has been reported that someone alleges I was informed after a Mass in 1984 that Father Shanley had molested a child. I have absolutely no memory of such a conversation, and those who have worked most closely with me can attest that such a report would have been acted upon.

There is no record of that having happened, and furthermore, I had no suspicion about Fr. Shanley concerning this in the ensuing years. The 1993 allegation was my first knowledge. I wish I had known in 1984, and I wish I had been aware of the 1966 report. It is only possible to act based on what is known, however.

I am certain that as time goes on, fresh revelations concerning cases will necessitate some explanation on the part of the Archdiocese. Never, however, has there been an intent to put children at risk. The fact that I have introduced radical policy changes indicates that deficiencies existed in the way we handled these cases in the past. Mistakes have also been made when facts which should have been before me were not. I often have made decisions based on the best information available to me at the time, only to find that new details later became available which some may argue I should have had previously. Obviously, I wish that I had been aware of all pertinent facts before making any past decisions. During the past five months and continuing into the present, our records have been and are being reviewed to ensure that all pertinent facts are available. It goes without saying that the Archdiocese is fully cooperative with the Attorney General, the District Attorneys, and the Department of Social Services.

On last Friday, I was briefed by the Commission assisting me in developing a revised policy and programs to ensure that the protection of children be our first priority in dealing with this issue as we go forward. I am most grateful to the Commission members for the progress they are making toward preparing final recommendations, and I am supportive of their suggestions regarding an enhanced role for the laity. Their work will be of invaluable help as we move forward. However difficult these past months have been, the fact that this issue is being dealt with in a far more effective way than before is most comforting.

Today is Pentecost. When the Holy Spirit came upon the early Church gathered in prayer in the Upper Room, the Church was transformed. On Pentecost Sunday in the many upper rooms of this Archdiocese we gathered around our altars in prayer. We who are the Church were gathered in that greatest expression of prayer which is the Eucharistic Sacrifice.

Pentecost is pre-eminently the feast of the Church. We stand, as the Archdiocese of Boston, in desperate need of the Holy Spirit's gifts. The work we must do together is being hampered by the division which bewilderment, hurt, distrust and anger have sown. We are the Church. That "We" must never be understood in an exclusive sense, however. It is not just "We the Laity," or "We the Hierarchy," or "We the Clergy," or "We the Religious," or "We the Prophetic Voice." It is all of us together.

In the Third Eucharistic Prayer, after the words of Institution, the celebrant prays: "Grant that we, who are nourished by his body and blood, may be filled with his Holy Spirit, and become one body, one spirit in Christ." That is my prayer as I write these words to you.

May our novena to the Holy Spirit conclude with our hearts open to receive a fresh outpouring of the Spirit's gifts. May the Spirit "fill every member of the Church with holiness so that, working together as the Body of Christ, we might be built up in faith, hope and love in order to proclaim the Gospel with joy."

Please know of my constant prayer for each of you who with me are this Archdiocese. In your kindness and in virtue of the unique communion that is ours, please pray also for me and for all of the priests who selflessly serve the Church with dedication and integrity.

Devotedly yours in Christ,

Bernard Cardinal Law
Archbishop of Boston

STATEMENT SIX, Bernard Cardinal Law,
remarks at mass, Cathedral of the Holy Cross,
November 3, 2002

Earlier this week, I was privileged and blessed to meet with a truly inspiring group of people who had been sexually abused as children by a priest. They had invited me to join them and their family members and friends who gathered with them as they continued their own efforts to deal with the devastating effects of the abuse they endured.

That meeting, although difficult and painful at times, was truly an occasion of grace for me and, I hope and pray, for all of those with whom I gathered.

It was suggested during our time together that it would be good for me to address, more publicly and frequently, a number of issues which came up in the course of our time together. After all, there are many other people who have been abused by other priests. I told them that I would be willing to do just that.

What follows now is a sincere attempt to honor the spirit of our meeting. I am indeed indebted to all of those who contributed so much by their presence, words and actions earlier this week.

It almost seems like an eternity away, yet it was in January of this year that the crisis of sexual abuse of children by clergy began to dominate our consciousness. Ten months later, I stand before you with a far deeper awareness of this terrible evil than I had at that time.

No one who has not experienced sexual abuse as a child can fully comprehend the devastating effects of this horrible sin. Nor is it possible for someone else to comprehend the degree of pain, of confusion, of self doubt, and of anger that a mother or father feels with the knowledge that her child, that his child, has been sexually abused by a priest. Who can know the burden of a wife or husband of someone who was abused as a child?

I do not pretend to fully comprehend the devastating consequences of the sexual abuse of children. Over these past 10 months, however, I have been focused in a singular way on this evil and on what it has done to the lives of so many.

As I have listened personally to the stories of men and women who have endured such abuse, I have learned that some of these consequences include lifelong struggles with alcohol and drug abuse, depression, difficulty in maintaining relationships, and, sadly, even suicide.

It is impossible to think of an act of sexual abuse of a child in isolation. There is inevitably a ripple effect from this evil act which spreads out and touches the lives of all of us.

Clearly, these evil acts have touched our life together as an Archdiocese. Our relationships have been damaged. Trust has been broken.

When I was a young man I was profoundly influenced by different priests. They represented all that was good to me. During my high school years, Father Mark Knoll, a Redemptorist priest, was a great mentor. During my college years, Bishop Lawrence J. Riley and Father Joseph Collins made a lasting impact upon my life. Like countless others, I placed great trust in them.

One of the insidious consequences of the sexual abuse of a child by a priest is the rupturing of that sacred trust. For some victim-survivors, not only is it difficult to trust priests again, but the Church herself is mistrusted. Many victim-survivors and their family members find it impossible to continue to live out their lives as Catholics, or even to enter a Catholic church building.

Once again I want to acknowledge publicly my responsibility for decisions which I now see were clearly wrong.

While I would hope that it would be understood that I never intended to place a priest in a position where I felt he would be a risk to children, the fact of the matter remains that I did assign priests who had committed sexual abuse.

Our policy does not allow this now, and I am convinced that this is the only correct policy. Yet in the past, however well intentioned, I made assignments which I now recognize were wrong. With all my heart I apologize for this, once again.

Apology in and of itself is not sufficient. I hope that the efforts that have already been made and which are in process in this Archdiocese to insure the protection of children as we move forward will serve as a motive to accept my apology.

Today, however, I would also ask forgiveness. I address myself to all the faithful. Particularly do I ask forgiveness of those who have been abused, and of their parents and other family members.

I acknowledge my own responsibility for decisions which led to intense suffering. While that suffering was never intended, it could have been avoided had I acted differently. I see this now with a clarity that has been heightened through the experience of these past 10 months.

I ask forgiveness in my name and in the name of those who served before me.

We turn first to God for the forgiveness we need. We must, however, also beg forgiveness of one another.

The dynamics of the evil of sexual abuse of children are very complex, and can often generate deep shame within those who have been abused.

There are time, strangely enough, when those who have been abused wonder whether they themselves were to blame, and there are times when their parents are plagued with self doubt about the manner in which they exercised their own parental responsibilities. I would want to say a word to such survivors and to such parents.

Realize that the sexual abuse of a child by an adult is always an act of exploitation. When the abuser is a priest, it is a profound violation of a sacred trust. In order to experience healing from the pain and all the sad consequences of such abuse, it is necessary to recognize that the blame lies with the perpetrator.

For us as a community of faith, forgiveness is always seen in the context of the forgiving, reconciling love of God made manifest by the cross of Christ. Christ draws us to Himself and draws us closer to one another. For whatever wrong we have done we turn to God for forgiveness, even as we extend forgiveness to one another.

The forgiving love of God gives me the courage to beg forgiveness of those who have suffered because of what I did. As I beg your forgiveness, I pledge my unyielding efforts to insure that this never happens again.

Finally, once again I urge all those who live with the awful secret of sexual abuse by clergy or by anyone else to come forward so that you may begin to experience healing. The resources of the Archdiocese through the Office of Healing and Assistance Ministry are available to you. Obviously, anyone with knowledge about past abuse should make this information available to appropriate public authorities. No one is helped by keeping such things secret. The secret of sexual abuse needs to be brought out of the darkness and into the healing light of Jesus Christ.

NOTES

Introduction
From Private to Public Confession

1. CNN/USA Today/Gallup Poll, Jan. 5–7, 2001; Opinion Research Corporation Poll, May 5–7, 2006. Archived by CNN at http://archives .cnn.com/2001/ALLPOLITICS/stories/01/10/cnn.poll.clinton and http://edition.cnn.com/2006/POLITICS/05/12/bush.clinton.poll/ index.html.

2. See, for example, "The Framing of Fundamentalist Christians: Network Television News, 1980–2000," by Peter A. Kerr, in *Journal of Media and Religion* (2003, Vol. 2, No. 4, pp. 203–235); David Firestone, "The Nation; What Hath God Wrought? Lieberman and the Right," *New York Times*, Sept. 3, 2000; Christian Smith, *American Evangelicalis: Embattled and Thriving* (University of Chicago Press, 1998), particularly pp. 131ff.; Amy Johnson Frykholm, *Rapture Culture: Left Behind in Evangelical America* (Oxford University Press, 2004), pp. 18–38.

3. Aaron Lazare, *On Apology* (Oxford University Press, 2004), pp. 24–26, 45–49.

Chapter 1
Grover the Good, Beishazzar Blaine, and the Rapacious Woman

1. "End of the Battle," in the *Chicago Daily Tribune*, July 12, 1884, p. 1.

2. Henry F. Graff, *Grover Cleveland* (Henry Holt, 2002), pp. 60–62.

3. Graff, p. 22.

4. "The Germans in Politics: Listening to Speeches in Favor of Cleveland," *New York Times*, Sept. 30, 1884, p. 5.

5. Jocelyn Noveck, "'Tis the season to be sorry: a look back at a year of notable apologies," CNN.com, Dec. 1, 2006.

6. John Locke, *Second Treatise*, 14.163.

7. "Corruption in Politics," *New York Times*, Nov. 30, 1884, p. 11.

8. Locke, *Second Treatise*, 14.163.

9. Grover Cleveland, *The Writings and Speeches of Grover Cleveland*, ed. George F. Parker (Cassell, 1892), p. 29.

10. H. Paul Jeffers, *An Honest President: The Life and Presidencies of Grover Cleveland* (William Morrow, 2000), p. 105.

11. Locke, *Second Treatise* 9.123

12. Jeffers, *An Honest President*, p. 108.

Chapter 2
In the Presence of the Elect (with the World Looking On)

1. Kinsely Twining's letter, widely circulated, was reprinted in *The Bookman: An Illustrated Magazine of Literature and Life*, vol. 20 (Dodd, Mead & Co., 1905), p. 443.

2. The Fourth Lateran Council prescribed (in *Omnis utriusque sexus*) that each member of the church confess individually to the parish priest, once a year, during Lent. There is not a great deal of evidence for how often this took place before the Fourth Lateran Council of 1215, but if we can assume that the Council was regulating an already common practice, confession had been an annual event for some time. The official teaching of the "seal of confession," which prohibited the priest from speaking of any of these private matters which might be confessed to him by a penitent, was first set down in 1151, in Gratian's compiled edicts of the Church, and was affirmed by the Lateran Council in 1215. But both of these written formulations probably grant the force of church law to a long-standing custom. See Peter Biller, "Confession in the Middle Ages," pp. 4–7; Alexander Murray, "Counselling in Medieval Confession, pp. 63–66; also Canon 21 of *Omnis utriusque sexus*, trans. H. Rothwell in *English Historical Documents, 1189–1327*, pp. 654–55.

3. Martin Luther, *Complete Edition of Luther's Latin Works*, trans. Andrew Thornton (Walter de Gruyter, 1967), p. 422.

4. Kenneth Scott Latourette, *A History of Christianity*, volume 2, pp. 709–11.

5. That Luther's assertion of justification by faith is not as simple as it initially sounded can clearly be seen in the sermons of sixteenth-century German Lutherans. They found themselves continually preaching on the doctrines of justification to their (presumably justified) congregations. Practically and pastorally, Luther's idea of conversion "defied easy comprehension. . . . It was necessary to spell out clearly what salvation by grace through faith meant." [Patrick T. Ferry, "Confessionalization and Popular Preaching," pp. 1149–50]

The themes of conversion and repentance were covered again and again, to congregations who in most cases had already professed to hold a justifying faith. Patrick Ferry points out that literally hundreds of these sermons aim to console hearers who seem to have been weighed down with guilt. "God will not have you to remain in the damning darkness along with the papists and turks," preached the sixteenth-century Lutheran pastor Simon Musäus. "He has not let you be baptized and come to the recognition of His Son, or established such a foundation and beginning of your salvation, for nothing. Do not doubt that His will is solely and completely to save you." [Ferry, pp. 1154–55] The promise of justification by faith was clearly fraught with uncertainty; neither baptism nor membership in a church body was adequate to ward off the fear that the hope of salvation was built on the sands of self-deception.

6. John Calvin, *Institutes of the Christian Religion* 3.1.4, 3.1.3, 3.2.7.

7. Ibid., 3.2.7.

8. Ibid., 3.2.12

9. For many modern evangelicals, the moment of conversion still remains a signpost pointing away from doubt. At an evangelistic rally at Liberty University in the late 1980s, the speaker recommended that anyone who doubted his or her salvation find a private place, say out loud, "I believe that Christ died for my sin," and then write the place, time, and date in the front of a Bible. When in doubt, the believer merely needed to look back at this affirmation to be assured of salvation.

10. Matthew 10:32–33, NIV.

11. Ibid.

12. Patricia Caldwell, *The Puritan Conversion Narrative*, p. 45; she credits Edmund S. Morgan's *Visible Saints* for this argument.

13. David D. Hall, *Worlds of Wonder, Days of Judgment*, p. 171.

14. In *The Works of Jonathan Edwards*, vol. 2, pp. 5–6

15. Jonathan Edwards, "A Faithful Narrative of the Surprising Work of God," § 1.

16. In *The Works of Jonathan Edwards*, vol. 1, pp. 360–61.

17. George Whitfield, "Marks of a True Conversion," Sermon 23 in *Selected Sermons of George Whitfield.*

18. Allan Nevins, *Grover Cleveland: A Study in Courage* (Dodd, Mead, 1948), pp. 79–80.

19. The "First Great Awakening" is the traditional name not only for this two-year revival, but for a general age of religious revival that began with Edwards and carried on through the 1940s. In *America's God*, Mark Noll characterizes the First Great Awakening as a "renewal

of pietistic popular Calvinism" that saw a transition from defining Christianity by doctrine to defining it by piety. The nature of the Awakening and its existence are both subjects for debate. In *Awash in a Sea of Faith*, Jon Butler denies that there was any such thing as a "First Great Awakening," calling it an "interpretive fiction"; rather, he sees the Whitefield campaign as simply another in a long series of episodic revolts against church hierarchy. Richard Bushman, on the other hand, sees the First Great Awakening as a discrete movement centered on the empowerment of laypeople, and thus as a preparation for revolution. Whitefield's revival techniques, rather than the larger social implications of the revivals themselves, are of central importance for this particular study.

20. Nancy Ruttenburg, "George Whitefield, Spectacular Conversion, and the Rise of Democratic Personality," pp. 429, 431, 442.

21. Noll, *History of Christianity*, p. 167; the attendance, according to Marilyn Westerkamp, was between 10,000 and 20,0000. See *Women in Early American Religion, 1600–1850*, p. 102.

22. Latourette, *A History of Christianity*, p. 453.

23. Hatch, *Democratization*, pp. 52–53.

24. Charles A. Johnson, "The Frontier Camp Meeting," pp. 98–101.

25. Finney's attitude towards revivals was certainly related to his tendency to view conversion largely as an act of human will; in William McLoughlin's words, "In his explanation of conversion according to the laws of mind, he had made a slight obeisance to the agency of the Holy Spirit. . . . However, this brief acknowledgment of the supernatural element in revivals was buried beneath such a mass of scientific certitude in the other direction that it was forgotten." (McLoughlin, *Modern Revivalism* [Ronald Press, 1959], p. 85) Finney's theology remains difficult to categorize. He preached an agency on the part of the sinner that would have scandalized Calvin and even called sinners to "change their own hearts" but consistently added to these exhortations the insistence that change could only come when God provides the agency. For a more detailed discussion, see Allen C. Guelzo, "An Heir or a Rebel? Charles Grandison Finney and the New England Theology," *Journal of the Early Republic* 17 no. 1: 61–94).

26. Charles G. Finney, *Lectures on Revivals of Religion* (Fleming H. Revell, 1868), p. 10.

27. Finney *Lectures*, pp. 122, 158–59.

28. Catherine A. Brekus, *Strangers and Pilgrims*, p. 288; also Guelzo, "An Heir or a Rebel?," p. 62. Guelzo points out that the anxious bench may also have been borrowed from frontier Baptist practice. (It was, however, definitely not Presbyterian.)

29. McLoughlin, *Modern Revivalism*, p. 122.

30. Jeffrey K. Hadden, "Religious Broadcasting and the Mobilization of the New Christian Right," p. 235.

31. Marsden, *Fundamentalism and American Culture*, p. 32.

32. Bruce J. Evensen, "'It Is a Marvel to Many People': Dwight L. Moody, Mass Media, and the New England Revival of 1877," p. 272.

33. Marsden, *Fundamentalism and America Culture*, pp. 35, 44.

34. Martin, *A Prophet With Honor*, p. 52.

35. Matin, *A Prophet*, p. 51.

36. McLoughlin, *Modern Revivalism*, p. 419.

37. E. Brooks Holifield has pointed out that the conversion narratives of the Puritan churches acted to affirm and extend the brotherly (and sisterly) relationships between members; he cites Cotton's descripiton of church members as owing each other the duties of "love, unity, equality, communion, and the bearing of each other's burdens," and concludes that the conversion narratives had both a vertical and a horizontal function. See "Peace, Conflict, and Ritual in Puritan Congregations" (*Journal of Interdisciplinary History* 23, no. 3: 155–56.

38. Romans 3:23, 3:10.

39. Nevins, *Grover Cleveland*, p. 169.

Chapter 3
Aimee Semple McPherson and the Devil

1. Edith Blumhofer, *Aimee Semple McPherson*, pp. 239, 247, 255–66, 278–80.

2. Daniel Mark Epstein, *Sister Aimee*, p. 288.

3. Blumhofer, *McPherson*, pp. 7, 282; Epstein, *Sister Aimee*, pp. 293–94.

4. *New York Times*, May 21, 1926, p. 14, and May 24, 1926, p. 3; *Los Angeles Times*, May 20, 1926, p. 2.

5. *Los Angeles Times*, June 24, 1926, p. 4 and July 11, 1926, p. 1; Blumhofer, *McPherson*, pp. 284–85.

6. *Los Angeles Times*, June 24, 1926, pp. 2, 4.

7. Ibid., p. 1; *New York Times*, June 26, 1926, p. 15, and June 27, 1926, p. 12; Blumhofer, *McPherson*, pp. 287–89; Lately Thomas, *The Vanishing Evangelist*, p. 102.

8. *New York Times*, June 27, 1926, p. 12.

9. Blumhofer, *McPherson*, p. 290; Lately Thomas, *Storming Heaven*, p. 54; *New York Times*, July 8, 1926, p. 8; *Los Angeles Times*, July 11, 1926, pp. 1, 3, July 15, 1926, p. 1, and July 21, 1926, p. 1.

10. *New York Times*, Sept. 17, 1926, p. 1.

11. *Los Angeles Times*, Dec. 30, 1926, pp. 1–2; *New York Times*, Jan. 11, 1927, p. 26.

12. *New York Times*, Feb. 20, 1927, p. 12; Blumhofer, *McPherson*, pp. 300–308.

13. Sarah Comstock, "Prima Donna of Revivalism," *Harper's Magazine*, Dec. 1927.

14. *New York Times*, July 27, 1927, p. 23.

15. Blumhofer, *McPherson*, p. 107.

16. Thomas *The Vanishing Evangelist*, p. 15.

17. Blumhofer, *McPherson*, p. 274.

18. Ibid., p. 183.

19. At a 1901 prayer meeting held by Charles Fox Parham in Topeka, a young woman named Agnes Ozman spoke in tongues—the first modern manifestation of glossolalia in American Protestantism. However, the Azusa Street revival was the event that Pentecostalists themselves pointed to as the foundation of the movement.

20. Sometimes these two confessions/conversions happen simultaneously, but the two-stage conversion (first to saving faith, and only later to Holy Spirit–filled blessing) is more common.

21. Grant Wacker, "The Functions of Faith in Primitive Pentecostalism," pp. 357.

22. Joe Creech, "Visions of Glory," pp. 406–7, 423.

23. Wacker, "Functions of Faith," p. 369.

24. James W. Carey, *Communication as Culture*, p. 16.

25. Tona Hangen, *Redeeming the Dial*, pp. 55–56; *Los Angeles Times*, Feb. 5, 1924, p. a16.

26. Barbara Green, *Spectacular Confessions*, p. 5.

27. Ibid., p. 7

28. Ibid., p. 198.

29. That is, by drawing its ministers only from denominationally-controlled theological schools, and carefully policing admission to those schools so that women cannot rise into the ranks of those qualified to be ordained.

30. Creech, "Visions of Glory," p. 415; Mark Chaves, "The Symbolic Significance of Women's Ordination," p. 94; Susie C. Stanley, "The Promise Fulfilled," p. 139; Isaiah 3:12.

31. Blumhofer, *Mcpherson*, p. 195; Quentin J. Schultze, *Christianity and the Mass Media in America*, p. 60.

32. *Los Angeles Times*, July 21, 1926, p. A1

33. Thomas, *Vanishing Evangelist*, p. 167; Blumhofer, *McPherson*, p. 294.

34. Blumhofer, *Restoring*, p. 3.

35. Damian Thompson, *The End of Time*, pp. 122–23.

36. Bobby C. Alexander, *Televangelism Reconsidered*, p.53.

37. *Baltimore Evening Sun*, Dec. 13, 1926; quoted in Blumhofer, *McPherson*, p. 296.

38. *New York Times*, Feb. 21, 1927, p. 8; *Los Angeles Times*, Nov. 8, 1926, p. A1; *New York Times*, Oct. 4, 1926, p. 25.

39. Winifred Johnston, "Newspaper Balladry," pp. 119–20.

Chapter 4
Confession Goes Public

1. Quoted in George Marsden, *Fundamentalism and American Culture*, pp. 158–59.

2. Grant Wacker, "The Holy Spirit and the Spirit of the Age in American Protestantism, 1880–1910," p. 46. George Marsden offers a helpful definition: fundamentalists were "traditional evangelicals" who had "declared war" on the "modernizing trends" that led mainline preachers to "tone down the offense to modern sensibilities of a Bible filled with miracles and a gospel that proclaimed human salvation from eternal damnation only through Christ's atoning works on the cross" (Marsden, *Reforming Fundamentalism*, p. 4). Joel Carpenter defines fundamentalism as prioritizing theological truth above all else, and lists the five distinctives of fundamentalist theology in *Revive Us Again*, pp. 4–6, 13–16.

3. "The Radiophone and Preaching," *Christian Century*, 22 March 1923, p. 344; "The Radio an Inconvenience to Religious Narrowness," 16 Aug. 1923, p. 129; "Religious Radio Programs Need Much Improvement," 16 Feb. 1944, p. 197; Schultze, pp. 118–19.

4. Robert Miller, "Radio and Religion," p. 137.

5. Robert Miller, *Harry Emerson Fosdick*, p. 384. Fosdick began preaching in 1924 from the headquarters of RCA, which he proudly called the "temple of established culture"; in 1927, he moved to NBC and began a weekly Sunday afternoon program called *National Vespers*.

6. Eugene Bertermann, "The Radio for Christ," *United Evangelical Action* (March, 1949) p. 3; William H. Foulkes, quoted in Jesse M. Bader, ed., *The Message and Method of the New Evangelism*, p. 230; Schultze, 'Christianity and the Mass Media in America,' pp. 63–64.

7. Christopher Lynch, *Selling Catholicism*, pp. 20–21; Coughlin was later dropped by the major networks after making a series of pro-Mussolini, pro-Hitler, and anti-Semitic remarks, but was able to take

his program to a number of local radio stations, keeping much of his listenership.

8. Ibid.

9. Fulton J. Sheen, "How to Have a Good Time," pp. 835, 840.

10. Lynch, *Selling Catholicism*, p. 24.

11. Ibid., p. 24. When Sheen's program ended in 1957, he returned at four different times in the next ten years to host other successful series. Incidentally, his long tenure earned him a place of honor in the folk song, "Did you ever think when a hearse goes by, / when the worms go in and the worms go out / your hair turns white, your skin turns green; / you start to look like Bishop Sheen."

12. Alexander, *Televangelism Reconsidered*, p. 59.

13. Lynch, *Selling Catholicism*, p. 135. On this issue mainline Protestants departed somewhat from the company of their Catholic colleagues; the *Christian Century*, the most widely distributed voice of mainline Protestantism, was sharply critical of Fulton Sheen for accepting commercial sponsorship.

14. Jeffrey Hadden, "Religious Broadcasting," p. 239.

15. Hal Erickson, *Religious Radio and Television in the United States, 1921–1991* (McFarland & Co., 1992), pp. 153–55.

16. Ibid., p. 47. Graham was profiled in November 1949; Roberts in May 1951.

17. Oral Roberts, *The Call*, p. 169.

18. Ibid., p. 95.

19. Ibid., pp. 170–71.

20. See chapter 6, "Shooting Your Allies."

21. Roberts, *The Call*, p. 182.

22. In the 1950s, popular Pentecostal TV broadcasts included not only Roberts's *Hour of Power*, seen on 136 channels, but A. A. Allen's healing services and Rex Humbard's Sunday services, televised from 1958 onwards in his specially-built Cathedral of Tomorrow, a church designed to incorporate TV equipment. Popular fundamentalist (non-Pentecostal) broadcasts included Tim LaHaye's *The LaHayes on Family Life*, which was syndicated nationwide beginning in 1956; Dr. Wally Criswell's Sunday-morning sermons from First Baptist Church of Dallas, which were televised from the early 1950s onward; and Donald Grey Barnhouse's fifteen-minute Bible study segments, *Man to Man*, which were televised beginning in 1956 See Erickson, *Religious Radio and Television*, pp. 64, 100, 112–13, 153.

23. I have chosen to avoid the term "evangelical" where possible, since it has a whole constellation of meanings. Technically, both Pentecostals and fundamentalists belonged to the "evangelical"

form of Protestantism preached by eighteenth- and nineteenth-century revivalists. However, in contemporary American political rhetoric, "evangelical" has also come to define a particular type of conservative Protestant believer, one who affirms the five fundamentals but takes a more active stance towards cultural engagement. I will call this "neoevangelicalism" in order to avoid confusion with the wider "evangelicalism," which has been around since the Great Awakening.

24. Robert M. Price, "A Fundamentalist Social Gospel," *Christian Century*, Nov. 28, 1979, p. 1183.

25. Billy Sunday, "Food for a Hungry World," pp. 790–91.

26. Mark Noll, "Where We Are and How We Got Here," *Christianity Today*, Oct. 29, 2006.

27. Stuart Barton Babbage, "Review of Current Religious Thought," *Christianity Today*, June 9, 1958, p. 35.

28. Douglas A. Sweeney, "Essential Evangelicalism Dialectic," *Church History* 60, no.1 (March, 1991), p. 71–72.

29. *Christianity Today* mission statement, archived online at http://www.christianitytoday.com/help/features/ctimission.html.

30. The book was critical of fundamentalism for failing to "apply [the fundamentals of the faith] effectively to crucial problems confronting the modern mind." Henry concluded, "It is an application of, not a revolt against, fundamentals of the faith, for which I plead." Henry represented the overlapping spheres that neoevangelicals occupied: he held a theological degree from the fundamentalist Northern Theological Baptist Seminary, and a Ph.D. from Boston University; he was a founding member of the National Association of Evangelicals, a neoevangelical association that brought Pentecostal and fundamentalist denominations together in partnership. In 1956, the NAE rolls included, among many other Pentecostal members, the Assemblies of God, the International Pentecostal Church of Christ, and the International Church of the Foursquare Gospel, the denomination founded by McPherson; they were joined by over a dozen fundamentalist member denominations, including the Christian Reformed Church in North America, the Evangelical Free Church of America, and the Open Bible Standard Churches. See Carl F. H. Henry, *The Uneasy Conscience of Modern Fundamentalism* (William B. Eerdmans, 1947), p. xviii.

31. Martin, *A Prophet with Honor*, pp. 108–9; Billy Graham, *Just As I Am*, pp. 134–35.

32. Martin, *Prophet*, p. 118.

33. Graham, *Just As I Am*, pp. 432–33.

34. Helen W. Kooiman, *Transformed,* pp. 137, 130.

35. Norman Vincent Peale's weekly program *What's Your Trouble?* was distributed by the National Council of Churches beginning in 1952; James Pike, Dean of the Cathedral of New York, hosted a weekly debate on ABC called *American Religious Town Hall* (1954–1957); CBS caried a long-running ecumenical program sponsored by the Federal Council of Churches called *Lamp Unto My Feet,* which (among other things) broadcast a series of ballets about David, Saul, and Bathesheba; and *Look Up and Live,* also broadcast on CBS, was produced by the National Council of Churches for six months out of every year, after which the National Council of Catholic Men took over for four months and the New York Board of Rabbis for the remaining two. See Erickson, pp. 114, 118–19, 142–43.

36. "The Scramble for Radio-TV," *Christianity Today,* Feb. 18, 1957, pp. 20–23; quoted by Schultze, *Christianity and the Mass Media in America,* p. 127. *Christianity Today* claimed that the "national constituency" of evangelicals numbered 36,719,000.

37. Jeffrey K. Hadden, "The Rise and Fall of American Televangelism," pp. 116–21.

38. "New Era for Christian Communication," *Christianity Today,* Oct. 1966, p. 3, quoted in Schultze, *Christianity and the Mass Media in America,* p. 67; "Outreach to the Masses," *Christianity Today,* Sept. 1968, p. 35, quoted in Schultze, p. 64; Schultze, p. 65.

39. Eric Caplan, *Mind Games,* p. 3. At the beginning of his study, Caplan helpfully defines psychotherapy as "the *deliberate and systematic* effort to relieve nervous and mental symptoms without recourse to somatic agents" (p. 2, italics in original).

40. The participating denominations were primarily those which later became known as "mainline," but to refer to a mainline-fundamentalist distinction before the 1920s is slightly anachronistic.

41. Caplan, *Mind Games,* pp. 117–19.

42. In his study Psychology and American Catholicism, Kevin Gillespie points out that the influence of psychotherapy both on medicine and on popular culture swelled again during World War II, when Jewish psychotherapists fleeing Nazi persecution gathered in the United States (pp. 14–15).

43. Peter Phillips Sheehy, *The Triumph of Group Therapeutics: Therapy, the Social Self, and Liberalism in America, 1910–1960,* p. 25.

44. Ibid., pp. 29–30.

45. Bernard D. Cohen, Mark F. Ettin, and Jay W. Fidler, *Group Psychotherapy and Political Reality: A Two-Way Mirror* (International Universities Press, 2002), p. 93.

46. Ibid., p. 115.
47. Ibid., p. 96.
48. Ibid., p. 118.

Chapter 5
Kennedy Misreads His Public

1. "Woman Passenger Killed, Kennedy Escapes in Crash," *New York Times,* July 20, 1969, pp. 1, 50.

2. "Kennedy Seeking to Bar Police From Prosecuting Him in Crash," *New York Times,* July 22, 1969, p. 18; "Hundreds of Messages Are Sent To Police Chief in Kennedy Case," *New York Times,* July 23, 1969, p. 22.

3. Adam Clymer, *Edward M. Kennedy: A Biography* (William Morrow, 1999), pp. 150–151.

4. This and subsequent extracts that follow in this chapter are from Edward M. Kennedy's televised address, broadcast from the home of Joseph P. Kennedy, July 25, 1969. A transcript of the full address is included in Appendix A.

5. Among many examples that could be offered: in the year before Kennedy's confession, J. L. Legrande wrote that Martin Luther King's acts of nonviolent civil disobedience were motivated by the "personal decision" that he was morally obligated to resist not only the evil, but the instrumentality responsible for it" ("Police Science," *Journal of Criminal Law,* vol. 58, no. 3 [1967]).

6. "Editorial Comment on Kennedy Speech," *New York Times,* July 27, 1969.

7. "Public Forgiving in Kennedy Poll," *New York Times,* Aug. 4, 1969.

8. Adam Clymer, *Edward M. Kennedy,* p. 158.

9. William H. Honan, *Ted Kennedy: Profile of a Survivor,* pp. 120–21.

10. Ralph G. Martin, *Seeds of Destruction: Joe Kennedy and His Sons,* p. 602. Kennedy had refused to be nominated for the presidency in 1968, after his brother's assassination, but had launched a bid for the post of party whip instead; he won the job in January 1969, in defiance of the tradition that usually awarded it to more senior Senators.

11. Clymer, *Edward M. Kennedy,* p. 225.

12. Ibid., p. 286.

13. "Democrats Urge Kennedy to Speak," *New York Times,* July 25, 1969, p. 44.

14. "Tragedy and Mystery," *New York Times,* July 25, 1969, p. 46.

15. Clymer, *Edward M. Kennedy*, p. 297.

16. The Fourth Lateran Council prescribed (in *Omnis utriusque sexus*) that each member of the church confess individually to the parish priest, once a year, during Lent. There is not a great deal of evidence for how often this took place before 1215, but if we can assume that the Council was regulating an already common practice, confession had been an annual event for some time. See Peter Biller, "Confession in the Middle Ages," p. 7; Alexander Murray, "Counselling in Medieval Confession," p. 63.

17. John Austin's classic legal work of 1832, *The Province of Jurisprudence Determined*, conceptualizes the foundation of ancient law as control, exercised by a "sovereign person or body," through legal demands, over "a member or members of the independent political society wherein that person or body is supreme." Law was thus an imperative speech act, existing outside and independent of relatively passive subjects, who were constrained by law's commands. The act of confession, as Kevin Crotty puts it, "further entrenches law: confession entails the acceptance—or at least the acknowledgment—of the law's authority." See John Austin, *The Province of Jurisprudence Determined*, 1:13; Kevin Crotty, *Law's Interior*, p. 92.

18. Crotty, *Law's Interior*, pp. 93–94; Pseudo-Quintilian, *Declaration* 34, trans. Crotty, section 2.3.

19. Augustine, *Confessions* I. i.1, trans. Henry Chadwick.

20. Charles Taylor, *Sources of the Self*, pp. 128–29.

21. Ibid., p. 129.

22. Ibid., p. 130.

23. Augustine, "The Free Choice of the Will," I. III. 8; Crotty, *Law's Interior*, pp. 107–8.

24. Biller, "Confession," pp. 4–7.

25. Canon 21 of the Fourth Lateran Council: "Let the priest absolutely beware that he does not by word or sign or by any manner whatever in any way betray the sinner. . . . For whoever shall dare to reveal a sin disclosed to him in the tribunal of penance we decree that he shall be not only deposed from the priestly office but that he shall also be sent into the confinement of a monastery to do perpetual penance."

26. Heggen writes, "In the *Libri Poenitentiales* especially, the idea is often given that a person can be more inwardly sure of the forgiveness of his sins and readmittance into the community of the church in the measure that he has performed heavier penances." (*Confession and the Service of Penance*, p. 36).

27. Ibid., pp. 36–37. As additional support for this theory, Peter Biller points out that, after 1220 or so, a new genre of confessional

literature emerged in Paris and grew in importance for the next century. This was the *quodlibet* (the "what-you-will"), a set of questions and answers for the use of the priest, intended not to prescribe appropriate penances (as earlier handbooks had done), but rather intended to make the confessional session itself as complete and correct as possible. Biller, "Confession," pp. 11–12; L. E. Boyle, *Pastoral Care* vol. 2, pp. 242–51.

28. The argument over when this third shift took place continues to occupy the scholarly literature on medieval confession. Heggen pegs it to the late thirteenth century, while both John Bossy and Mary Mansfield argue for a later shift, post-1400. See Heggen, *Confession*, pp. 36–37; Biller, "Confession," pp. 15, 30; and Mansfield, *Humiliation*, p. 129.

29. Thomas Tentler, *Sin and Confession on the Eve of the Reformation*, p. 117.

30. Biller suggests that this change was brought about, in part, by the teaching of Jean Charlier de Gerson of the University of Paris (1363–1429). Gerson's emphasis on Christian mysticism, as a way of avoiding overreliance on rationalism, brought the orientation of the heart more into view. See Biller, "Confession," pp. 16, 23.

31. John Bossy, "Moral Arithmetic: Seven Sins into Ten Commandments," p. 217.

32. The late medieval writings of Peter Lombard and Raymond of Penaforte both fall within this "contritionist tradition." In the *Sentences*, Book IV, Distinction xvi., no. 1, Lombard writes that contrition is the gateway into paradise; Raymond of Penaforte defines penance itself as "repenting past evils," shifting the emphasis even further towards the attitude of the heart. See Thomas Tentler, *Sin and Confession on the Eve of the Reformation*, p. 105.

33. Among other refinements, sorrow over sin was refined into two types: contrition, or pure sorrow over the mere presence of sin; and attrition, sorrow which was merely brought about by fear of punishmen. The sixteenth-century Council of Trent declared that while contrition alone could bring forgiveness, attrition could also open the door to grace, provided that it was combined with the sinner's full participation in the sacrament of confession. Protestant reformers had declared that no fallen man could ever hope to achieve complete and full confession; the Council of Trent responded by constructing a way for sinners to reach a judicial, if not actual, assurance that they had satisfied God's requirement of repentance. When the priest declared absolution, the confession was declared adequate. See Council of Trent, Session XIV, c. 4; W. David Myers, *"Poor, Sinning*

Folk," pp. 108–1011; also Heggen, *Confession,* p. 43; Charles Gobinet, *The Instruction of Youth in Christian Piety,* p. 51.

34. "Court Transcript," *New York Times,* July 26, 1969.

35. Wilson, *Pardon and Peace,* p. 48.

36. Augustine, *Confessions* IX.ii.2.

37. Augustine, *Confessions* IV.2.2, VIII.6.13, IX.2.2, IX.5.13.

38. "People of Massachusetts Rush to Support Kennedy," *New York Times,* July 26, 1969, pp. 1, 10.

39. Ralph G. Martin, *Seeds of Destruction,* p. 596.

40. Adam Clymer, *Edward M. Kennedy,* p. 153.

41. Ibid., p. 286.

Chapter 6
Jimmy Carter, Traitor to the Cause

1. Peter G. Bourne, *Jimmy Carter: A Comprehensive Biography from Plains to Postpresidency,* p. 346.

2. Robert Scheer, "*Playboy* Interview," *Playboy,* Nov. 1976. In Don Richardson, ed., *Conversations with Carter,* pp. 38–39.

3. Ibid., pp. 57–58. A transcript of the full question and answer is included in Appendix B.

4. "Carter Admits to 'Adultery in My Heart,'" *Los Angeles Times,* Sep. 20, 1976, p. A2; "Carter tells of temptations and religious beliefs," *Augusta Chronicle,* Sept. 21, 1976, p. 10A; "Carter, on Morals, Talks With Candor," *New York Times,* Sept. 20, 1976, pp. 1, 26;

5. "Carter's Comments on Sex Cause Concern," *New York Times,* Sept. 23, 1976, p. 36.

6. Ibid., p. 36.

7. Richardson *Conversations with Carter,* p. 33.

8. Bourne, *Jimmy Carter,* p. 348.

9. Ibid., p. 348.

10. A week later, *Playboy* editor G. Barry Golson remarked, acidly, that this was a "curious" remark, given that Rockefeller had been interviewed in *Playboy* by Robert Scheer the previous year. ("When Carter and Playboy Spoke in Plains," *New York Times,* Sept. 30, 1976)

11. Mark 2:15–17.

12. Michael James McClymond, *Embodying the Spirit: New Perspectives in North American Revivalism* (The Johns Hopkins University Press, 2004), p. 152.

13. Matthew Avery Sutton, *Aimee Semple McPherson and the Resurrection of Christian America* (Harvard University Press, 2007), p. 215, also pp. 241–42.

14. Marsden, *Fundamentalism and American Culture*, p. 159.

15. "The first generation of pentecostals generally maintained a rigid separation between Christianity and politics," Sutton writes; see *Aimee Semple McPherson*, pp. 215ff.

16. Qtd. in Marsden, *Reforming Fundamentalism*, in his discussion of fundamentalist influence during the Eisenhower administration (pp. 153–156).

17. Karl Marx and Frederick Engels, "Proletarians and Communists" (§ 2), *Manifesto of the Communist Party*, trans. Samuel Moore and Frederick Engels (Kerr, 1881).

18. J. I. Packer, *"Fundamentalism" and the Word of God* (Eerdmans, 1958), p. 17. Packer, British by birth and Oxford-trained, was deeply connected to American evangelicalism; he wrote for Eerdmans, a Michigan publishing company, signed the Chicago Statement on Biblical Inerrancy in 1978, and eventually took a Canadian teaching job.

19. Packer, *"Fundamentalism" and the Word of God*, pp. 18–21.

20. Mark Noll, *A History of Christianity in the United States and Canada*, pp. 376–78.

21. C. I. Scofield, *The Scofield Reference Bible* (Oxford University Press, 1909), study note, Romans 11:26.

22. Donald Grey Barnhouse, *The Invisible War* (Zondervan, 1965), p. 273.

23. Ibid., pp. 274–77.

24. Hal Lindsey with C. C. Carlson, *The Late Great Planet Earth* (Zondervan, 1970), pp. 33, 41.

25. Ibid., p. 43. Lindsey's schema also fit well into the anti-Communist rhetoric of neoevangelicals; in his reading of Ezekiel 38–39, the U.S.S.R. was identified as the "northern enemy" that would attack Israel and bring on Armageddon.

26. Erickson, *Religious Radio and Television*, pp. 53–54.

27. Fundamentalists and neoevangelicals tended to view Pentecostals with theological suspicion, fearing that the Pentecostal insistence on divine revelation through tongues and prophecies might undercut Scripture's claim to sole authority. But in fact Pentecostals *did* ascribe to the inerrancy of Scripture, despite their willingness to add to it, and the rhetoric of Pentecostal leaders often matched the antimodernist pronouncements of fundamentalists. Like fundamentalists, Pentecostals placed the experience of submission to the Word

of God, personal confession of sin, and conversion at the very center of their theology.

28. The message has persisted, although the timeline has changed. In 2004, Pat Robertson told President George W. Bush that, should Bush abandon his support of Israel, Christians would abandon the Republican party, since any diminishment of Israel's power could only result from "Satan's plan to prevent the return of Jesus Christ." Robertson's speech, made during a trip to Jerusalem, is archived online at http://www.newsmax.com/archives/articles/2004/10/3/214501.shtml.

29. Humanist Manifesto I (1933). Archived online at http://www.americanhumanist.org/about/manifesto1.html.

30. Humanist Manifesto II (1973). Archived online at http://www.americanhumanist.org/about/manifesto2.html.

31. Footnote 11, *Torcaso v. Watkins*, 367 U.S. 488 (1961).

32. Tim LaHaye, *How To Win Over Depression* (Zondervan, 1974), pp. 71, 86–87.

33. Onalee McGraw, *Secular Humanism and the Schools: The Issue Whose Time Has Come* (Heritage Foundation, 1976), p. 76.

34. Tim LaHaye, *The Battle for the Mind* (Fleming H. Revell, 1980), p 9.

35. Charles E. Garrison, *Two Different Worlds: Christian Absolutes and the Relativism of Social Science* (University of Delaware Press, 1988), p. 38.

36. Francis Schaeffer, *A Christian Manifesto* (Crossway Books, 1981), pp. 55–56.

37. Bill Gothard, *Advanced Seminar Textbook* (Basic Life Principles, 1986), p. 20.

38. Bill Gothard, "A Clear Conscience," in *Syllabus: Institute in Basic Youth Conflicts* (Institute in Basic Youth Conflicts, 1975), pp. 2–29.

39. Pseudo-Quintilian, *Declaration* 34.2.3.

40. Kevin Crotty, *Law's Interior*, p. 116.

41. Marx and Engels, "Proletarians and Communists" (§ 2).

42. Bill Moyers, "A Talk with Carter, May 16, 1976," *Los Angeles Times*. In Richardson, *Conversations with Carter*, p. 15.

43. William Martin, *A Prophet*, p. 463.

44. Kenneth E. Morris, *Jimmy Carter: American Moralist*, pp. 160–61.

45. Bill Moyers, "A Talk With Carter, May 16, 1976," *Los Angeles Times*. Richardson, ed., *Conversations with Carter*, pp. 13–14.

46. "Carter's Comments," *New York Times*, p. 36.

47. "Carter and Playboy," *Augusta Chronicle*, Sept. 23, 1976, p. 4.

48. William Safire, "The Weirdness Factor," *New York Times*, Sept. 30, 1976, p. 41.

49. Michael Lienesch, *Redeeming America: Piety and Politics in the New Christian Right*, p. 186.

50. Bourne, *Jimmy Carter*, pp. 263, 279–80, 334.

51. "Carter's Comments," *New York Times*, p. 36.

52. "Playboy Interview," in Richardson, *Conversations with Carter*, pp. 53–54.

53. Bourne, *Jimmy Carter*, pp. 315–16, 345.

Chapter 7
Jim Bakker Shoots His Allies

1. Michael D'Antonio, *Fall from Grace: The Failed Crusade of the Christian Right* (Rutgers University Press, 1992), p. 171; Jim Bakker, *I Was Wrong* (Thomas Nelson, 1996) pp. 2–3.

2. "Jim Bakker Resigns from PTL," *Charlotte Observer*, March 20, 1987, p. 1.

3. Ibid. The full text of the newspaper story is included in Appendix C.

4. Sheehy; *The Triumph of Group Therapeutics* (Ph.D. diss., 2002), pp. 224–26.

5. Jane M. Shattuc, *The Talking Cure: TV Talk Shows and Women* (Routledge, 1997), p. 30.

6. "Points West: For Bruised Spirits, Bitter Medicine." *New York Times*, Sept. 7, 1988.

7. Bernard M. Timberg, *Television Talk: A History of the Television Talk Show* (University of Texas Press, 2002), p. 6.

8. Ibid., p. 4.

9. Ibid., p. 13.

10. Jane M. Shattuc, *The Talking Cure*, p. 4.

11. Ibid., p. 95.

12. Patrician Joyner Priest, *Public Intimacies: Talk Show Participants and Tell-All TV* (Hampton Press, 1995), pp. 58–60, 65.

13. Timberg, *Television Talk*, p. 135.

14. Shattuc, *The Talking Care*, pp. 56–57.

15. Timberg, *Television Talk*, p. 139.

16. Peter S. Hawkins, "American Heritage," in *One Nation Under God*, ed. Marjorie Garber and Rebecca L. Walkowitz (Routledge, 1999), p. 269.

17. Pat Robertson, Bakker's former boss at CBN, wrote in his autobiography that whenever Jim wept, the "phones in the studio started ringing," people "called in weeping," and contibutions skyrocketed.

18. Larry Martz, *Ministry of Greed* (Newsweek, 1988), p. 21.

19. T. J. Jackson Lears, "From Salvation to Self-Realization: Advertising and the Therapeutic Roots of the Consumer Culture, 1880–1930," in *The Culture of Consumption*, ed. Richard Wrightman Fox and T. J. Jackson Lears (Pantheon, 1983), pp. 3–4. Mimi White brings this argument into the 1980s and provides an extensive discussion of the therapeutic elements of the Home Shopping Network in *Tele-Advising: Therapeutic Discourse in American Television* (University of North Carolina Press, 1992), pp. 8–12.

20. Jerry Falwell and Elmer Towns, *Capturing a Town for Christ*, p. 74.

21. Hadden, "Rise and Fall," p. 121.

22. Ben Armstrong, *The Electric Church*, pp. 8–10.

23. Mark A. Shibley, "Contemporary Evangelicals: Born-Again and World Affirming," p. 68.

24. Heather Hendershot, *Shaking the World for Jesus: Media and Conservative Evangelical Culture*, p. 146.

25. Matthew 24:23–24, 36–44.

26. Michael Lienesch, *Redeeming America: Piety and Politics in the New Christian Right*, p. 2.

27. Clyde Wilcox, "The Christian Right in Twentieth-Century America: Continuity and Change," p. 668.

28. Ann Rowe Seaman, *Swaggart: The Unauthorized Biography of an American Evangelist*, pp. 262–63. The title of the book (not to mention its content) demonizes the "liberals" who are "raping" America without even having to specify how their policies are damaging the nation.

29. Thomas C. O'Guinn and Russell W. Belk, "Heaven on Earth: Consumption at Heritage Village, USA," pp. 229–30.

30. Harding, *The Book of Jerry Falwell*, p. 160.

31. Jimmy Swaggart, "Divine Imperatives for Broadcast Ministry," in *Religious Broadcasting* (November,1984), p. 14; quoted in Schultze, *Christianity and the Mass Media in America*, p. 64.

32. "Ownership of property is biblical," Jerry Falwell wrote in 1980. "Competition in business is biblical. Ambitious and successful business management is clearly outlined as a part of God's plan for His people." This is not, as Thomas O'Guinn and Russell W. Belk suggest, a Pentecostal expression of prosperity as proof of God's blessing (and to characterize Jerry Falwell as in any way Pentecostal is to entirely misunderstand his brand of neoevangelicalism). Rather, this is a traditional evangelical expression of the dynamic relationship between converted behavior on the part of individuals and a

properly functioning society. See O'Guinn and Belk, "Heaven on Earth," p. 229.

33. Ezra Bowen, "Looking to Its Roots," *Time*, May 25, 1987.

34. Richard N. Ostling, "T.V.'s Unholy Row," *Time*, Monday, Apr. 6, 1987.

35. "Bakker Scrubs Plans to Tell His Side," *Charlotte Observer*, May 3, 1987, p. 1d.

36. David Brand, "God and Money," *Time*, Aug. 3, 1987.

37. Robert Tilton, *The Power to Create Wealth*, pp. 17, 29, 32, 111–22.

38. Robert Tilton, *How to Kick the Devil Out of Your Life*, pp. 35, 70, 91.

39. Jim Bakker, *You Can Make It!* (PTL Enterprises, 1983), p. 88.

40. Quoted in Hawkins *American Heritage*, p. 265.

41. Edith L. Blumhofer, *Restoring the Faith: The Assemblies of God, Pentecostalism, and American Culture*, pp. 170ff., 256.

42. Quoted in Charles Shepard, *Forgiven* (Atlantic Monthly, 1989), p. 79.

43. *Charlotte Observer* reporter Charles Shepard eventually won a Pulitzer prize for his coverage of the PTL scandal.

44. "Bakker Asserts He Resigned," *New York Times*, March 24, 1987.

45. "Preachers' Battle Transfixing the South," *New York Times*, March 26, 1987.

46. Ostling, "T.V.'s Unholy Row."

47. Ibid. Falwell lost the case, but kept his reputation, since he had visibly tried to keep his name out of *Penthouse*; he had clearly learned a lesson from the Carter debacle of 1976.

48. "Bakker, Evangelist, Resigns His Ministry Over Sexual Incident," *New York Times*, March 21, 1987.

49. Oral Roberts, on *Something Good Is Going to Happen to You*, March 1987.

50. "A Really Bad Day at Fort Mill," by Richard N. Ostling. In *Time*, Mar. 30, 1987.

51. Ezra Bowen, "Looking to Its Roots," *Time*, May 25, 1987.

52. "Falwell denies tricking Bakker," *Augusta Chronicle*, May 28, 1987.

53. Ibid., p. 1.

54. "PTL will bounce back, Falwell says," *Augusta Chronicle*, May 31, 1987, p. 8a.

55. Jon D. Hull, "At Home with Jim," *Time*, June 8, 1987.

56. "Free this week, can evangelist make a comeback?" *Charlotte Observer*, Nov. 27, 1994, p. 1a.

57. Jim Bakker, with Ken Abraham, *I Was Wrong*, pp. 3, 14–15, 21.

58. Ibid., p. 461.

59. "Jim Bakker preaching a new version of the gospel," *Charlotte Observer*, April 25, 1998.

60. "Jim Bakker flattered by positive response in Branson," *Charlotte Observer*, April 14, 2003; "Jim Bakker returns to television with new, small-scale series," *Seattle Times*, July 3, 2006.

61. January 4, 2007 broadcast of the "Christ's Ambassador," fundraising talk show.

Chapter 8
Jimmy Swaggart's Model Confession

1. From the transcript of Jimmy Swaggart's "Apology Sermon," preached Feb. 21, 1988. A full transcript of the sermon is found in Appendix D.

2. Michael J. Giuliano, *Thrice-Born: The Rhetorical Comeback of Jimmy Swaggart*, pp. 1–2.

3. "Swaggart Is Subject of Investigation by His Church," *New York Times*, Feb. 20, 1988.

4. "Swaggart Is Silent on Inquiry," *New York Times*, Feb. 21, 1988.

5. Richard N. Ostling, "Now It's Jimmy's Turn," *Time*, Mar. 7, 1988.

6. "Lousina Presbytery refuses to reconsider Swaggart's punishment," *Augusta Chronicle*, Mar. 2, 1988, p. 14; "Church officials to tackle Swaggart issue," *Augusta Chronicle*, Mar. 23, 1988, p. 5; "Church elders bar Swaggart from preaching for a year," *Augusta Chronicle*, Mar. 30, 1988, p. 1.

7. "Swaggart plans to defy church, resume preaching in May," *Augusta Chronicle*, Mar. 31, 1988.

8. "Church Defrocks Swaggart for Rejecting Its Punishment," *New York Times*, Apr. 9, 1988.

9. "Swaggart Says He Has Sinned; Will Step Down," *New York Times*, Feb. 22, 1988.

10. Ibid.

11. "Swaggart's Troubles Show Tension of Passion and Power in TV Evangelism," *New York Times*, Feb. 28, 1988.

12. "A Fiery Swaggart Returns to Pulpit," *New York Times*, May 23, 1988.

13. Giuliano, *Thrice-Born*, pp. 99, 107.

14. Ibid., p. 131.

15. "Church Orders 2-year Rehabilitiation for Swaggart"; Ostling, "Now It's Jimmy's Turn."

16. "Swaggart Makes TV Appearance, Saying He'll Tell His Sin Someday," *New York Times*, March 7, 1988.

17. Giuliano, *Thrice-Born*, "Scandals Emptied Pews of Electronic Churches," *New York Times*, March 3, 1991, p. 3

18. "Swaggart Plans to Step Down," *New York Times*, Oct. 15, 1991.

19. "No Apologies This Time," *Time*, Oct. 28, 1991.

20. Randall Balmer, "Still Wrestling with the Devil," *Christiantiy Today*, Mar. 2, 1998.

21. Ibid.

Chapter 9
Clinton and the Three Public Confessions

1. "Clinton Accused of Urging Aide to Lie," *Washington Post*, Jan. 21, 1998, p. 1.

2. Interview with Jim Lehrer, *Newshour*, January 21, 1998, provided by Federal News Service. A full transcript of this first statement can be found in Appendix E.i.

3. Transcript of interview on NPR special news report, Jan. 21, 1998.

4. *Roll Call*, Jan. 21, 1998.

5. "President Imperiled as Never Before," *Washington Post*, Jan. 22, 1998, p. 13.

6. "Clinton Forcefully Denies Affair, or Urging Lies," *Washington Post*, Jan. 27, 1998, p. 1.

7. Ibid.

8. "Clinton Denied Initiating Job help for Lewinsky," *Washington Post*, Mar. 5, 1998, p. 1.

9. "Time Line," in *Washington Post*, Sept. 13, 1998, p. 32.

10. Deposition of President Clinton, 10:30 a.m., Jan. 17, 1998; released Mar. 13, 1998. A transcript of the portions of the deposition having to do with the President's relationship to Monica Lewinsky can be found in Appendix E.ii.

11. "Follow the Wording," *Washington Post*, April 26, 1998, p. 1.

12. "Clinton Denounces Leak as 'Illegal,'" *Washington post*, Mar. 6, 1998.

13. "Clinton Dismisses Attacks," *Washington Post*, May 1, 1998, p. 1.

14. Public statement of President Clinton, Aug. 17, 1998; transcript provided by the Federal Document Clearing House. A full transcript of the entire statement can be found in Appendix E.iii.

15. Ronald Lee and Matthew H. Barton, "Clinton's Rhetoric of Contrition," pp. 225–26.

16. From the White House transcript of President Clinton's speech in Oak Bluffs, MA, Aug. 28, 1998.

17. From the Associated Press transcript of President Clinton's Prayer Breakfast Speech, Friday, September 11, 1998. The full text of this confession can be found in Appendix E.v.

18. Bill Clinton, *My Life*, pp. 23, 30

19. Ibid., p. 39.

20. Ibid., p. 46.

21. Ibid., p. 241–42.

22. "Clintons Find Solace, Support at Church," *Washington Post*, Jan. 26, 1998, p. 9.

23. Ibid.

24. "Aide, Clinton Were Close," *Washington Post*, Jan. 25, 1998, p. 1.

25. "The Prodigal Who Didn't Come Home: Why the President's 'Apology' Misfired," *Christianity Today*, Oct. 5, 1998.

26. Official website of Jerry Falwell Ministries, http://www.falwell.com/index.cfm?PID=13737.

27. LaHaye, *Battle for the Mind*, pp. 182–83, 198.

28. Ibid., p. 188.

29. Shibley, "Contemporary Evangelicals," p. 80.

30. Ronald Reagan's 1983 speech to the National Association of Evangelicals, in which he called the Soviet Union an "evil empire," demonstrates the successful infiltration of secular political discourse by the language of religious morality.

31. "Prayer Breakfast Sways Ministers," *Washington Post*, Sept. 12, 1998, p. 10.

32. "Pray for the President," transcript of a sermon delivered by Gordon MacDonald on Sept. 13, 1998, to the congregation of Grace Chapel, Lexington, Mass.

33. Ibid.

34. "Testing of a President: Spiritual Help; New Minister Joins Clinton's 2 Counselors," Sept. 18, 1998.

35. "Testing of a President: The Counselors; Clinton Selects Clerics to Give Him Guidance," *New York Times*, Sept. 15, 1998.

36. MacDonald, "Pray for the President."

37. "Testing of a President: The Conservatives; Christian Coalition Moans Lack of Anger at Clinton," *New York Times*, Sept. 20, 1998.

38. Ibid.

39. Richard Schechner, "Oedipus Clintonius," *TDR*, 43, no. 1 (Spring, 1999), p. 7.

40. Andrew Ferguson, "It's the Sex, Stupid," in *Time*, Feb. 2, 1998; "White House Sex Allegations Don't Trouble Most People," *Washington Post*, Jan. 26, 1998, p. 1.

41. "Lewinsky: 2 Coasts, 2 Lives, Many Images," *Washington Post*, Jan. 24, 1998, p 1.

42. "Lewinsky's Former Teacher Discloses Affair," *Washington Post*, Jan 28, 1998, p. 22.

43. "Aide's Interest in Clinton Was Well-Known," *Washington Post*, Jan. 29, 1998.

44. "Aide, Clinton Were Close,Friends Told," *Washington Post*, Jan. 25, 1998, p. 1

45. "President's Popularity Hits New High," *Washington post*, Feb. 1, 1998, p. 1.

46. "Willey's Story Gets a Shrug From Public," *Washington Post*, Mar. 19, 1998, p. 01.

47. Grand jury testimony of President Clinton, August 17, 1998; released to the public, Sept. 21, 1998. A transcript of the relevant sections of the testimony can be found in Appendix E.iv.

48. Crotty, *Law's Interior*, p. 94; Culombe v. Connecticut, 367 U.S. 568, 602 (1961).

49. Crotty, *Law's Interior*, p. 97.

50. Ibid., p. 100.

51. David Horowitze, "Clinton's Amen Chorus," *FrontPageMagazine. com*, Oct. 12, 1998.

52. Toni Morrison, "The Talk of the Town," *The New Yorker*, Oct. 5, 1998, p. 32.

53. Linda Schulte-Sasse, "Fixing the Nation's Problem: When a Sweet Bird of Youth Crosses the Line," *Cultural Critique* 43 (Autumn 1999), p. 22.

54. "Testing of a President: The Supporters; Blacks Stand by a President Who 'Has Been There for Us,'" *New York Times*, Sept. 19, 1998.

55. Ibid.

56. Schulte-Sasse, "Fixing the Nation's Problem," p. 35.

57. Orlando Patterson, "What is Freedom Without Privacy," *New York Times*, Sept. 15, 1998; Barbara Leah Harman, "In Internet Age, Not Even President Has Privacy," *New York Times*, Sept. 19, 1998.

58. Transcript of interview with Jim Lehrer, *Newshour*, January 21, 1998.

59. "Willey's Story Gets Shrug."

60. "President's Popularity Hits New Highs," *Washington Post*, Feb. 1, 1998, p. 1.

61. "Willey's Story Gets Shrug."

62. Kate M. Kenski, "The Framing of Network News Coverage During the First Three Months of the Clinton-Lewinsky Scandal," in *Images, Scandal, and Communication Strategies of the Clinton Presidency* (Praeger, 2003) pp. 252–53.

63. "President's Popularity Hits New Highs," *Washington Post*, Feb. 1, 1998, p. 1.

64. "Starr's Report Paints a Many-Sided Portrait," *New York Times*, Sept. 14, 1998.

65. Lee and Barton, "Clinton's Rhetoric of Communication," p. 232.

66. Ibid.

67. Public Gives Clinton Blame, Record Support," *Washington Post*, Feb. 15, 1999, p. 1.

Chapter 10
Unaware of Change

1. David France, *Our Fathers: The Secret Life of the Catholic Church in an Age of Scandal*, pp. 206–10.

2. "Nine Allege Priest Abused Them, Threaten to Sue Church," *Boston Globe*, May 8, 1992, p. 1.

3. Ibid.

4. "Some Fault Church on Sex Abuse By Priests," *Boston Globe*, May 11, 1992, p. 1.

5. "Sexual Abuse by Priests is a 'Betrayal,' 'Rare,' Law Says," *Boston Globe*, May 14, 1992, p. 29.

6. Ibid.

7. "Law Raps Ex-Priest Coverage," *Boston Globe*, May 24, 1992, p. 23.

8. In his original confession, Swaggart said, "Many times I have . . . chastised [the media] for what I thought and believed was error. . . . This time I do not. I commend them. I feel that the media . . . have been fair and objective and even compassionate." He listed by name Ted Koppel, three local TV channels, and investigative reporter John Camp, and praised all of them.

9. "More Suits Filed Against Ex-Priest," *New York Times*, July 26, 1992.

10. "Bishops Pledge to Fight Sexual Abuse by Priests," *New York Times*, Nov. 20, 1992.

11. France, *Our Fathers*, p. 217.

12. "Church allowed abuse by priest for years: Aware of Geoghan record, archdiocese still shuttled him from parish to parish," *Boston Globe*, Jan. 6, 2002.

13. "Officials avoided confronting priest," *Boston Globe*, Jan. 24, 2002.

14. Cardinal Bernard Law, press conference, Jan. 9, 2002. The full text of Law's statement can be found in Appendix F.i.

15. "A 'grieving' Law apologizes for assignment of Geoghan: Orders priests, others to report pedophiles," *Boston Globe*, Jan. 10, 2002.

16. "Why won't Law back disclosing past sex abuse?" *Boston Globe*, Jan. 18, 2002.

17. Cardinal Bernard Law, press conference, Jan. 24, 2002. The full text of Law's statement can be found in Appendix F.ii.

18. France, *Our Fathers*, pp. 309–310.

19. Bernard Law, "Open Letter," Jan. 26, 2002. The full text of the letter is found in Appendix F.iii.

20. "Most Catholics in poll fault Law's performance," *Boston Globe*, Feb. 8, 2002.

21. Lance Morrow, "Let Priests Marry," *Time*, Mar. 25, 2002.

22. "Church allowed abuse by priest for years."

23. Bernard Law, "Open letter to priests of the Boston Archdiocese," April 12, 2002. The complete text of this letter can be found in Appendix F.iv.

24. "Abuse victims decry cardinal's letter as insult," *Boston Globe*, April 13, 2002.

25. Bernard Law, "Open letter to the Archdiocese of Boston," Pentecost, May 19, 2002. The complete text of this letter can be found in Appendix F.v.

26. "Globe is denied access as punishment for story," *Boston Globe*, June 14, 2002.

27. "In meeting with victims, Law begs forgiveness: Private talk marked by tears and anger," *Boston Globe*, Oct. 30, 2002.

28. France, *Our Fathers*, p. 534.

29. Bernard Law, "Remarks at Mass, Cathedral of the Holy Cross," Nov. 3, 2002. The complete text of the statement can be found in Appendix F.vi.

30. "More clergy abuse, secrecy cases: Records detail quiet shifting of rogue priests," *Boston Globe*, Dec. 4, 2002.

31. Seidler, "Contested Accommodation," p. 851.

32. Andrew M. Greeley, "The Failtures of Vatican II After Twenty Years," (America 146, Feb. 1981), pp. 86–89.

33. Jaroslav Pelikan, "The Enduring Relevance of Martin Luther 500 Years after His Birth," *New York Times Magazine*, Sept. 18, 1983, pp. 43–45, 99–104.

34. Wallace, "Catholic Women," p. 31.

35. John Seidler, "Contested Accommodation," p. 852.

36. Patrick Carey, *Catholics*, pp. 116, 119.

37. Seidler, "Contested Accomodation," p. 857.

38. Gallagher, "Marriage and Sexuality," p. 239–40.

39. *"Humanae vitae:* Encyclical of Pope Paul VI on the Regulation of Birth," July 25, 1968.

40. Patrick Carey, *Catholics*, p. 132.

41. Francis Randolph, *Pardon and Peace: A Sinner's Guide to Confession*, pp. 9–10.

42. Ibid., pp. 13–14, 19.

43. Randolph, *Pardon and Peace*, pp. 32–33.

44. Law, "Open letter," May 19, 2002.

45. Law, "Open letter," Jan. 26, 2002.

46. Law, "Press conference," Jan. 9, 2002.

47. Law, "Open letter," Apr. 12, 2002.

48. "More Suits Filed Against Ex-Priest."

49. "Nine Allege Priest Abused Them."

50. Ibid.

51. Seidler, "Contested Accommodation," p. 859.

52. "Some Fault Church on Sex Abuse By Priests."

53. "The apologies aren't enough," *Boston Globe,* Jan. 25, 2002.

54. "Archbishop in name only," *Boston Globe,* Jan. 29, 2002.

55. "Stung by sex-abuse cases, Catholics call for reform," *Boston Globe,* Feb. 4, 2002.

56. Morrow, "Let Priests Marry."

57. "Catholic lay leaders urge broad reforms: Ask for rethinking of ministry, secrecy," *Boston Globe,* March 10, 2002.

58. "Church loses the last word," *Boston Globe,* April 14, 2002.

Conclusion
Predictions

1. "'I Am Guilty of Sexual Immorality . . . a Deceiver and a Liar,' Haggard Confesses," *Christianity Today Online,* posted 11/05/2006.

2. Ibid.

3. "Minister's Own Rules Sealed His Fate." *New York Times,* Nov. 19, 2006.

4. "Ousted Pastor 'Completely Heterosexual.'" *New York Times,* Feb. 7, 2007.

5. "Minister's Own Rules Sealed His Fate."

6. LaHaye, *Battle for the Mind*, p. 174.

7. "Some Tormented by Homosexuality Look to a Controversial Therapy." *New York Times*, Feb. 12, 2007.

8. "The Preacher and the Prostitute," *People*, Nov. 20, 2006, pp. 71–74.

9. Mark Foley, statement of Sept. 29, 2006.

10. Statement by Mark Foley's attorney, David Roth, Oct. 3, 2006.

11. "Acquaintances Question Alcoholism." *Washington Post*, Oct. 3, 2006.

12. "Senator's Link to 'D.C. Madam' Exposed," *Associated Press*, July 10, 2007; "Senator's Number on 'Madam' Phone List," *Washington Post*, July 10, 2007.

13. "Senator's Link to 'D.C. Madam' Exposed."

14. "Vitter tries to move forward," Gannet News Service, July 19, 2007.

WORKS CITED

Alexander, Bobby C. *Televangelism Reconsidered: Ritual in the Search for Human Community.* Atlanta: Scholars Press, 1994.

Armstrong, Ben. *The Electric Church.* Nashville: Thomas Nelson Publishers, 1979.

Augustine. *Confessions*, trans. Henry Chadwick. Oxford: Oxford University Press, 1998.

Austin, John. *The Province of Jurisprudence Determined.* New York: Noonday Press, 1954.

Bachman. John W. *The Church in the World of Radio-Television.* New York: Associated Press, 1960.

Bader, Jesse M., ed. *The Message and Method of the New Evangelism: A Joint Statement of the Evangelistic Mission of the Christian Church.* New York: Round Table Press, 1937.

Bakker, Jim. *You Can Make It!* Charlotte, NC: PTL Enterprises, 1983.

Bakker, Jim, with Ken Abraham. *I Was Wrong.* Nashville: Thomas Nelson Publishers, 1996.

Barnhart, Joe E., with Steven Winzenburg. *Jim and Tammy: Charismatic Intrigue Inside PTL.* Buffalo, NY: Prometheus Books, 1988.

Biller, Peter. "Confession in the Middle Ages: Introduction." In *Handling Sin: Confession in the Middle Ages*, ed. Peter Biller and A. J. Minnis. York: York Medieval Press, 1998, pp. 3–33.

Blumhofer, Edith L. *Aimee Semple McPherson: Everybody's Sister.* Grand Rapids: William B. Eerdmans Publishing Co., 1993.

————. *Restoring the Faith: The Assemblies of God, Pentecostalism, and American Culture.* Chicago: University of Illinois Press, 1993.

Bossy, John. "Moral Arithmetic: Seven Sins into Ten Commandments." In *Conscience and Casuistry in Early Modern Europe*, ed. Edmund Leites. Cambridge: Cambridge University Press, 1988, pp. 214–34.

Bourne, Peter G. *Jimmy Carter: A Comprehensive Biography from Plains to Postpresidency.* New York: Scribner, 1997.

Bratt, James D. "The Reorientation of American Protestantism, 1835–1845." *Church History*, 67, no. 1 (March 1998), pp. 52–82.

Brekus, Catherine A. *Strangers and Pilgrims: Female Preaching in America, 1740–1845.* Chapel Hill: University of North Carolina Press, 1998.

Brereton, Virginia Lieson. *Training God's Army: The American Bible School, 1880–1940.* Indianapolis: Indiana University Press, 1990.

———. *From Sin to Salvation: Stories of Women's Conversions, 1800 to the Present.* Indianapolis: Indiana University Press, 1991.

Butler, Jon. *Awash in a Sea of Faith: Christianizing the American People.* Cambridge, MA: Harvard University Press, 1990.

Caldwell, Patricia. *The Puritan Conversion Narrative: The Beginnings of American Expression.* Cambridge: Cambridge University Press, 1983.

Calvin, John. *The Institutes of the Christian Religion,* trans. Henry Beveridge. London: Arnold Hatfield, 1599.

Caplan, Eric. *Mind Games: American Culture and the Birth of Psychotherapy.* Berkeley: University of California Press, 1998.

Carey, James W. *Communication as Culture: Essays on Media and Society.* Winchester, MA: Unwin Hyman, 1988.

Carey, Patrick W. *Catholics in America: A History.* Westport, CT: Praeger, 2004.

Carpenter, Joel. *Revive Us Again: The Reawakening of American Fundamentalism.* New York: Oxford University Press, 1997.

Cleveland, Grover. *The Writings and Speeches of Grover Cleveland,* ed. George F. Parker. New York: Cassell Publishing Company, 1892.

Clinton, Bill. *My Life.* New York: Alfred A. Knopf, 2004.

Clymer, Adam. *Edward M. Kennedy: A Biography.* New York: William Morrow, 1999.

Cohen, Bernard D., Mark F. Ettin, and Jay W. Fidler. *Group Psychotherapy and Political Reality: A Two-Way Mirror.* Madison, CT: International Universities Press, 2002.

Creech, Joe. "Visions of Glory: The Place of the Azusa Street Revival in Pentecostal History." *Church History,* 65, no. 3 (Sept., 1996): pp. 405–24.

Crotty, Kevin. *Law's Interior: Legal and Literary Constructions of the Self.* Ithaca: Cornell University Press, 2001.

D'Antonio, Michael. *Fall From Grace: The Failed Crusade of the Christian Right.* New Brunswick, NJ: Rutgers University Press, 1992.

Edwards, Jonathan. *The Works of Jonathan Edwards,* vols. 1 and 2. Peabody, MA: Hendrickson Publishers, 1998.

Epstein, Daniel Mark. *Sister Aimee: The Life of Aimee Semple McPherson.* New York: Harcourt Brace Jovanovich, 1993.

Erickson, Hal. *Religious Radio and Television in the United Stats, 1921–1991: The Programs and Personalities.* Jefferson, NC: McFarland, 1992.

Evensen, Bruce J. "'It Is a Marvel to Many People': Dwight L. Moody, Mass Media, and the New England Revival of 1877." *New England Quarterly,* 72, no. 2 (June 1999): 251–74.

Falwell, Jerry, and Elmer Towns. *Capturing a Town for Christ.* Chicago: Fleming H. Revell, 1973.

Ferry, Patrick T. "Confessionalization and Popular Preaching: Sermons against Synergism in Reformation Saxony," *Sixteenth-Century Journal,* 28, no. 4 (Winter, 1997): 1143–66.

Finney, Charles G. *Lectures on Revivals of Religion.* Chicago: Fleming H. Revell Company, 1868.

Foucault, Michel. *History of Sexuality,* vol. 1, trans. Robert Hurley. New York: Vintage, 1980.

France, David. *Our Fathers: The Secret Life of the Catholic Church in an Age of Scandal.* New York: Broadway Books, 2004.

Gallagher, John. "Marriage and Sexuality: Magisterial Teaching from 1918 to the Present," In *Change in Official Catholic Moral Teachings: Readings in Moral Theology,* no. 13, ed. Charles E. Curran. New York: Paulist Press, 2003, pp. 227–47.

Garrison, Charles E. *Two Different Worlds: Christian Absolutes and the Relativism of Social Science.* Newark: University of Delaware Press, 1988.

Gillespie, C. Kevin. *Psychology and American Catholicism: From Confession to Therapy?* New York: Crossroads, 2001.

Giuliano, Michael J. *Thrice-Born: The Rhetorical Comeback of Jimmy Swaggart.* Macon: Mercer University Press, 1999.

Gobinet, Charles. *The Instruction of Youth in Christian Piety.* Dublin, 1973.

Gothard, Bill. *Syllabus: Institute for Basic Youth Conflicts.* Oak Brook, IL: Institute in Basic Youth Conflicts, 1975.

Gothard, Bill. *Advanced Seminar Textbook.* Oak Brook, IL: Institute in Basic Life Principles, 1986.

Graff, Henry F. *Grover Cleveland.* New York: Henry Holt, 2002.

Graham, Billy. *Just As I Am: The Autobiography of Billy Graham.* San Franscisco: HarperSanFrancisco, 1997.

Greeley, Andrew M. "The Failures of Vatican II after Twenty Years,." *America,* no. 146, (Feb. 1981): 86–89.

Green, Barbara. *Spectacular Confessions: Autobiography, Performative Activism, and the Sites of Suffrage, 1905–1938.* New York: St. Martin's, 1997.

Griffith, R. Marie. *God's Daughters: Evangelical Women and the Power of Submission.* Berkeley: University of California Press, 1997.

Guelzo, Allen C. "An Heir or a Rebel? Charles Grandison Finney and the New England Theology," *Journal of the Early Republic,* 17, no. 1 (Spring, 1997): 61–94.

Hadden, Jeffrey K. "Religious Broadcasting and the Mobilization of the New Christian Right," *Secularization and Fundamentalism Reconsidered: Religion and the Political Order,* vol. 3, ed. Jeffrey K. Hadden and Anson Shupe. New York: Paragon House, 1989, pp. 230–51.

Hadden, Jeffrey K. "The Rise and Fall of American Televangelism," *Annals of the American Academy of Political and Social Science*: Religion in the Nineties 527, (May, 1993): 113–30.

Hadden, Jeffrey K. and Anson Shupe. *Televangelism: Power and Politics on God's Frontier.* New York: Henry Holt, 1988.

Hall, David D. *Worlds of Wonder, Days of Judgment: Popular Religious Belief in Early New England.* Cambridge, MA: Harvard University Press, 1989.

Hangen, Tona J. *Redeeming the Dial: Radio, Religion, and Popular Culture in America.* Chapel Hill: University of North Carolina Press, 2002.

Harding, Susan Friend. "Imagining the Last Days: The Politics of Apocalyptic Language," *Bulletin of the American Academy of Arts and Sciences*, 48, no. 3. (Dec., 1994): 14–44.

———. *The Book of Jerry Falwell: Fundamentalist Language and Politics.* Princeton: Princeton University Press, 2000.

Hatch, Nathan O. *The Democratization of American Christianity.* New Haven: Yale University Press, 1989.

Hawkins, Peter S. "American Heritage." In *One Nation Under God? Religion and American Culture,* ed. Marjorie Garber and Rebecca L. Walkowitz. New York: Routledge, 1999, pp. 258–79.

Heggen, F. J. *Confession and the Service of Penance,* trans. Peter Tomlison. Notre Dame, IN: University of Notre Dame Press, 1968.

Heimert, Alan, and Andrew Delbanco, eds. *The Puritans in America: A Narrative Anthology.* Cambridge, MA: Harvard University Press, 1985.

Hendershot, Heather. *Shaking the World for Jesus: Media and Conservative Evangelical Culture.* Chicago: University of Chicago Press, 2004.

Henry, Carl F. H. *The Uneasy Conscience of Modern Fundamentalism.* Grand Rapids, MI: William B. Eerdmans, 1947.

Holifield, E. Brooks. "Peace, Conflict, and Ritual in Puritan Congregations," *Journal of Interdisciplinary History*, 23, Religion and History, no. 3 (Winter, 1993): 551–70.

Honan, William H. *Ted Kennedy: Profile of a Survivor.* New York: Quadrangle Books, 1972.

Jeffers, H. Paul. *An Honest President: The Life and Presidencies of Grover Cleveland.* New York: William Morrow, 2000.

Johnson, Charles A. "The Frontier Camp Meeting: Contemporary and Historical Appraisals, 1805–1840," *The Mississippi Valley Historical Review*, 37, no. 1 (June 1950): 91–110.

Johnston, Winifred. "Newspaper Balladry," *American Speech*, 10, no. 2 (Apr., 1935): 119–21.

Kenski, Kate M. "The Framing of Network News Coverage During the First Three Months of the Clinton-Lewinsky Scandal." In *Images,*

Scandal, and Communication Strategies of the Clinton Presidency, ed. Robert E. Denton, Jr., and Rachel L. Holloway. Westport, CT: Praeger, 2003, pp. 247–69.

Kooiman, Helen W. *Transformed: Behind the Scenes with Billy Graham.* Wheaton: Tyndale House Publishers, 1970.

LaHaye, Tim. *The Battle for the Mind.* Old Tappan, NJ: Fleming H. Revell, 1980.

Latourette, Kenneth Scott. *A History of Christianity,* vol. 2: *Reformation to the Present,* rev. ed. New York: Harper and Row, 1975.

Lawless, Elaine J. "'The Night I Got the Holy Ghost. . .'": Holy Ghost Narratives and the Pentecostal Conversion Process," *Western Folklore,* 47, no. 1 (Jan., 1988): 1–19.

Lazare, Aaron. *On Apology.* Oxford: Oxford University Press, 2004.

Lears, T. J. Jackson. "From Salvation to Self-Realization: Advertising and the Therapeutic Roots of the Consumer Culture, 1880–1930." In *The Culture of Consumption: Critical Essays in American History, 1880–1980,* ed. Richard Wrightman Fox and T. J. Jackson Lears. New York: Pantheon Books, 1983, pp. 3–38.

Lee, Ronald, and Matthew H. Barton. "Clinton's Rhetoric of Contrition." In *Images, Scandal, and Communication Strategies of the Clinton Presidency,* ed. Robert E. Denton, Jr., and Rachel L. Holloway. Westport, CT: Praeger, 2003, pp. 219–46.

Lienesch, Michael. *Redeeming America: Piety and Politics in the New Christian Right.* Chapel Hill: University of North Carolina Press, 1993.

Lindsey, Hal, with C. C. Carlson. *The Late Great Planet Earth.* Grand Rapids, MI: Zondervan, 1970.

Luther, Martin. *Complete Edition of Luther's Latin Works,* trans. Andrew Thornton, OSB. Berlin: Walter de Gruyter, 1967.

Lynch, Christopher Owen. *Selling Catholicism: Bishop Sheen and the Power of Television.* Lexington: University Press of Kentucky, 1998.

Mansfield, Mary C. *The Humiliation of Sinners: Public Penance in Thirteenth-Century France.* Ithaca: Cornell University Press, 1995.

Marsden, George. *Fumdamentalism and American Culture: The Shaping of Twentieth-Century American Evangelicalism, 1870–1925.* New York: Oxford University Press, 1980.

Marsden, George. *Reforming Fundamentalism: Fuller Seminary and the New Evangelicalism.* Grand Rapids, MI: William B. Eerdmans, 1987.

Martin, Ralph G. *Seeds of Destruction: Joe Kennedy and His Sons.* New York: G. P. Putnam's Sons, 1995.

Martin, William. *A Prophet With Honor: The Billy Graham Story.* New York: William Morrow, 1991.

Marx, Karl, and Frederick Engels. *Manifesto of the Communist Party.* Trans. Samuel Moore and Frederick Engels (1888). In *Marx/Engels Selected Works,* vol. 1 (Moscow: Progress Publishers, 1969), pp. 98–137.

Mavity, Nancy Barr. *Sister Aimee.* New York: Doubleday, Doran and Co., 1931.

McClymond, Michael James. *Embodying the Spirit: New Perspectives on North American Revivalism.* Baltimore: The Johns Hopkins University Press, 2004.

McGraw, Onalee. *Secular Humanism and the Schools: The Issue Whose Time Has Come.* Washington, DC: The Heritage Foundation, 1976.

Miller, Robert M. *Harry Emerson Fosdick: Preacher, Pastor, Prophet.* Oxford: Oxford University Press, 1985.

Miller, Spencer, Jr. "Radio and Religion," *Annals of the American Academy of Political and Social Science,* 177 (Jan., 1935): 135–40.

Morris, Kenneth E. *Jimmy Carter: American Moralist.* Athens: University of Georgia Press, 1966.

Murray, Alexander. "Counselling in Medieval Confession." In *Handling Sin: Confession in the Middle Ages,* ed. Peter Biller and A. J. Minnis. York: York Medieval Press, 1998, pp. 63–77.

Myers, W. David. *"Poor, Sinning Folk": Confession and Conscience in Counter-Reformation Germany.* Ithaca: Cornell University Press, 1996.

Nevins, Allan. *Grover Cleveland: A Study in Courage.* New York: Dodd, Mead, 1948.

Noll, Mark A. *A History of Christianity in the United States and Canada.* Grand Rapids, MI: William B. Eerdmans, 1992.

———. *America's God: From Jonathan Edwards to Abraham Lincoln.* Oxford: Oxford University Press, 2002.

———. "Where We Are and How We Got Here." *Christianity Today,* Oct. 29, 2006.

———. *The Work We Have To Do: A History of Protestants in America.* New York: Oxford University Press, 2002.

O'Guinn, Thomas C., and Russell W. Belk. "Heaven on Earth: Consumption at Heritage Village, USA," *Journal of Consumer Research,* 16, no. 2 (Sept., 1989): 227–38.

Olsen, Jack. *The Bridge at Chappaquiddick.* Boston: Little, Brown, 1970.

Opie, John, Jr. "James McGready: Theologian of Frontier Revivalism." In *Church History,* 34, no. 4 (Dec., 1965): 445–56.

Packer, J. I. *"Fundamentalism" and the Word of God.* Grand Rapids, MI: William. B. Eerdmans, 1958.

Pelikan, Jaroslav. "The Enduring Relevance of Martin Luther 500 Years after His Birth." *New York Times Magazine* (Sept. 18, 1983): 43–45, 99–104.

Price, Robert M. "A Fundamentalist Social Gospel." *Christian Century*, Nov. 28, 1979: 1183.

Priest, Patricia Joyner. *Public Intimacies: Talk Show Participants and Tell-All TV*. Cresskill, NJ: Hampton Press, 1995.

Pullum, Stephen J. *"Foul Demons, Come Out!": The Rhetoric of Twentieth-Century American Faith Healing*. Westport, CT: Praeger, 1999.

Randolph, Francis. *Pardon and Peace: A Sinner's Guide to Confession*. San Francisco: Ignatius Press, 2001.

Richardson, Don, ed. *Conversations withe Carter*. Boulder, CO: Lynne Rienner Publishers, 1998.

Roberts, Oral. *The Call: An Autobiography*. New York: Doubleday, 1972.

Rothwell, Harry, ed. *English Historical Documents, 1189–1327*. London: Routledge and Kogan Paul, 1975.

Rubenstein, Richard L. "God and Caesar in Conflict." In *Secularization and Fundamentalism Reconsidered: Religion and the Political Order*, vol. 3, ed. Jeffrey K. Hadden and Anson Shupe. New York: Paragon House, 1989, pp. 201–14.

Schaeffer, Francis. *A Christian Manifesto*. Westchester, IL: Crossway Books, 1981.

Schulte-Sasse, Linda. "Fixing the Nation's Problem: When a Sweet Bird of Youth Crosses the Line." *Cultural Critique*: The Politics of Impeachment, vol. 43 (Autumn, 1999): 13–37.

Schultze. Quentin J. *Christianity and the Mass Media in America: Towards a Democratic Accomodation*. East Lansing: Michigan State University Press, 2003.

Scofield, C. I. *The Scofield Reference Bible*. New York: Oxford University Press, 1909.

Seaman, Ann Rowe. *Swaggart: The Unauthorized Biography of an American Evangelist*. New York: Continuum, 1999.

Seidler, John. "Contested Accommodation: The Catholic Church as a Special Case of Social Change." *Social Forces*, 64, no. 4 (June, 1986): 847–74.

Shattuc, Jane M. *The Talking Cure: TV Talk Shows and Women*. New York: Routledge, 1997.

Sheehy, Peter Phillips. *The Triumph of Group Therapeutics: Therapy, the Social Self, and Liberalism in America, 1910–1960*. Ph.D. dissertation, University of Virginia, 2002.

Sheen, Fulton J. "How to Have a Good Time." In *American Sermons: The Pilgrims to Martin Luther King Jr.*, ed. Michael Warner. New York: Library of America, 1999, pp. 835–40.

Shepard, Charles C. *Forgiven: The Rise and Fall of Jim Bakker and the PTL Ministry*. New York: Atlantic Monthly Press, 1989.

Stanley, Susie C. "The Promise Fulfilled: Women's Ministries in the Wesleyan/Holiness Movement." In *Religious Institutions and Women's Leadership: New Roles Inside the Mainstream,* ed. Catherine Wessinger. Columbia: University of South Carolina Press, 1996, pp. 139–57.

Sunday, Billy. "Food for a Hungry World." In *American Sermons: The Pilgrims to Martin Luther King Jr.* New York: Library of America, 1999, pp. 787–93.

Sutton, Matthew Avery. *Aimee Semple McPherson and the Resurrection of Christian America.* Cambridge, MA: Harvard University Press, 2007.

Sweeney, Douglas A. "The Essential Evangelicalism Dialectic: The Historiography of the Early Neo-Evangelical Movement and the Observer-Participant Dilemma." *Church History,* 60, no. 1 (March, 1991): 70–84.

Taylor, Charles. *Sources of the Self: The Making of the Modern Identity.* Cambridge, MA: Harvard University Press, 1989.

Tentler, Thomas. *Sin and Confession on the Eve of the Reformation.* Princeton: Princeton University Press, 1977.

Thomas, Lately. *The Vanishing Evangelist: The Aimee Semple McPherson Kidnapping Affair.* New York: The Viking Press, 1959.

———. *Storming Heaven: The Lives and Turmoils of Minnie Kennedy and Aimee Semple McPherson.* New York: William Morrow, 1970.

Tilton, Robert. *How to Kick the Devil Out of Your Life.* Dallas: Robert Tilton Ministries, 1988.

———. *The Power to Create Wealth.* Dallas: Robert Tilton Ministries, 1988.

Timberg, Bernard M. *Television Talk: A History of the TV Talk Show.* Austin: University of Texas Press, 2002.

Wacker, Grant. "The Functions of Faith in Primitive Pentecostalism." *Harvard Theological Review,* 77, no. 3/4 (Jul.–Oct., 1984): 353–75.

Wacker, Grant. "The Holy Spirit and the Spirit of the Age in American Protestantism, 1880–1910." *The Journal of American History,* 72, no. 1 (June 1985): 45–62.

Wallace, Ruth A. "Catholic Women and the Creation of a New Social Reality." *Gender and Society,* 2, no. 1 (March, 1988): 24–38.

Westerkamp, Marilyn J. *Women in Early American Religion, 1600–1850: The Puritan and Evangelical Traditions.* New York: Routledge, 1999.

Whitefield, George. *Select Sermons of George Whitefield.* J. C. Ryle, ed. London: Banner of Truth, 1964.

Wilcox, Clyde. "The Christian Right in Twentieth-Century America: Continuity and Change." *Review of Politics,* 50, no. 4 (Autumn 1988): 659–81.

Wilson, Alfred, C. P. *Pardon and Peace.* New York: Sheed and Ward, 1947.

TEXT PERMISSIONS

INDEX